FELTON
WAPITI HUNTIN TRIPS
#8 - #12

All inquiries should be addressed to:

Book Domain LLC.
543 E Louise Dr Phoenix, Az 85050

Ordering Information:
Amount Deals. Special rebates are accessible on the amount bought by corporations, associations, and others. For points of interest, contact the distributor at the address above.

Printed in the United States of America.

ISBN-13   Paperback   978-1-964100-40-1
           eBook   978-1-964100-41-8

Library of Congress Control Number: 2025902912

FELTON
WAPITI HUNTIN TRIPS
#8 - #12

TERRY LARKIN

BOOK DOMAIN LLC
Publish to Perfection

Felton 8

THE KOSTMAN BROTHER'S

CHAPTER 1

It had been a long hot five day ride back home from the coast. Sure they did some more training, like tracking, untracking, and retracking the Marshal through all the backwoods and countryside they rode through. They had even practiced shooting at pine cones, or better yet, those salty ass corn biscuit's.

It was late afternoon or early evening when they came riding back into Prineville. Everyone was staring at them as they rode by, Wapiti looked down at his clothes, then remembered it had been at least two days since they'd washed up.

Shawn rode up to the front of the Courthouse, where Judge Monson was standing on the boardwalk and waiting to hear how the last huntin trip had gone, and where were the Carpenter Brother's?"

"Somewhere out in the Pacific Ocean." Shawn answered, taking his last pull off his flask, tipping it upside down to show it was empty. "Now if you don't mind Your Honor, we're thirsty, hungry, and tired."

"Understandable Marshal, Wapiti…But how and why are they out in the ocean?" Judge Monson very questionably asked

"They evaded capture by riding up and into a ship that was loading up with cattle bound for China." Shawn said, looking down the street towards Carmen's restaurant. "So I doubt they'll be back for a couple years."

"While you two were out gallivanting around the countryside, Butch Cassidy and the Sundance Kid were seen over in Baker City. Somehow they think they stole over a half million in cash and at least enough gold to fill four full wagon loads of gold out of the new Oregon trust and Loan bank." Judge Monson started to explain.

"How the hell did they get out of town with that much gold and no-one saw them?" Shawn asked with a big smile on his face.

"Nobody knows…When they searched for them, they found them and the Larkin brothers all past out in their rooms at the Baker City Grand Hotel." Judge Monson answered

"Did you say the Larkin Brothers were involved?" Shawn asked

"YA, Why?" Judge Monson answered

"Cause if Randy Larkin had anything to do with it, you'll never find it or what they did with it. That Youngman has a knack of out smartin the average Lawman." Shawn answered, with a serious look on his face. "If they found them asleep in a high class hotel like that one…You'll never find anyone who could testify and prove they weren't there all night."

"You think maybe you and Wapiti need to go check it out?" Judge Monson asked

"Trust me Your Honor…you, me, nor anyone else will ever find any of that gold." Shawn said, turning his horse down the road towards the Livery, with Wapiti right behind him.

"He's right, Your Honor, about the robbery. If Randy Larkin had anything to do with it, you'll never find it or find any proof he or his brothers were involved." Wapiti said, riding past the Judge. Then up the street to the Livery.

"Marshal, just how and where would they hide four large wagon loads of gold at in the middle of the night?" Wapiti asked, dismounting and leading his horse inside the Livery.

"I don't have a clue, and truthfully I don't care. "Shawn said, calling out for Gordy. "Hell, knowing Randy he probably did the robbery just to prove it could be done...Then," He said, as he started chuckling, "Then he probably shared it with all the City's resident's."

"But Why?" Wapiti asked, as Gordy came walking out of the office and Jose came running thru the door with two large bottles of cold beers in his hands. Giving one to both Shawn and Wapiti.

"Did You Have To Shoot Anyone This Huntin Trip Marshal?" Jose asked excitedly.

"Thanks Jose, no son, we didn't have to shoot anyone this trip." Shawn answered looking down at him, then back at Wapiti. "Like I said, Randy would do something like that just for shit' and giggles...Just to prove the bank could be robbed."

Starting to chuckle a little, Wapiti too thanked Jose for the beer and took a big drink. "He would, wouldn't he! Steal all that gold I mean, just for something to do, then leave a small, maybe ten plus pound bags of gold at every house around town. Who's going to tell ANY Lawdog they found a bag of gold outside or inside through a broken window at their house in the morning." He said, starting to laugh.

"I sure as hell wouldn't." Gordy said, grabbing the rope to the pack horse so he could unload it. "I'd just repair the window, then go out of town after a couple months and cash it in."

"Just like in Pendleton, when their Aunt put the entire U.S. Cavalry Fort and railyard workers asleep. Then fired up every loco-motive and hossler engine's, sending them in every possible direc-tion out of town making it look like the outlaws did actually go out on one of those trains, she drove it right out the front gate with all that gold. Remember Marshal?" Wapiti said, starting to remove his saddle

"Yes I Do!" Shawn said, chuckling too. "If I'd have given a damn about that gold, I could have found it within a couple hours, if I gave a damn, but I didn't, and still don't."

"How, and why didn't ya?" Gordy asked

"There was only one set of wagon tracks over the morning dew. I followed them briefly out the main entrance of the Fort and across the street up an Alleyway between the house's." Shawn cheerfully started explaining "That newly made Brigadier General Dan Love, had taken control of that gold away from me the second we rode through the gate. The way I figured it, they lost it, they could find it. I was sick and tired of worrying about that gold, and wanted to move on to bigger and deadlier Outlaw's."

"So how'd she put the Fort to sleep?" Gordy asked

"It was a promotion party for Colonel Dan Love to Brigadier General. Their Aunt Patty catered the party. She put a BUNCH of sleeping solution in the cake and ice cream. All I remember was starting on my second piece of cake and seeing the Larkin brother's and the Mex walking away before I passed out. But in the morning, they were all back and passed out at the General's table with the rest of us." Shawn said.

"How'd she get enough of that stuff to put the entire Fort and train yard workers asleep?" Gordy asked, with a big smile on his face, starting to untie the packsaddle.

"Don't have a clue, and I don't care." Shawn said, putting his saddle on the closest saddle rack. "I'd love to stay and talk Gordy but I have to flip Wapiti for first shower. Then get something better than my cookin to eat."

Wapiti flipped a silver dollar in the air, and told Shawn to call it. "Tails!" Shawn yelled out, as Wapiti caught the coin and placed it on the back of his hand. Removing his top hand revealed the eagle with its wing's spread out.

"Hot Damn, I get first shower." Shawn shouted out, picking up his gear, he headed towards the door. "Gordy, give the horses all a good lookin over please, there's no tellin' when we might have to pull out."

"Sure thing Marshal." Gordy answered, watching them walk out the door.

Walking outside, Shawn briefly stopped and looked up and down the street, then headed across towards their shack.

The word had gotten out how the Carpenter brothers had gotten away. Some people were chuckling about it, and some were saying they wouldn't want to go to spend two plus months at sea then wind up in a country they didn't, or couldn't speak their language. But then with fifty thousand dollar at thirty plus to dollars to one of theirs, not to mention all the gold they had, that was well into the tens of thousands of dollars as well. So they could buy themselves a nice place and learn the language within a couple years.

Shawn was too tired to stop and talk about it with anyone. Within just a couple minutes they had crossed the street, walked in between the buildings and over to their shack. Dropping his saddle bags and their dirty laundry bag. Leaning his rifle up against the wall, he quickly grabbed a clean pair of clothes and headed towards Carmen's back door and the bathing room.

Wapiti too grabbed a clean change of clothes and followed him towards the restaurant. But he stopped off at the wash basin and washed up. Walking in the back door of the restaurant he walked into the dining area, looking around he saw an empty table, he could also see everyone had stopped talking and were staring at him.

When the waitress came up, she started to hand him a menu. "No thanks, I'll have the T-bone steak, all the fixins, and a cold beer please." Wapiti said, sitting down in a chair and smiling at the Young lady.

"Right away, Deputy." She answered walking away.

"You Ain't Drinking No Beer In Here Chief, I Don't Care Who You Think You Are!" a man said, who was sitting with three of his friends at the table next to him. "Indian's Aren't Allowed To Have Alcohol, they get too drunk and cause too much trouble."

"Looks like you're the ones trying to cause the trouble." Wapiti calmly said, looking the four men over. Two men on the front corner were obvious loggers, the two on the back corner were cowboys. All four men stood up and formed a line in front of him, with the two loggers in the middle and the cowboys on the outsides.

"Look guys, we just got back from a long two weeks out there in the mountains. I'm tired, I would just like to be able to eat my dinner in peace, then go catch up on some much needed rest, please." Wapiti calmly asked. Looking up at the four men.

"If you think we're going to let them serve you any alcohol, your crazy Chief!" the Cowboy to his right shouted out. While all the other customers started getting up out of their chairs and moving to the outside walls. Out of the way from whatever was about to happen.

Wapiti leaned over the table onto his forearms. "Gentlemen, if I have to get up out of this chair, you four men will be paying for ALL THE DAMAGE in this fine establishment!"

"The only thing that's going to get broke around here is you BOY!" the Logger to his right shouted out.

"Like I calmly just asked… do you gentlemen promise to pay for all the damages for all the broken furniture and dishes during this little demonstration of 'WHY,' I will drink a beer anytime I desire." Wapiti calmly stated, leaning back in his chair, continuing to look the size of the men over.

"Gladly, No problem, we have more than enough money, we all just got paid!" the Four Men proudly shouted out. Looking around the room at everyone, then back at Wapiti as he slowly stood up, walked around the side of the table till he was facing all four men just over three feet away.

Wapiti waited for about three seconds as they chuckled and were looking at each other wondering if he was really going to take him on. So with their attention briefly off him he reached out and grabbed the Cowboy to his right with both hands, doing a full back spin turning around swinging motion he threw him into the other Cowboy sending them both stumbling over chair's and crashing to the floor, one on top of the other. Ducking down under the fist of the Logger to his right. He brought his own right up into and under the sternum of the logger to his left, making the man feel like his heart had just exploded in his chest and he fell lifeless to the floor. As his face instantly turned to a deep purple from lack of ability to breathe. Spinning around on his left foot he brought his right fist around, drilling the man dead center of his face, breaking his nose, blackening both eyes, and knocking the man out cold as his body crashed down on top of a table behind himself, breaking two legs on that side and sending dishes and food flying around as he fell to the floor. Seeing the other two Cowboys standing up and starting to come at him. He did another two-seventy spin on his left foot and caught the first Cowboy on the right on the side of his head with his right foot, giving him a severe concussion sending his lifeless body flying over one table and crashing down on the floor between the next closest table. Turning to face the last man, Wapiti quickly ducked under the man's right blow allowing him to bring his left up under the man's left rib cage, causing the man to lift his head up and body backwards in pain. Bringing his right fist from down low, to up under the man's chin with everything he had. Nearly ripping the man's head off sending him flying upwards and backwards crashing down onto a table at least five feet away, breaking it into as his lifeless body laid knocked out cold.

Wapiti looked down at the four men laying around on the floor, then around the room at everyone else. Walking over to a table, Wapiti picked up a large pitcher of water, and started dumping it on their faces waking them up with a big smile on his face. "Good Morning Gentlemen, now how stupid do you feel right now…Four of you, and only one little ole me. You men don't only look, but you must feel foolish because you did it in front of all these people here." Wapiti was explaining, when the waitress returned with his beer. Thanking her, he opened it up and took a big drink. Slowly wiped his mouth off and continued. "Counting you four, I'm now up to thirty five scalps, or as you whites like to call it…notches on my gun. How many more do I have to take on before you all start respecting me and my people. Since I've been a Deputy U.S. Marshal, I've seen far more drunkin stupid things done by you White Eyes, than I've ever seen done by drunkin stupid Indians. To begin with… we don't carry pistols, so No-One gets shot during our drunken brawls." He said, continuing to look around the room at everyone, then back to the four slowly staggering to stand back up and get their eyes to focus on what was going on around them.

For the first thirty seconds or so, the four men couldn't remember what had happened to them and wondered why their heads hurt like hell. They were all dazed and confused, their eyes were all blurry making it hard to see anything or anyone clearly, and through the ringing in their heads they could hear Wapiti talking, as they started looking back at each other, then around the room at all the people staring at them with fear in their eyes. What had just happened, how did that Buck Indian take all four of them out in less than thirty seconds and not ONE of them even laid a hand on him. They were all beginning to wonder and remember, three continuing to hold their acking heads and one still trying to breathe. But all four were listening to what Wapiti was saying.

"Now gentlemen, we had an agreement from the beginning of our little miss understanding, that you would pay for all broken merchandise. That table has two broken legs, and those two both have at least one. Then there's all the broken dishes on the floor as well." Wapiti was explaining while pointing them out. "Carmen, could you please come out here and tell these four gentlemen how much they owe in damages please."

"Deputy, damages like these down at one of the Saloon cost's about fifty buck's." one of the logger's started saying, as all four men started reaching in their pockets for their wallets. "But there, you don't have the dishes, so we'll throw in another fifty, will that cover it Ma'am." He continued, taking money from the others, adding it up, he handed it to Carmen.

Carmen took the money, looked at it, then around the room at all the damage, then around at all the people standing watching everything that had happened. "I thank you men for the money and the entertainment... This will more than cover the damages. But I do have one request of each of you...you either shake Deputy Wapiti's hand and apologize to him, or you will never be allowed in My Restaurant ever again, Do I Make Myself Clear Gentlemen!" she demanded, glaring into each man's eyes.

"Yes Ma'am," all four men answered. Still trying to get the acking heads to stop hurting and spinning. Slowly, all four men stood full up, took one more look at each other, then around the room. Then, one by one they apologized to Wapiti and shook his hand. Then politely excused themselves and headed towards the door.

"I don't know why you people don't leave Deputy Wapiti alone, he has more than proved himself to be a good honorable man." Carmen proudly said. "He's been living here almost four months and I've never seen him drunk. You men like a cold beer after a hard day's work, why not him too." She concluded, then walked back into the kitchen.

Shawn came walking out of the shower room drying his hair off with a towel. "What'd I miss?" he asked, looking around the room.

"Deputy Wapiti beat up four men all by himself, Marshal!" Jose said, with excitement in his voice and his eyes. "You should have seen it, Marshal, four men, two almost as big as you, not one of them even hit him once and he Knocked Them All Out."

"What really happened?" Shawn asked, looking around at all the people slowly walking back over to their tables and setting back down.

"Just like the boy said." A man closest to the Marshal stated while chuckling out at the same time..

"Four Men, WHY, he don't have a mark on him!" Shawn spat out, looking around the room.

"Like the boy said, he didn't give them a chance to Marshal." Another man started explaining. "Truthfully, it was over with before it really even got started. Wapiti took every man out with one blow from his powerful fists or his feet."

"Where are the four men at now?" Shawn asked, looking around the room. "I'd like to meet 'em."

"Their over at the Doc's office, I do believe…I think they're all over there looking for some kind of pain pill to make the hurting in their heads go away." Another man said, chuckling. "Young Deputy Wapiti there knocked each one out cold. Then had the pleasure of waking each one back up by dumping cold water in their faces. It kinda reminded me of some of the fight's I've seen you in Marshal. Only with you, someone gets to hit you a couple times, but not with

Young Wapiti there." The man continued pointing at Wapiti. "He cleaned their clock before they knew what hit 'em."

"I bet they're still trying to figure out what did hit them." Another man yelled out, chuckling a little. "How many scalps you up to now Wapiti?" Shawn asked. Proudly, puffing his chest up for the effect.

"Thirty five." Wapiti answered proudly

"The last time we were up to your village, Chief Joseph gave you a head dress with twenty four feathers in it, one for every enemy soldier defeated in the line of duty and earning everyone's respect along the way…He's only been on the job for four months now, I bet by years end, his feather's will reach the ground." Shawn said, with a big smile on his face. "Well Wapiti, the tub's yours."

"Thanks Marshal, but I haven't eaten yet." Wapiti said, setting back down at the table and the waitress put his plate of food down in front of him.

"What can I get you Marshal?" the waitress asked, "Or do you need a menu."

"What Wapiti's having looks good. But you'd better bring two more beers to please?" Shawn answered

"Right away Marshal." The waitress said, walking away.

"What started the fight?" Shawn asked Wapiti.

"Me, ordering a beer, those men said Indian's weren't allowed to have alcohol off the reservation." Wapiti said, smiling and taking another big pull off the bottle, emptying it. Then he set the empty bottle on the table. "I think I changed their minds again, just like in that little town last week."

"I didn't get to see that fight either." Shawn said, loud enough for everyone to hear him. "Seems like no-one wants to bother you till I'm not around to help out…This makes three times now in the last couple weeks. Three, four men at a time, just like tonight, they too were over with before they began." He was bragging up till the waitress returned with the beers.

Then, taking them both, he opened one and handed it to Wapiti. "Anyone going to say he can't have this beer." Shawn loudly asked

"Knock it off Marshal." Wapiti quietly said, in between bits.

"OOHH, Alright…I just hope next time I get to see the fight, instead of just hearing about it." Shawn said, still speaking in a loud enough voice so everyone could hear him.

"How long you think the Judge will give us off till we have to go back out again?" Wapiti asked

"I hope not for a couple days at least." Shawn said, just as the waitress set his food down in front of him. "Is there anything else I can get either of you?" the Waitress asked

"No thank you." Wapiti answered

"I'll take another beer please." Shawn said, cutting into his T-bone Steak.

"Yes Sir Marshal, I'll be right back." The waitress said, then headed back towards the kitchen.

Wapiti quickly finished his dinner and headed for a nice hot bath. Shawn too quickly ate his dinner, finishing up just a couple minutes after Wapiti, getting one more cold beer he took it with him out the shack.

Setting down at the small table outside he slowly started drinking his beer. Taking out his pocket watch, he looked at it. It was just past seven-thirty. After only a few more minutes, Shawn stood up, took a couple more big pulls off the bottle till it was empty. Setting the bottle in a half full crate of empty bottles, then walked over to his nice soft bed and fell quickly sound asleep.

It had only taken Wapiti twenty minutes most to finish his bath, get another beer and head back out to their shack. Quietly walking up on the wooden porch, he sat down and slowly enjoyed his last beer and the cool night breeze. He could hear men arguing over in Moser's Saloon. It only took Wapiti about twenty minutes to slowly drink his last beer for the night. But it was so peaceful and relaxing watching the sun slowly go down behind the mountains to the west. Taking his last drink off the bottle, he reached down and put the empty in the crate next to the wall. Standing up, he stretched his arms full out, then quietly walked over to his bed trying not to wake the Marshal. But it didn't work, he had only taken a couple steps inside the shack when Shawn rolled over to see who it was. Then quickly fell back asleep, with Wapiti doing the same.

The next thing either one could remember was waking up to the smell of coffee inside the shack. Which meant Carmen had sent one of the kids out with a hot plate and a pot of coffee. They both looked at each other, then over at the coffee pot setting on the table a couple feet away. They both wanted a cup, but neither one wanted to get out of bed to get it.

After a couple minutes, they both decided to get up and have a cup of Carmen's coffee. Neither one knew what she did different, but her coffee was the best in the State and Wapiti said so, filling up both cup's.

"I have to agree with you Wapiti." Shawn said, "Why don't you bring that out on the front porch." He said, walking towards the door.

"Sure thing Marshal." Wapiti answered, following him out the door to the little table. Setting the hot plate and coffee down on the table, Wapiti sat down.

Within a couple minutes Griselda came walking up asking them what it was they wanted for breakfast and where did they want to eat it at?

"I'll take a large stack of pancakes, three eggs over easy, and both sausage and bacon please." Shawn said

"I'll have the same thing." Wapiti said, and I think we'll eat out here. "What do you think, Marshal?"

"Out here sounds good to me." Shawn answered, looking back at Griselda.

"Ok, I'll be right back with it as soon as Mom gets it cooked." Griselda answered, then she ran back towards the restaurant.

"When do we have to go see the Judge?" Wapiti asked

"He likes it when I come in right after lunch around one o-clock." Shawn answered

"What time is it now?" Wapiti asked

"Hell if I know." Shawn spat out, taking his pocket watch out and looking at it. "It's almost nine-thirty." He said, putting his watch back inside his pants pocket. Then, he refilled their coffee cups.

"It sure is a nice morning, not too hot, but peaceful and relaxing." Wapiti said

"I have to agree with you." Shawn answered. Looking between the buildings towards the bank across the street. In some cases they could hear the people talking, but couldn't make out exactly what they were talking about.

The two had been enjoying the relaxing morning for about five minutes when Jose and Griselda both brought out their food and a fresh coffee pot and hot plate. Thanking them for it, Shawn tipped each one a silver dollar.

It only took them maybe ten minutes to eat, but it was a nice relaxing ten minutes that they both enjoyed eating at their own pace, instead of the hurry up mode they'd been in over the last couple weeks.

They were just finishing up when Sheriff Twick Shaver came walking towards them. "Good morning Marshal, Wapiti. How you two doing this morning?"

"Alright!" Shawn said, picking up another empty cup, he blew out and filled it up for Twick. "So what's up with you Sheriff."

"Not much, just thought I'd come over and talk with you men to see what you've been up to." Twick asked

"Just chasing Outlaw's." Shawn said, taking a bite of food. "How have things been going around here?"

"The usual Saloon fight's, a couple small-time cattle rustler's... other than that, it's been boring around here." Twick answered

"You been keeping up with your target practice?" Shawn asked

"Yeah, Gordy and I come over at least a couple evening's every week. I'm getting faster and better at hitting the paper targets, but how do I know I can shoot a real person?" Twick asked

"Just remember one thing...If you don't shoot them first, they're going to shoot you." Shawn said, with a serious look on his face. "He who hesitates even just one second, is the dead one Sheriff."

"That's what Gordy keeps reminding me." Twick answered "How many people have you had to shoot it out with so far Wapiti?"

"Just one, Tom Skerritt, over in La Grande last month." Wapiti answered

"He was suppose to be one of the fastest guns out there." Twick said, looking back and forth between the two.

"I heard that too, so I was ready when he pulled his pistol and I was able to shoot it out of his hand." Wapiti said, assuredly. "Then I was warned about a snub nose 38 he kept in his back, so when he reached for it, I shot him in his right shoulder making him drop the gun to the floor, then I warned him, if he tried to pull that knife in his boot on me while I was handcuffing him, I shove it up his ass and it'd hurt to shit for a few weeks

"What about the men in his Gang, didn't any of them try to back his play?" Twick asked

"He was down to just having a young scared kid with him when I caught up to him. I knew I wouldn't have to worry about him. Cause he was frozen in place and staring at me with nothing but fear in his eyes. I figured he'd make his play for his pistol as he was standing up, I was right…He started to pull it when he was about half way up. Thanks to all the Marshal's practicing, I pulled my pistol and shot his out of his hand." He started joking about it, like he couldn't believe I was that fast, talking to all the people in the room hoping to draw my attention towards the crowd of people and not at him. All the while he's reaching for the 38 in his back. Continuing to repeat how fast I thought I was, why, if I'd give him a second chance the outcome would be different next time. Then the local Deputy came in hollering about "What the hell is going on in here!. Tom took the chance that maybe it had taken my attention away from him, so he tried to pull the pistol on me, so I shot him in his right shoulder… then I told him if he tried to grab for his knife while I was walking across the room, my third bullet would be center mass." Everyone in the room knew Center Mass, meant dead center heart shot.

"So did he go for the knife?" Twick asked chuckling, but respectably.

"NO … he threw it on the floor." Wapiti answered

"How'd you know about the 38 and the knife?" Twick asked

"One of their members had gotten shot, so they split up into two groups. One of the two men I first caught up with told me about them." Wapiti answered.

"That was nice of him." Twick said "I haven't been tested with my gun yet, but I have had the pleasure of breaking up some Saloon fights. But only two men at a time, not three and four at a time like you can Wapiti." He chuckled, reaching over and slapping him on the shoulder. "I just wish I could get to see one of your fights.

Everyone hears stories from the spectator's how fast you take everyone out. They say you're a sight to see…! How about it Marshal, are they as much fun to watch as everyone says they are?"

"Like you, I only hear the stories. But a couple times I got to hear the rucass start, but by the time I got there to see what was happening, they've all been over with." Shawn said "Out there on the trail we've come across some camp sight's where the kids are playing Cops and Robbers. They draw sticks to see who gets to be U.S. Deputy Marshal Wapiti!" Shawn said, braggingly.

"I know, they're doing it here too!" Twick said, with excitement in his voice. "Like the Marshal here, you're becoming a legend."

"Just doing my job." Wapiti said, with a big smile on his face. "I have to admit it, I do like it when small groups of men come at me and tell me I'm not welcome…I like changing their minds."

Twick looked at his pocket watch, it was just after ten-thirty. "OH SHIT! Court started five minutes ago. I need to get over there or Judge Monson will be mad as hell and you know it Marshal." Then shaking both men's hands, he took off running towards Main Street.

"He's right, Judge Monson don't like it when you're not there to testify when your case comes up. Cause then he has to postpone the case to a later date. Fact, in some cases if he don't know all the facts, he don't think it's as bad as it really was, so he dismisses the charges all together."

"Why don't you just re-arrest them?" Wapiti asked

"CAN'T, all charges have been dropped. So, he's innocent of all charges. Regardless of what they were." Shawn stated, pouring a small shot of whiskey in his coffee.

"What are you thinkin about this morning, Marshal?" Wapiti asked, trying not to laugh.

"Don't you worry about what I'm thinking about!" Shawn said, smiling behind his coffee cup, before taking a drink.

"Alright Marshal." Wapiti answered, still smiling and standing up. "I'll get the gun cleaning kits so we can get some of the dust out of our guns."

"That sounds like a good idea." Shawn said, following Wapiti into the shack. Where they both grabbed their pistol's and rifle's and headed back outside, set back down and started cleaning the gun's when Jose came running up.

"Mom wants to know if you guys need anything Marshal?" Jose asked

"How about a pitcher of cold tea please." Shawn answered, then looked over at Wapiti. "Cold tea sound good to you?"

"Yeah, it does." Wapiti answered, briefly looking over at them. Then, went back to running the long rod up and down the barrel of his rifle.

"Ok. I'll be right back." Jose said, turning and running back towards the restaurant.

Neither one said much while they cleaned their gun, till Jose returned with the pitcher of cold tea and three cup's. "Can I get my pistol and clean it Marshal?" he asked

"I cleaned it after the last time we practiced, so it don't need cleaning." Shawn answered

"OH, OK." Jose said, with disappointment in his voice.

"I'll let you clean it the next time." Shawn said

"Can we practice shooting today Marshal?" Jose excitedly asked.

"Maybe tomorrow son, today I don't want to do anything but rest and relax after our last huntin' trip." Shawn answered, pouring a large shot of whiskey into his tall glass of cold tea.

"It looks like he has some serious thinkin' to do too." Wapiti said, with a big smile on his face.

"BITE ME!" Shawn said, looking over at Wapiti with a disgusted look on his face.

Wapiti just smiled at him and started cleaning his pistol. Which only took them about ten minutes to finish and Shawn took his pocket watch out. It was just about eleven o-clock.

CHAPTER 2

"Jose, could you do me a favor?" Shawn asked, putting his pistol back in his holster and picking up his rifle.

"Yes Sir Marshal, what do you need me to do?" Jose asked

"Wake me up around twelve-thirty so we can make it over to see the Judge by one." Shawn said, walking back inside the shack.

"Sure thing Marshal, Wapiti…are you going to lay down too?" Jose asked

"A nap does sound real good." Wapiti said, standing up and picking up his rifle. Then reaching into his pocket he pulled out a silver dollar and handed it to him. "Would you please bring us another pitcher of cold tea when you wake us up. It would be nice to have something cold to drink when we get up."

"Yes Sir Wapiti." Jose said, walking back towards the restaurant.

Shawn and Wapiti headed for their beds and laid back down. Within ten minutes, Shawn was sawing timber with his snoring.

Wapiti was tired, but he really couldn't fall asleep. He was thinking about what the Marshal had told all the people in the restaurant yesterday. The last four months that he'd been on the job have been exciting…He was right, it had been. Was the last thing he could remember thinking about when Jose was shaking his foot and telling him it was time to wake back up.

"UUHH" Wapiti mumbled rolling back over, wondering to himself how long he had slept. Setting up, he reached for the cup of cold tea Jose was handing him. "I brought the Marshal a cup too. But I bet he will want this cold beer here more." Jose said, walking over towards Shawn who was waking up and setting up.

"Marshal, I brought you and Wapiti that pitcher of cold tea, but I also brought you a cold beer." Jose said, handing it to him.

"No son, I can't drink that and go see the Judge with beer on my breath. But I can put a shot in my ice tea and he won't be able to smell it." Shawn said "But thanks for the thought, cause any other time I would want that cold beer."

Jose quickly filled the Marshal cup and gave it to him. "Thanks," Shawn said, taking a big drink. Then stood up, walked over to the table and refilled his cup. Then took out his flask and poured a couple shot's worth in, stirred it around with his finger. Then licking his finger, with a big smile on his face. "Now I'm ready to out-think the Judge… Come on Wapiti." He said walking towards the back of the building a few more building's down to come out across the street from the Court House.

Stepping up on the boardwalk, he looked up and down the street. There was actually a lot of foot traffic as well as horses and wagons. Taking a couple small drinks out of his cold tea, he started across the street trying not to spill any. Even though he had to dodge two trotting horses and one near runaway wagon, he spilt very little ice tea in the crossing and he showed it to Wapiti.

"I lost about a third of a cup when that old lady lost control of her Chariot." Wapiti chuckled out, looking at the wet spot down the front of his shirt. "There should be a law against old people who can't control their horses any more. They shouldn't be able to drive a wagon anymore…They could kill someone."

"You'll live, come on." Shawn said, walking over to the Court House, then inside and upstairs to the Judge's office.

Knocking on the door, he slowly opened it and looked inside. "Ruth, you in here?" Shawn called out, slowly walking in.

"Back Here Marshal." Ruth yelled back, walking back out of the Judge's office and back into hers. Deputy Wapiti, Marshal it's good to see you again. I hear tell you let prey get away from you Marshal." She said, with a big beautiful smile on her face.

"If you call living two, to three months out on that ocean, then winding up in a land of people you can't talk to. They got away without doing any time. Stop and think about...their stuck on a floating island out there in that big, vast Pacific Ocean. They ain't going to see anything but water for as far as their eyes can see, no land in any direction for months on end. Since there's only enough beds on the ship for the crew, the Carpenter Brothers just might be sleeping in the hay storage area...If you call that getting away, then they got away." Shawn said, smiling and looking around at every-one, including the Judge who was setting at his desk with a big smile on his face.

"Hearing you put it like that Marshal, I almost have to agree with you. Please come in." Judge Monson said, standing up and extending his hand to both men. Then asked if they needed any-thing to drink.

"No thanks, we brought our own." Shawn said, holding his large glass of cold tea up.

"It's probably spiked with whiskey knowing you Marshal." Judge Monson said, with a disgusted look on his face. "Now then, this Butch Cassidy and Sundance Kid thing that went down over in Baker City last week." The Judge started talking, but Shawn cut him off.

"Over a week ago Your Honor. If none of that gold has shown up yet, it never will." Shawn stated

"How can you be sure they didn't hide it and are just waiting for the right time to come back and safely get it out of town. Didn't you say you knew the young men that they were known to be with?" Judge Monson asked

"Yes I did, Your Honor. If they'd had the serial numbers from the cash that was stolen you might be able to find them. But if Randy Larkin figured it out, he had to have a hell of a lot of help to move that much gold in one night." Shawn said, taking a small drink. "Think about it, Your Honor, where and how would they hide that much gold. THEN, you know they're watching you, so Where, When, and How do you try and cash it in ANYWHERE." Shawn stated

"So where do you think the gold is then Marshal?" Judge Monson asked

"Knowing Randy, he probably split it up into smaller bags and gave some to everyone in town." Shawn boastfully said. "So how did they get in the vault anyhow?"

"Supposedly they dug a tunnel off the side of one of their opium tunnels that runs down under Baker City, it went up the outside of their new large underground safe and vault room on the backend. Then broke through the cement wall, cut the lock off the steel doors from the inside." Judge Monson explained.

"Well there's who stole it, them Chinamen!" Shawn shouted out. "Think about it, Your Honor, it took weeks to dig that tunnel. That job had to be planned out a couple weeks in advance. If it was me, I'd be looking into who was in charge of digging those tunnel's and start with his and all his family's house's to see if they hid that gold under their floor boards." "They Did That, and came up with nothing." Judge Monson said.

"Well then I don't know what to tell ya Your Honor, But I'll be damned if I'm going on a wild goose chance looking for something that no-one else can seem to find. So what else has been going on around the State." Shawn asked, taking a big drink off his ice tea.

"There's a new Gang of Outlaws been robbing trains, stage coaches, and bank's from Pendleton to Ontario over the last month." Judge Monson said, pulling the wanted posters out that had a picture of what each one looked like. "These three are the Kostman Brothers. Jim, Mike, and Kevin respectfully. They haven't killed anyone yet, but they have shot a couple drivers and half dozen plus passenger."

"Ontario, Can't the Marshal out of Boise cover that area?" Shawn asked

"He cover's Idaho, and YOU cover Oregon Marshal." Judge Monson stated. Looking back and forth between Shawn and Wapiti. "By the way, Deputy…I'd like to commend you on how you handled that situation over in the restaurant last evening. You Did It Without Using Your Gun Too!" He said, staring straight into Shawn's face.

"Now Your Honor, Those Men CHOSE To Fight Hand To Hand, No Gun's Involved…I wish they all did." Shawn stated, staring right back into Judge Monson's face. "Those four young men last night, that was a respectable thing. Those men had no respect for Deputy Wapiti. It wasn't an Outlaw situation, it wasn't a life or death situation, so gun's thank God were ever used."

"I know, you've only killed men that were shooting at you first. But in the four month's since Wapiti has come on board you've only killed one man." Judge Monson politely and calmly said.

"That man was trying to…" Shawn started saying, but the Judge cut him off.

"I Know Marshal, and yes, I'm very grateful you were there or Deputy Wapiti might not be with us." Judge Monson again said it gratefully and sincerely.

"Your Honor these robbery's started in Pendleton and have hit every City in conception. Their heading for Idaho." Shawn said, running his finger over the pathway that the Gang was taken on the large map of the State on the wall.

"I think they live somewhere this side of Pendleton. They started out at a Pendleton bank, then the next evening robbed the train passengers at Meacham when the train stopped to take on more water. Then a couple days later they hit a bank in La Grande, then hit a west bound stagecoach just outside North Powder that had three different banks' money on board heading for Portland." Judge Monson was explaining.

"What Idiot Banker Would Send His Money Veya Stage Over The Train Nowadays?" Shawn disgustedly asked

"I hear ya Marshal." Judge Monson said "I'd choose the train vault over a stagecoach everytime. Now, back to our robber's. A couple days later they hit a bank in Baker City. Then three days ago they hit a bank in Ontario. Now they should have enough money to live well and lay low for five to six months if they spend it wisely.

"Then by your own calculations they headed for somewhere in Idaho to lay low. Why else go the extra seventy plus miles from Baker City to rob one more bank and then head back this way to lay low." Shawn said, still looking the map over and taking his last drink of cold tea. "Ruth Darlin, do you have any more cold tea made up?"

"Yes Sir," Ruth answered, smiling over at him, and standing up. "Deputy Wapiti, would you like some more cold tea too?'

"Yes please Miss Twidwell." Wapiti said

"I'll be right back, gentlemen." Ruth said, walking out of the room and over to a cold storage, storage cabinet and took out the gallon jar of tea and brought it back, quickly re-filling everyone's glass, including hers. Which emptied the container, so she picked her pad of paper back up and set back down in her chair.

"I'll still bet they're heading back this way to lay low now Marshal. That way when they run out of money in five, six months like you said. Then, they could start all over again at the beginning starting back in Pendleton." Judge Monson was pointing out.

"That would mean they'd have to live at least this side of Hermiston, cause whoever drew these poster's did a good job. These faces would be easily recognizable, if the wrong person were to see them out and about." Shawn said, looking the poster's back over. "I personally think it's a waste of time, but you're the Boss." he said, picking up his cold tea glass, he poured a good healthy shot of whiskey into his cup and started to swirling it around to mix it up.

It instantly pissed Judge Monson off. "FELTON, it ain't even two o-lock in the afternoon and you're already drinkin'!"

"Not enough to do any harm." Shawn said, taking a small drink.

"He claims it helps him think better, Your Honor." Wapiti said with a small chuckle

"With as much as he drinks, he should be a Law Professor by now!" Judge Monson stated

"It's still a little weak." Shawn says, opening his flask back up and dumped another good shot's worth in. Then took another small sip. "That'll do just fine… Now, back to you Your Honor, I Know More About The Law Than That New Bone Head Public Defender Does…! So, you really want us to go chasing after a Gang that is probably going to lay low for awhile, according to your own thinking. Don't you think we'd be wasting our time, or better yet. Your Honor, how about you let me and Wapiti rest up for a couple days then we'll gladly go chasing after these three men." Shawn said, picking up the three wanted posters. But at least give us a couple days to rest up before we have to ride clear to the other side of the state."

"You can tie your horses to the stage from here to the Rail Head in Madras. Put your horses in the livestock car, get yourselves your own sleeper berth to catch up on your sleep going up to The Dalles. Then do the same thing on the train to Pendleton." Judge Monson said graciously.

"There won't be no sleeper car on the train from Madras to The Dalles. They only have one, maybe two passenger cars. The rest are empty flatbed rail hauling cars going back to be reloaded." Shawn said "One more thing Your Honor, you really think they'll be riding their horses back across one and sixty plus miles of ruff country in just a couple days." Shawn said

"Just then one of the Ticket Agent's from the Train Station came walking thru the front door. "Your Honor, I Have A Wire For You!" he called out, walking through Miss Twidwell's office and into the Judge's Office handing it to him.

"NO, but like you said those posters are excellently drawn, according to this wire, these three men were seen boarding the train in Huntington early this morning around seven A.M. The Ticket Agent says they bought three one-way tickets to Portland."

"Why come back to Huntington to board the train?" Wapiti asked

"Cause there's nothing there." Shawn said, looking at the map. "That's smart, there wouldn't be too many people around there that early in the morning. Less chance of anyone seeing and recognizing them."

"So they've been on the train heading this way for approxamintly seven hours." Shawn said looking back up at the map. "We can take this evening's stage to Madras, get in there in time to hopefully catch the train before it pulls back out heading north again. Figure from Huntington to The Dalles is approximately two hundred and seventy miles, give or take. Figure the train will average twenty miles an hour over the Blues. That's about thirteen and a half hours time, then figure in your major stop's. Baker City, La Grande, Pendleton, Boardman, add an hour for each one of them, so four more, makes seventeen. Then they have a half dozen smaller stop's to take on water. Figure thirty minutes each, that's another three. So all toll they should reach The Dalles in about twenty hours, give or take.

Taking out his pocket watch. "It's three o-clock now. So two hours before the stage pulls out, then four hour to Madras. That's thirteen hours, figure, ninety miles from Madras to The Dalles. Again, twenty mile an hour, that's four and a half. That brings us up to seventeen hrs. There's three water stop's, so that's another one and a half two hours. Which puts us getting into The Dalles about an hour ahead of them if we're lucky." Shawn said, turning and looking at the Judge. "But it all hinges on us catching that train in Madras… We miss it, and we miss them!"

"The evening stage, it'll be dark before we get there.' Wapiti said. "Just how the hell are we suppose to get any sleep being thrown around inside the dusty cab on a stagecoach?"

"It's only a little over four hour ride, you'll survive for that long… Miss. Twidwell." Judge Monson said, turning his head to face her. "I don't know when the next north-bound train will be pulling out. So you get down to the tele-graph office and tell them to send a message to the Madras Train Depot. Tell them that the late train don't leave town till the Marshal and Deputy are on board. You tell them they'll be there as fast as they can get there."

"Yes Sir, Your Honor." Ruth answered, standing up. "I'll get over there as fast as I can. Marshal, would you like me to do anything for you?"

"No thanks darlin. If the Judge wants use to catch the next stage we need to get going ourselves to get our gear together." Shawn said, looking at her with a big smile on his face. Shawn pulled out his pocket watch and looked at it. "It's going on three o-clock, the evening stage is suppose to pull out around five. We can rent a couple of good horses from the Livery in The Dalles when we get there if we need them."

"Alright Your Honor, I'll go on this wild goose chase of yours on one condition." Wapiti said, glaring directly into the Judge's eyes as he stood up.

"What's your request?" Judge Monson asked, not liking the way Wapiti was talking to him, and the look in his eyes, they made him feel uneasy inside.

"This ain't a request, it's a demand." Wapiti said sternly, still glaring into the Judge's face. "We haven't had more than a couple hours of relaxation time off since I signed on four months ago. When we get back from this little excursion of yours, we get two full days and three night off before we have to go chase anymore Outlaw's."

"I'll see what I can do about that. Like I told the Marshal earlier, he's the only U.S. Marshal in the state of Oregon. Yes, there's a half dozen of you U.S. Deputy Marshal's, But Shawn here is the only Full Marshal. So that means he get first crack at trying to bring in our serial robber's or killer's." Judge Monson said, looking back and forth between the two men. "But I promise I'll try and get you both a couple days off just as soon as I can Wapiti." Judge Monson said, apologetically.

"Now you know why my death count is so high." Shawn said, walking towards the door with Wapiti, but looking back at the Judge. "I always get the ones that have nothing to lose, if they do come in sitting up, then the Judge there is just going to hang them anyhow, so why come in alive at all."

"You men just be safe out there." Judge Monson yelled out, watching them close the door behind them.

They both stopped just outside the door, and looked up and down the street. Then, they started crossing it to the other side. Then walked in between the buildings and back over to their shake. Where they both packed up a backpack full of clean clothes and any other gear they might need. Then they walked over to the wash basin, pumped it full of water, and washed their hands and face off. Then they walked thru the back door of the restaurant and over to an empty table and sat down.

They had barley set down and one of the waitresses was at their table, handing each one a menu and a cold beer. "Do you men know what you want, or should I give you a couple minutes?' she asked, looking back and forth between the two men.

"I want a medium rare T-Bone steak with all the fixin's." Wapiti said, handing her the menu back and opening his beer.

"That sounds good to me too." Shawn said, handing her his menu. "Could you please ask Carmen to give us a couple cold beers to take with us when we leave?"

"Yes Sir Marshal. I'll wait till you finish your meals, then I'll put four in a burlap bag for you to take with you." The waitress answered, walking away.

"You really think we're going to catch up with those men in The Dalles before they go thru and end up somewhere around Portland?" Wapiti asked, looking around the room at everyone still staring at him like he was diseased. They were all afraid of him, but respectfully afraid of him.

Shawn couldn't help but start chuckling at everyone and telling Wapiti the very same thing about the respect they now have for him. "A No Good Stinkin Redskin has earned everyone's respect as a true Lawman, and they hated to admit it."

"It's alright Marshal, they don't scare me." Wapiti said, looking around the room.

"Maybe not, but you sure as the hell have them all scared of you." Shawn said, loud enough that everyone could hear him. "After yesterday's little brawl, you took the fight out of them."

That is exactly what they all were thinking of as they all started talking again. They all wished they had been in here last night and seen the fight. Would ANYONE in here this afternoon tell him he couldn't have a cold beer with his dinner.

It only took the waitress ten minutes and she was setting their food down in front of them. Shawn took his pocket watch out and looked at it. "It was just a little before four, so they could take their time and enjoy their meal."

"You never answered my question Marshal…You really think we'll be able to catch up with those men before they get to the Portland area and get lost in the crowd of people?" Wapiti asked "They've already been on the train all day."

"Yeah, but it's a long slow ride thru the canyon's and up over the Blue's till they get to Pendleton." Shawn said

When they were about half way through their dinner, the waitress brought them each over a new beer. "Thank You Very Much Young Lady." Shawn said, taking the last drink off his beer. Then he exchanged bottles with her.

Wapiti also thanked her and gave her his empty bottle in exchange for the new cold beer. Opening it up, he took a big drink. Setting the bottle on the table, he looked over at the Marshal. "You Really Think We're Going To Catch Up With Them!" He said, shaking his head in disbelief, taking another bite of steak.

"You just got thru tellin' the Judge you wanted to rest and relax for a couple days." Shawn said

"You call riding a dusty, jumpin up and down stage coach for three plus hours, then waiting around at the train station for the train if they didn't get it stopped. If they did, then we get to try and sleep on a two person bench seat. What part of that is comfortable and relaxing." Wapiti stated, swallowing his food, then washing it down with a drink off his beer.

"If we have to wait for the train in Madras, we'll get a hotel room." Shawn said

Finishing up dinner, Shawn looked at his pocket watch. It was twenty minutes to five. "Well let's get over to the Stage Coach Station and see how many people we have to contend with." He said, putting a couple dollars down for a tip for the waitress.

Wapiti did the same thing, then picked up his pack he headed towards the door. Still muttering under his breath just how much of a waste of time this is going to be. "They may have bought tickets for all the way to Portland, but they could get off anywhere in between as well. This was like looking for a needle in the haystack." He continued saying as they crossed the street to the Stagecoach Office.

They both looked around at the people waiting on the stage, some setting, and some standing. Shawn walked up to the Agent. "Two for the Stage to Madras and put it on my Marshal's account."

"Marshal, I only have one seat left." The Ticket Agent calmly said.

Shawn started looking around the room at everyone. "Who's all waiting for the Stage to Madras?"

"That Lady and her two children, and those two men sitting right there." The Agent said pointing.

Shawn looked at the two men, they were both wearing nice three piece suits. Looking down on the floor between them he saw a shiny silver briefcase. "I remember that briefcase." He said walking towards the men.

The smaller of the two reached down for and grabbed the briefcase, while the bigger one stood up and got in the Marshal's way, preventing him from getting too close to the briefcase. "What can I do for you Marshal?" the bigger man asked

"That's one of those fancy new dynamite proof briefcases, isn't it?" Shawn asked, looking both men over.

"What if it is?" the Guard said, looking down at Shawn's pistol.

"What say we all step outside for a little talk?" Shawn said, reaching around the Guard and grabbing the other man by the arm leading him outside. With the Guard and Wapiti right behind them.

Walking over to the edge of the building where no-one else could hear them. Shawn took one more quick look around, then started speaking in a low voice. "Now I know you have something very valuable inside that fancy briefcase. That's why you have this man to protect you, I respect that. But I need two seats on that Stage, either I guard you till we get to Madras where you can wait at the local Sheriff's office for him to catch up, OR, you both can wait here for the next stage around ten o-clock tonight."

"We'll take the later Coach." The man with the briefcase said. "But they charge ten dollars a ticket to change ticket's."

Reaching in his pocket, Shawn took out his wallet and took out a twenty dollar bill and gave it to the man. "I sure do appreciate this gentlemen. Fact, here's an extra twenty, go over to Carmen's Mexican/ American Restaurant and have dinner on me."

"Thanks Marshal." The man said, taking the money. "Glad we could help you."

They all four walked back inside and up to the Ticket Agent with Shawn leading the way. "Alright, they're taking the ten o-clock Stage. Now who's driving my Stage?"

"HELL IF I KNOW MARSHAL." The Agent yelled out. "They come and go faster than you do…most likely some rookie in one seat or the other."

"That's ok, now give me my tickets. If I don't turn them back in with my paperwork for each case, they don't reimburse for anything I don't have a receipt for." Shawn stated

"Yes Sir Marshal, Right Away Marshal." The Ticket Agent said, nervously filling out the paperwork for both seats, and handed Shawn the receipt as fast as he could get it done.

"Now You're Not Going To Charge These Men Any Ticket Exchange Charge Either!" Shawn demanded, looking over at the shorter man with a small smile on his face.

"I'm sorry Marshal, but it's company policy." The Ticket Agent, calmly said.

"What kind of policy is that?" Shawn said, in a serious, but a chuckling voice at the same time walking towards the door. "Come on Wapiti."

"Yes Sir Marshal." Wapiti said, following behind him and out to the boardwalk. Where the Stage Coach was pulling up along the outside. One man on top of the wagon was tossing luggage and mail bags off.

"How long till you pull out?" Shawn called up to the man.

"Don't know Mister," the man answered "My man riding shotgun is over at the Doc's with a severe headache."

"Well I'm Marshal Felton, I can ride shotgun if you need me to." Shawn said

"Sorry Marshal, didn't see who you were." The man said, standing on his knees, looking down at the Marshal, tossing two more Duffle bags off the top of the Stage.

"Sure would be nice if you did, Jake was one of them boy's over." Starting to chuckle, the Driver continued. "Three of those men's heads were damaged so bad, they still can't see straight or walk straight. Doc Becky said they all had bad concussions and needed to lay down for their brains to heal up."

"That's what happens when you try to tell someone they can't have something." Shawn said, with a big smile on his face. Opening the Stage door for the Lady and her two children to climb aboard.

"Wapiti, Tell them other two men we have room for them if they want to come on this Stage." Shawn yelled towards the men walking out the front door of the office.

"I Want To Be Able To Stretch Out A Little." Wapiti yelled back

The two men heard the Marshal's request of Wapiti to ask them. "I'd really like that Marshal." The one with the briefcase said, walking towards the Stage.

"I ain't going to be cramped up in there like those fish in a can that the Marshal eats." Wapiti said, pointing. "I want to be able to stretch out a little and maybe take a nap. So you two take the next Stage Please."

"Yes Sir, Deputy." The man said, stopping in his tracks and grabbing the arm of his guard to stop him too.

Within five minutes they were all loaded up and heading out of town. Wapiti was setting on one side of the StageCoach and the young twenty something lady and her two children were seating on the other side. Both kids were staring at Wapiti and hugging up against their mother.

"Sorry Deputy Wapiti, they're really bashful, I'm Janetta and these are my daughter's, Lori,5, and Susan 4…Girl's, this is U.S. Deputy Marshal Wapiti, he's one of the good guys." Janetta started explaining.

"But Daddy says some Indians scalp white people." Lori said, still staring up at Wapiti's face and long hair. "How come you have long hair like a girl?" she asked

"LORI, you shouldn't ask him that." Janetta quietly, but sternly said.

"It's alright Ma'am." Wapiti said, smiling. "My people believe no question is stupid. Kids speak anything and everything that comes into their heads. Sometimes it can be embarrassing for the parent's."

"Yes it can." Janetta shyly answered

"Don't worry about it Ma'am." Wapiti said, with a big smile on his face. Reaching inside his saddlebags, he pushed the paper bag of candy sticks, grabbing onto as many as he could, pulling them out he leaned over towards the girls with at least five different colors of hard candy sticks in his hand. "Here, pick a piece." He said

Both girl's started smilingly, slowly, and shyly reached out and took a piece of candy. Then quickly put their arms back around their Mom. "Girls, what do you say to Deputy Wapiti?"

"Thank you Deputy Wapiti" both girls said at the same time.

"My people wear their hair long for Spiritual Strength and Wisdom from the Heavenly Father." Wapiti said

"How does the length of his hair make him stronger Momma?" Susan asked, looking up at her.

"It's hard to explain sweetheart, but people show their love and respect to Heaven in many different ways." Janetta calmly said, smiling. "Isn't that the way you see it too Deputy?"

"Yes Ma'am it is." Wapiti answered "Girls, here's each of you one more piece of candy, if you promise not to be too loud and let me try to get a nap. If you're good, I'll give you each another piece when I wake up. He said, handing the girls each another piece of candy.

"I want the red one." Lori said, reaching to take it ahead of Susan.

"I want the red one." Susan yelled back, reaching for it too.

"It's alright girls." Wapiti said with a big smile on his face, he opened up his saddle bag. "I have plenty more of all kinds." Taking out a second red one he gave one to each girl.

"Thank you Deputy Wapiti, we promise we'll be quiet so you can take a nap." Both girls happily answered.

"But Momma, how's he going to sleep with the Stagecoach bouncing around so much?" Lori asked

"I'll do the best I can." Wapiti said, turning a little sideways, putting his pack up against the wall for a pillow and he did his best to try and fall asleep.

CHAPTER 3

"I'm Bob Jenson." The Coach Driver said, slapping down the rein's on the backs of all six horses and headed down the street. "It's a pleasure to meet you Marshal."

"Likewise." Shawn said, holding his hand out to shake his hand, holding the double barrel shotgun with the other. "So you men been having any trouble with hold ups?"

"YEP, at least one stage every couple of weeks between this way, or between Madras to Bend." Bob said, pulling out a fifth of whiskey. "Hope you don't mind if I drink and drive Marshal, sometimes that luke warm water don't wash this thick dirt down your throat."

"No, I don't mind as long as you share." Shawn said, with a big smile on his face.

"So who you chasing after that the Judge is making them hold the night train up for you?" Bob asked

"Three Kostman Brothers have been robbing everything from Pendleton to Ontario." Shawn answered.

"You're going all the way to Ontario to try and catch up with them. Why don't one of the Marshal's over in Idaho try and catch them?" Bob asked, slapping the rein's on the horses again.

"They were seen buying three tickets back to Portland this morning in Huntington. So the Judge wants us to try and head them off in The Dalles." Shawn said, taking the bottle from the driver and taking a small pull off it. "Don't mean to tell a man how to do his job, but aren't you running these horses a little fast for a thirty mile trip."

"No, a couple months back they stationed three replacement teams at a young widow's place at Rimrock Spring's." Bob said, taking one last small drink before putting the bottle back down beside his seat.

"That was nice of somebody." Shawn said

"Tell ya the truth, I think the Head honcho for the Stage Coach Company is having a thing with her on the side that his wife doesn't know about, and she thinks he's single, or at least that's what she's told me." Bob said, with a disgusted look on his face.

"Why hasn't anyone told her he's married?" Shawn asked

"They're all afraid of losing their jobs if they tell her." Bob answered

Shawn was surprised at how much traffic was on the road and at the speed Bob was running the stage they were flying by anyone and everyone that they had came across. A couple times he drove the Stage directly down the center of the road forcing the south bound wagon off the road. The northbound driver had no clue as to what was going on until they quickly passed them, causing their horses into running off the other side of the road.

Not only was he running everyone off the road, but he was dusting them all out as well. Shawn suggested that he slow down a little bit. But Bob said if they didn't make Madras by nine o-clock at the latest, he would be docked a quarter of his wages.

"What, don't they pay you by the trip?" Shawn asked

"YEAH, I get fifty bucks each way." Bob answered "I get four hours each way, that includes stopping and changing horses at Rimrock Spring's."

"With the two of us, it shouldn't take us much more than thirty minutes to change out the team. So you can slow these down just a little bit, if you don't mind." Shawn said

"I never thought you'd be afraid of a runaway Stagecoach." Bob chuckled, slowing the team down to a medium trot. "I usually run them hard like that for about an hour then slow them down to a slow trot for the rest of the way to the Stage Stop."

"It's a good thing they only have to travel fifteen miles at that speed, running them that hard for that long, you could kill a good horse." Shawn stated

"The trip used to take five plus hours with one team, cause you couldn't run them this hard your right. But now, changing the team out like we do, they cut our travel time down. So now we have no choice but to run them hard." Bob said.

They had been running along at a good medium pace out across the valley floor, in and out of the timber for a good hour and the traffic was letting up as everyone started pulling over to make camp for the night. The sun was just barley above the mountain ridge tops when all of a sudden on a blind corner the road was blocked with a large downed tree.

Bob started pulling back on the brake with everything he had, he knew the horses would stop themselves. The problem was getting that Coach slowed down and stopped before they ran up over the backs of the horses in front on them. Shawn was holding on to the seat with his right hand and the shotgun in is left, the horses just barely got stopped before they crashed into the tree, and the Stagecoach slid sideways for the last thirty feet before it came to a stop.

"TOSS THE SHOTGUN, OR I'LL DROP YOU." They heard a voice say, so Shawn instantly tossed the shotgun into the brush and started looking for whoever it was that was out there.

When he saw them, one riding down the hill to his left, and two directly in front of them. The one doing the talking was one of the two in front of them. "We Don't Need No Shootin Gentlemen!" Shawn said, pulling his coat over his lap and putting his hands in the air.

"That's very wise old man." The leader said. "Throw down the strong box, and what kind of passenger's do we have on board." He continued speaking, riding closer to the Stage.

"Bob, throw the box off." Shawn said calmly, looking the three men over, as Bob threw the cash box to the ground.

The one coming down the hill was maybe fifteen years old if he was lucky, by the look in his eyes this was his first robbery, Shawn thought. The other two, mid to late twenties, and this wasn't their first time. "We only have a family of four inside the Coach."

"Come on, Everyone Outside." The leader shouted, riding up to within ten feet of the Stage.

"You and the girl get out of here, move to the back of the Coach if you can." Wapiti whispered to Janetta, slowly opening the door. "Tell them I'm Sick and have been throwing up."

"WE'RE COMING OUT!" Janetta yelled out. Then she slowly stepped down out of the coach followed by her two girl's.

"I thought you said four people were inside?" the Leader yelled out. "Come on, get out of there."

"My husband is very sick with the pox, he has big blisters all over his body." Janetta said, holding the girls close to her side and slowly walking backwards.

"That's far enough Ma'am, I can see you don't have much." Their leader said, looking her over. "But then again, gold is up over twenty five an ounce, and your ring has what looks like a very large diamond on it...Starting to ride closer to her.

"Just stop right there Mister, Ma'am, please just toss him the ring." Shawn said, nodding his head, working his right hand closer to his pistol under his coat. The two main Outlaws were barely ten feet away, riding side by side, only five feet apart.

"Alright, you two jump down off there too." Their leader told them.

"Bob, you go down your side, and I'll go down mine." Shawn said, slowly leaning over. "Alright Mister, just don't get gun happy, we're coming down."

"Now You Daddy!" the leader said, turning his eyes in the direction of the Stage door, looking into the darkness of the Coach.

That was exactly what Shawn was waiting for, him to take his eyes off me. Throwing the coat aside with his left hand, he pulled his pistol, firing two quick shots, shooting the pistols out of the hands of both Outlaws, before they knew what hit them. Then he quickly turned and faced the Youngman on his left and told him to drop it, OR, he would drop him.

The kid was frozen in place and wasn't sure of what had just happened "HHHHHHHH,,,WWHHAATT." He started to say.

"I said drop it, or I'll drop you!" Shawn demanded, one more time.

"UUUHH   YYEESSS   SSIIRRR MMAARRRSHHSHAAALLLL." He stammered, stuttering and dropping his pistol to the ground. Then slowly, he held his hands up. While the other two were cursing up a storm from the pain that came with a hole thru the middle of their hands "Now I could have just killed all three of you for this stupid stunt you thought you were going to get away with." Shawn started explaining, as Wapiti stepped out of the Coach with his pistol drawn.

"You all three should have just been killed!" Shawn demanded again, looking over at the teenager. "Is that what you want son, to be DEAD!" he yelled at the kid.

"NNNOOO SSSIIIRRR." The Youngman said, staring at the barrel of the Wapiti's .44 pistol. It was the biggest barrel he had ever seen. "PPPLLEEAASSEE MMAARRSSSHHAALLL, DDDOONN'TTT SSHHOOTT...!"

"I'm not going to shoot you son, put your arms down, Not you two, get them up in the air." Shawn demanded from them. "Wapiti, I have some handcuffs in my saddle bags here." He said, throwing them to the ground at his feet.

"Yes Sir Marshal." Wapiti said, taking three pair out and walked over to the two closest men first. "Put your hands behind your backs gentlemen." He told them.

"Just how the hell are we supposed to guide our horses with our hands cuffed behind us and what are we supposed to hold on to?" Their leader was shouting out as Wapiti cuffed his hands behind his back.

"I'll tie your horses off to the Coach and lead you boys in." Shawn said. Then looking over to the teenager. "When did you hook up with these two?"

"They stayed at my parent's house a couple days ago...they made it sound fun and exciting." The Youngman nervously started explaining.

"FUN AND EXCITING, you should be dead right now... does that sound Fun and Exciting!" Shawn yelled at the Youngman again. "Where you from son?' Shawn asked calmly

"Just outside Madras, my Dad has a half section I help him farm." The Youngman answered, looking around at everyone, and seeing Wapiti walking towards him.

"Bet you wish you were back there right now, don't ya?" Shawn asked

"Yes Sir, I do." He answered, putting his hands behind his back.

"Hold up Wapiti." Shawn said, waving him back with his free hand. "Can you promise me, if I let you go home, that you'll never do anything stupid like this again?"

"YES SIR MARSHAL, I PROMISE!" the Youngman started saying and apologizing for it at the same time. "This wasn't any fun Marshal, I've learned my lesson. Please believe me…I don't want to go to prison."

"Alright son, I'll let you go this one time. BUT if I EVER, catch you robbing anyone again, I'll see you're charged with armed robbery. That's three to five years of making little rocks out of big rocks, UNDERSTAND!" Shawn said, looking straight into his eyes. He could see the fear in them from the beginning. But with his last remark, there was a little sparkle of hope in his watery eyes. It was all the Youngman could do not to start crying like a child, he was scared for his life.

"Thank you so much Marshal!" the Youngman started saying. "I promise you I'll never do ANYTHING like this ever again if you let me go Marshal, I Promise…!"

"Alright then, get on your way." Shawn told the Youngman.

"We promise we'll never try anything like this again either Marshal." Both the other men started saying. "Promise, we see what could happen, you changed our minds too."

"Like Hell, I wasn't born yesterday. I bet when I get you back to Madras and run your names, I'll bet you both have done time already for robbery." Shawn said, jumping down off the Stage Coach.

"YEAH, once I did prison time, but you shootin' me in my gun hand changed my mind about robbing anymore again Marshal."

The leader kept saying. "Like you said, we should be dead right now."

"Shut up Mister." Shawn said, grabbing their reins in one hand, he lead the horses over to the back of the coach. Taking their two lariat's, he removed the bridle's off the horses and tied one end of the rope to the halter and the other end to the back of the stage. "Wapiti, you and Bob see if you can move that tree?"

Then looking back up at the two Outlaw's. "Using these lariat's like this will enable us to travel faster without your horses getting tangled up with the Coach." Starting to chuckle. "But you boys are going to be eating dust all the way to Madras."

"It'd be quicker to tie one of their lariats around one end of the tree, tie the other end off to the kid's horse, it would be easier and faster to pull it out of our way." Wapiti said, looking over at the log, then back at the Marshal.

"Youngman, use your horse and rope and do what Deputy Wapiti needs you to do." Shawn said, looking back over to the teenager.

"Yes Sir Marshal," he said, untying his rope. He rode over and put the loop around the bigger end which was off the ground already from the branch's holding it up. Then Wapiti and Bob got on the back side to push. With the help from the horse, they pushed and he pulled the tree around and over towards the other side of the road out of their way.

"Thank you Youngman," Shawn said, walking over to him as he rolled his rope back up. Holding his hand out, he shook the Youngman's hand. "Don't make me regret this son!"

"NO SIR MARSHAL, I Promise." The Youngman said. "I'll never steal anything as long as I live. I learned my lesson, Marshal."

"I hope so, now get out of here before I change my mind." Shawn said, turning and walking back to the Stagecoach to see everyone was back on board and ready to leave. "You men had better hang on because our driver has to make up for lost time." He said, climbing back up into the driver's seat and the Coach headed down the road at a slow trot.

"I said let's go." Shawn said, with a big smile on his face, looking back at the two Outlaw's trying to hang on to the small rim around their saddle's seat, squeezing tightly with their legs.

"SLOW DOWN!" they started shouting at the Marshal.

It had only been a couple miles further to the Stage Stop. "Let's hurry up and get these animals changed out and get out of here as fast as we can." Shawn said, jumping down off the Coach as it came to a stop. "Come on Wapiti, help me catch the new team out of the corral."

"Take the team in the middle Corral." They heard a lady's voice tell them.

"Thanks Ma'am," Shawn said, waving back to her, as he and Wapiti walked into the corral and quickly attached all the lead ropes to their halters, then led them back to the Stage. Where Bob was in the process of unhooking the horses.

"Bob hasn't told me why you men are running almost an hour behind time?" the Lady said

"Those two men back there tried to hold us up Ma'am." Shawn said

"Shawn, meet the Widow Lady." Bob said, starting to remove the harnesses from the old team.

"It's a pleasure to meet you Ma'am, sorry to hear about your husband." Shawn said, helping to change all the harnesses out as fast as they could.

"I've never been married Marshal, but my first BO. Dad caught us up in the hayloft enjoying a recently new found way of enjoying each other companionship, if you get my meanin'." The Widow Lady said.

"Yes I do Ma'am." Shawn said, smiling. "I remember a few of those hayloft's when I was a younger."

"Well, any how Dad's first barrel he fired in the air to get our attention, WHICH of course it did. My Bo jumped up, pulled his pants up while running for the open door jumping down to the ground below. When he was about thirty yards or so, my Dad shot him in the ass with rock salt."

"I bet that hurt like hell." Shawn said, chuckling a little.

"Well Sir, the story got out that Dad killed that Youngman instead of just wounding him. So after that no boy's or men would come near me. So they started calling me the Widow Lady…and it stuck. Tell ya the truth, very few people even know my real name."

"Mind if I ask what it is Ma'am?" Shawn asked, putting another collar over a horse's head.

"Not at all, it's Karen." She said "But I prefer The Widow Lady. That way none of the men that come through here don't try anything with me, if you understand what I'm saying Marshal?"

"Yes Ma'am I can." Shawn said, turning and facing her. "It's a respect thing, they feel sorry for you so they leave you alone in the way I believe you're talking about."

"It is, and they do. Sure, some of them offer me good money. But with the tip's, this little Café makes me a good living." Karen said. "Speaking of which, what can I fix you folks to eat before you pull out."

"We Could Use Something Cold To Drink." One of the Outlaw's shouted out.

"I'll get to ya," Shawn yelled back at them. "Could you make us some hamburgers and deep fried tators to go please?"

"Right away Marshal." Karen said, walking back inside.

"How we supposed to eat with our hands cuffed behind our backs?" the Leader asked

"Who said I was feeding you. As far as I'm concerned, you men can wait till we get to Madras." Shawn said, walking up to the men. "Now, I'm going to uncuff one of your hands, you will bring them around in front of yourselves so I can recuff you. This way you can hang on easier."

"Yes Sir Marshal, thank you." They both started saying and turning their hands in the direction of the Marshal.

Reaching up, Shawn unlocked the cuff of one hand of the Leader. When he brought them back around to the front, Shawn wrapped the open cuff around the saddle horn and locked it down. "This will detour you from trying to jump off your horse on the way back. Cause if you do happen to fall off, you'll get drug for a long way before we notice you." Then Shawn quickly did the same to the other Outlaw.

"How about something to drink Marshal?" both Outlaw's asked again.

"Alright," Shawn said, walking over to the Stagecoach and took down the water bag and walked back over to the men and handing it up to them.

The second man grabbed the bag first and started to take a big drink of the warm water. But he quickly spit it back out. "This water's almost hot enough to take a bath in, could you please refill it with fresh water Marshal?" he asked

"You're lucky I'm in a good mood today." Shawn said, taking the bag back. Starting to dump the water out walking over to the pump and started pumping it. Then quickly refilling the bag and walked back over to the two Outlaw's.

"Here, try this." Shawn said, handing the man the water bag.

He quickly started taking a long drink off the bag, when the Leader was reaching over with his free hand trying to get the water bag for himself. Turning his head away, he quickly took a second drink. Then he handed it to the Leader.

He too took a big long drink right off. Being behind the Coach had been a dusty ride and they were covered from head to toe in dust now. They kept passing the bag back and forth between themselves while Shawn, Wapiti and Bob continued switching out the team of horses.

They were just finishing up when Karen came back out with eight hamburgers in one back and the same number of fried tator orders in the other. Walking over to the Coach, she handed the bags to Janetta. "Here's a couple Sasburilla's for you and the girls to drink Ma'am."

"Thank you Ma'am, how much do I owe you?" Janetta asked, opening her purse.

"I get reimbursed for the Marshal, Deputy and all prisoner's from the State. I'll just say you folks were part of the Marshal's group. What they don't know, won't hurt them." Karen said, with a big smile on her face. "How about you give me two of those hamburger's and I'll give them to the Outlaw's to eat."

"Ok," Janetta said, handing her two hamburgers. "You sure you don't want me to pay you for me and the girl's." She said, reaching back into her purse.

"Really, it's no problem." Karen said, walking back to the Outlaw's and giving each man one.

Both men started eating, but had only had a couple bite's when Bob shouted out that they were ready to pull out. "Let us finish our hamburgers at least." The leader shouted out.

"Sorry boys, but because of you this Stage is a good hour behind time. So I advise you to hang on tight." Shawn said, grabbing what was left in the two bags and climbed back aboard the stage. Thanking Karen one last time, the Stagecoach headed back down the road at a slow trot while they both ate their dinner.

It may have only taken ten minutes to eat, but in those ten minute it had gotten darker. But the near full moon was giving them enough light to see the road. So, no sooner did Bob finish his hamburger and he slapped the rein's down hard on the backs of the horses and they leaped into a full out run.

Catching everyone but him off guard. Shawn was in the process of taking a drink off his flask. But he went flying backward and the bottle came flying straight back into his face. Both Outlaw's were lucky they each already had one hand one the saddle horn, or they would be getting drug right now. Within the next hundred feet the dirt and dust started coming up off the road from the Coach's wheel's started hitting them in their eyes, mouth and up their noses with a massive, burning stinging feeling from every grain of sand and dirt hitting them. They both reached for their hats with their free hands to hold over their faces to protect themselves. Leaning forward, riding blind, they held on for life. All three girls came flying across the inside of the Stage ending up on top of Wapiti.

Janetta and the two girls quickly climbed off Wapiti, everyone was laughing about what had just happened and was he alright?"

"I'm fine." Wapiti said, rubbing his head. "But which one of you kicked me in the head?"

"I think it was me," Susan said, smiling shyly. "I was standing up in my seat, then I went flying through the air flipping over with my head in your lap and my feet somewhere up around your head."

Within a manner of minutes the Stagecoach was traveling at a steady speed. With the help of the leaf spring's, so each girl crumbled on each side of Janetta using her thigh as a pillow. The ride inside was really pretty smooth, the seat cushions were nicely done.

They were soft and comfortable to lay on for the outside two seats. But with Janetta being in the middle she couldn't stretch out as well.

"Why don't one of you girls come over and lay down in this seat, that way we all will have our own little corner of the Coach to ourselves." Wapiti says in a joking, but spooky voice. Reaching over and grabbing Susan's toes. "If part of your body comes into my corner, then I can take it."

"NO!" Susan says, pulling her foot back. Smiling and giggling at the same time.

"Remember, I've got the candy." Wapiti said, holding up a couple pieces.

"I'll Move!" Lori said, jumping down out of their seat, tripping and falling face first into the seat cushion, bloodying her top lip, and she started crying a little.

Both Janetta and Wapiti reach for Lori at the same time. But with her being on Wapiti's side of the coach, he picked her up first and started looking her over. "You alright?"

"YEAH," Lori shyly said, touching her bloody lip with her fingers and looking at it and showing it to Wapiti. "See, I have an owy!"

"I see that, why don't you let your Mommy kiss it all Better." Wapiti said, standing Lori up on her feet.

"I'm ok, can I please have a red candy stick?" Lori asked, smiling up at Wapiti.

"Sure Darlin, why don't you just sit right over here first." Wapiti said, picking her up and setting her in the other corner. "Now, let's see what colors of candy I have." He said, opening his saddle bag' "Looks like I have green, blue."

"I Want Blue!" Susan said, jumping up in her seat.

"Settle down girls." Janetta said, reaching to stop her from falling off the seat with one arm and reaching for the piece of candy with the other arm.

"Here." Wapiti said, handing her the piece of candy. "Kids can be a handful at times."

"When do I get my red candy?" Susan asked

"Susan, that's not a nice way of asking for candy." Janetta started saying.

"But Lori already got her piece." Susan said pointing over at her sister.

"Just a second sweetheart." Wapiti said, continuing to look through the paper bags. "I have green, yellow, orange, another yellow."

"I want red!" Susan said

"I'm looking, but I don't see any more red." Wapiti said, looking inside the paper bag. "All's I have left are green, yellow, purple, pink, and orange."

"What's green taste like?" Susan asked

"Like a tart green apple, they're really good." Wapiti said, handing her one.

"OK, thank you Deputy Wapiti." Susan said, sitting down in her seat and within a few seconds the two girl could only think about eating that long piece of hard candy.

"Thank you Deputy." Janetta said "They're both overly excited about meeting you, and then seeing the Marshal shoot the pistol's out of the hands of those two Outlaw's. Their friends at school will never believe them."

"Yes they will Mommy, cause you can tell them it's true." Lori said. "You're not supposed to lie, HUH, Deputy Wapiti."

"That's right honey, now leave Deputy Wapiti alone. I'm sorry Deputy." Janetta said, with a flustered look on her face.

"It's alright Ma'am. I enjoy joking with the kids. Believe it or not, it actually helps calm their parents down too." Wapiti said, handing her the bag of candy. "What flavor would you like?

"I'll take a pink one." Janetta said, pulling one out of the bag, then handing it back to Wapiti. "Thank you."

"You're very welcome Ma'am." Wapiti said, taking the bag back and putting it away.

"These are good Mommy." Both girls said, sucking on the candy stick.

"They sure are, that was nice of Deputy Wapiti to share with us." Janetta said.

"Daddy says you should always share." Lori answered

"That's right sweetheart. We should always share." Janetta said

Within five minutes both the girls were sound asleep, and Wapiti and Janetta weren't far behind.

CHAPTER 4

"Don't you warn folks before you do that?" Shawn shouted at him. "Besides, I don't think we need to be going this fast…Can you even see the road?" he asked, getting a better seat and a better and stronger grip on the side rail.

"Sure I can Marshal, can't you see that darker line going down the middle of the valley here. Hell, there ain't much more than one or two small turns in the road from here to Madras."

"You sure about that?" Shawn asked, staring into the dusky conditions they were riding thru.

"Sure I am Marshal. I make this run five times a week." Bob answered, slapping the horses again.

"I don't care if you do, I would much appreciate it if you'd slow this Coach down." Shawn said.

"OOOH, ALRIGHT!" Bob said, slowly the horses to a medium trot.

"Thank you." Shawn said, repositioning himself on the bench seat again. Then took a pull off his flask, handing it over to Bob when he finished.

"Thanks Marshal, but I have my own, remember." Bob said, taking a small pull off the flask anyway.

"I carry a smaller flask so I don't drink too much." Shawn said, taking the flask back.

"This bottle stay's with the coach so whoever is driving can have a couple drinks and no-one can see." Bob said, with a big smile on his face. "Rule number one to all new drivers…You empty it, you replace it at the next stop."

"What happens if they forget?" Shawn asked

"They get the shit kicked out of themselves." Bob quickly answered, starting to chuckled. "Whoever the next drive is, if he reaches down and finds the bottle empty, at his next stop he wires the home office out of Madras, then the other Driver's go over to his house at what would be the middle of the night for him, sometimes that can be twelve noon if you drove all night like I'm doing tonight. But all the other driver's, and there's ten driver's to cover this run and down to Bend, north to Warm springs, then there's a team that comes from Maupin which is fifty-four miles, so in the middle of nowhere they put in a stagestop. It's ran by a single mother and her two boy's. She's actually a very beautiful and desirable lady. Now, she runs a class A meal and her boy's take care of their livestock, she has a milk cow, this years calve and the one from last year getting fattened up to be butchered for next winter's meat. Her and many other small restaurants around here, since the meat only lasts about a week, each member, and they have over fifty-two, they each butcher their steer when their day comes up in line drawn out of the hat. Anyway, back to beautiful Barbra, more than one rich businessman has gotten off that north or south bound coach until the next one comes through about twelve hours later. I'm here to tell you she gets as much as the top ladies at the cathouse in Terrebonne." starting to chuckle again. "There's been more than one coach accidentally on purpose break down in Terrebonne, the ladies go get something to eat, while the men customers, they pay us extra money to show why we were broke down. They also have to get Dave to sign a work order, because we have to show work paid out for the reason. So

Dave get's a third of the actual bill, on top of our normal change team out time, so the men on that specific coach can spend a couple hours inside playin with the ladies. There again, many young men stay until the next coach comes through.

As the moon got higher, it was easier to see the road, even for Shawn. But the speed they were traveling at was plenty fast enough as far as he was concerned. So he wasn't going to say anything to Bob about how clear the night really was.

After a good two and a half hours of mostly silent traveling they could see the street lights that lit some of the main street of Madras. After another twenty or so minutes they could see the train all lit up, sitting on the tracks waiting for them before it could pull out.

Take us by the Sheriff Office first Bob, if you could please?" Shawn asked

"No problem Marshal, it's just a couple doors up from the Stage Stop." Bob said, slowing the team down to a walk the rest of the way in.

Shawn pulled out his pocket watch and looked at it as they rode past the first street lantern, it was just about nine-thirty. "Looks like we're a little late."

"That's alright, they can't dock my wages when I can prove we were robbed." Bob said, smiling and pointing his thumb towards the two Outlaw's tied to the back of the Coach. "With them and you as my evidence, I just might get some kind of reward."

"Reward for what?" Shawn asked, looking down the endless street ahead of them.

"WHY, because not one of my passengers was injured during the hold up." Bob said. "That should be worth something."

"They weren't hurt cause I was there, you had nothing to do with the outcome of what happened out there." Shawn said

"I kept the passenger's calm during the entire episode." Bob proudly said, pulling into the station.

"Episode my ass." Shawn chuckled, looking over at Bob, waiting for the Stage Coach to come to a complete stop. "You don't even have a gun, so how the hell did you have anything to say what happened during that little so called episode back down the road... But I'll see to it they don't dock you your wages."

"Much appreciated Marshal." Bob said, holding his hand out to shake the Marshal's hand as the Stage Coach came to a stop. "Truthfully, I'm glad we had you around. Not that they'd gotten away with much. But you never know what some of those robber's will do to a beautiful young lady. I hate to say it, but in ten years of driving Stage Coaches I've seen plenty of young Lady's drug off into the bush's and sexually molested and there wasn't a damned thing anybody could do to stop them either."

"I've seen the outcome you're talking about too many times over the last thirty plus years of being a Lawman of sort's...I'll tell ya Bob, if it was up to me, I'd castrate all the rapists. But the Judges just tack on another year or two. Well, it's been good traveling with you Sir, but we need to get going. I don't know just how long they've already held that train up for us and I have to turn those two over to the town Sheriff Deputy."

"What two men Mister...Bob, why, you so late. We were just about to send out a search party." They heard a man say.

"Deputy, I'm U.S. Marshal Shawn Felton," Shawn said, getting down from the stage and opening the door. "I've got two prisoners tied up outback there." He said, pointing with his rifle.

Wapiti was the first one out, carrying Lori in his arms and speaking in a low voice. "Just let me help Janetta get these girls inside and I'll be right back to help you Marshal."

"Sounds fine Wapiti, I'll meet you over at the jail house." Shawn said, walking towards the back of the Stage Coach where he got his first look at the two Outlaw's. They each were caked with two inches of dust.

"I told you boys you'd get a little dusty on the way in." Shawn chuckled, walking up to them with his handcuff key in his hand. "If I were you Deputy, I'd get the Fire Department out here to wash these boys off before letting them lay down in one of the beds..

"Right now I'd take a water trough to jump in." the second man said, as Shawn unlocked the cuff from around the saddle horn and recuffed his hands behind his back. Helping him off his horse, Shawn walked over to the Leader and did the same thing.

They both started jumping up and down trying to knock some of the dust off themselves and everyone within ten feet down wind of them started getting covered in dust too. A few of them started cursing them out because of it. Shawn just laughed and turned them towards the jail house a couple doors down. "Come on you two. Deputy, I want you to hold these men on charges of attempted armed robbery. When the next jail Coach heading for Prineville comes thru put them on it. They can sit in jail and wait till I get back to testify against them."

"Yes Sir Marshal, I'll be sure to do that. Now you and Deputy Wapiti need to get over to the train. They've been holding it up for over four hours and some of the people are getting a little hot under their collar if you get my meanin'." The Deputy said, stopping just outside the Jail House.

"They'll be alright." Shawn said, looking around at everyone. "Wapiti, you got all our gear?"

"Yes Sir Marshal." Wapiti said, walking up beside him and handing him his pack. "It's a good thing the station is only a couple more blocks away." He said, walking beside the Marshal.

Walking up the street they could see at least fifty people under the lantern's standing on the landing waiting to board the train. When they were within a block they started hearing some of the voices and they were all cursing the fact that the train had been held up for almost five hours. They were supposed to pull out at four-thirty, and it's after ten now. Some understood they were waiting on the marshal and Deputy Wapiti, but waiting this long was ridiculous.

Then they had all heard the Stagecoach had pulled in well over a half hour ago. So what could possibly be still holding them up, when were they going to get there.

They had just stepped off the boardwalk and started crossing the street over to the Depot. When the first person saw them. "It's about time Marshal!" a man yelled out. "Now we can load up and get hell out of here."

"Sorry folks, but we had to deal with an attempted Stage Coach robbery or we'd have been here over an hour ago." Shawn spoke out loud enough so everyone could hear him.

"I can't believe they held up this train for a worthless Redskin." Someone in a group of men spat out.

"I think he should have to ride on top of one of the flat cars as opposed to inside any passenger car." They heard another voice from the same group shout out. While everyone else slowly started loading up into the train, but looking in their direction.

Shawn and Wapiti purposely walked in their direction. When they were about a half block away from the half dozen plus young men Shawn spoke up. "How many of you, against us two, says he rides in the passenger car and all the loser's ride the flat cat...What Do Ya Say Wapiti, Me and You Against, let's see here." He says, starting to count the men. "Six, seven, eight, nine... Nine against two...I like them odd's."

"Your Dreamin Old Man!" a man in a nice dress suit, shouted out. While Shawn and Wapiti walked up to the group.

"You Guys Ain't Going To Do Anything And You Know It. So Shut Your Mouths And Get Aboard!" the Head Porter Yelled out.

Everyone started agreeing with him telling the men to shut their mouths and get aboard so they could finally get out of town, or they WOULD be the one's riding the flat car.

"Son Of A Gun!" Shawn said, pushing his way into and through the group of men. "I knew these guys were nothin but MOUTH…! Get Out Of My Way, before I knock you out of my way."

Everybody stopped and stepped aside to let the Marshal and Wapiti board first. Some of the people were commenting that from what they'd been hearing and reading about Deputy Wapiti's hand-to-hand combat was something to see, so he could have any seat his heart desired.

Walking through the crowd of people they both climbed up the steps to the train. "That way Marshal." The Porter said, pointing down the Aisle way. "I'll bring you gentlemen a cold bottle of beer just as soon as we get rolling Marshal, is there anything else I can get for you and Deputy Wapiti?"

Shawn stopped and looked over at the Porter. "You have a dining car on this train?"

"Yes Sir Marshal, just keep going two cars towards the front." The Porter answered, pointing in the opposite direction.

"Thank you Youngman." Shawn said, stepping back around the Porter and headed towards the Dining car with Wapiti right behind him. Everyone already in the car went totally quiet when they started walking down the Aisle through both cars. Those who were standing in the Aisle, quickly stepped out of their way and in between the bench seat's so they could pass.

Excusing themselves and thanking everyone as they walked through the car to the dining car next. Walking it the same thing happened, everyone in the car went totally quiet and started staring at them. "Is there a empty table in here?" Shawn asked

"Right back here Marshal." A Porter yelled out. "You people get out of their way, right here Marshal, Deputy, what can I get you gentlemen to drink?"

"Couple cold beers and a menu please." Shawn answered, slowly working his way back to the table. Still thanking everyone for stepping aside. When they got to the table, they quickly sat down looking around at everyone still staring at them. "Why don't the rest of you set down before we start rolling and you don't accidentally end up on the floor."

Everyone agreed with him and they all quickly and quietly took their seats and waited for the Porter to return. Which only took a couple minutes and he returned with two beers and menus and gave them to Shawn and Wapiti. "Gentlemen, we have a Prime Rib dinner with all the works. Sixteen ounce is five-ninety five and the twelve ounce is three-ninety five."

"We'll each have a medium-rare sixteen ounce please." Wapiti said, handing the menu back, opening up his beer. After taking a long drink off the cold bottle he set it down on the table. "Now that hits the spot." He said

Within five minutes the train was heading down the track, while three Porters took care of everyone in the car. Other Porter's also came and went with food and drinks to some of the passenger's in the other cars.

It only took them about thirty minutes to finish eating so Shawn suggested they grab a couple beers and go to one of the other cars so someone else could come inside the dining car. "Alright," Wapiti answered, holding his arm up to get one of the Porter's attention.

It took less than a minute and the Porter that had been waiting on them was at their table asking what else could he get for them. Wapiti handed the man a twenty dollar bill, this is for our dinner and drink plus your tip. Then handing him another five dollar bill. "This is for two more beers, but could you please bring them to us in one of the other passenger cars?"

"Yes Sir Deputy, right away. You two go find yourselves a seat and I'll find you." The Porter said, taking the money and picking up the rest of their dirty dishes and headed towards the kitchen car.

They both stood up and Wapiti led the way back up and out of the dining car towards the passenger cars. Walking into the first car they could see over half the people were sound asleep, and all the seat's were full up with two people in each bench seat. Continuing on to the second passenger car they saw two empty seats.

So they each sat down in one and did their best to stretch out and tried to fall asleep. Wapiti sat and stared out the window into the darkness of the night. The sound of the train clicking and clacking its way down the track. He could see the near full moon floating across the sky along with a few bright stars. He was almost ready to fall asleep when he heard the train whistle blow and the train started slowing down.

Looking around, he could see a Porter laying a blanket over a small child. "Excuse me Sir, Why are we stopping." Wapiti asked, whispering.

"Just taking on some water, Deputy." The Porter answered, walking over to him. "If you'd like to stretch your legs, we'll be here for about twenty minutes."

"Thanks, but I'm going to try and get some sleep." Wapiti answered, laying back over, looking back out into the darkness of the night. He could see light flickering off in the distance towards the Engine. After maybe twenty minutes most, the train was clicking and clacking its way back down the track and Wapiti quickly fell asleep.

Before he knew it the whistle was blowing again scarring him up out of his seat, looking to hit anyone attacking him. The Porter started laughing at him. "Just stopping for more water." the Porter said

"How much longer till The Dalles." Wapiti asked

"Should only be just over an hour." The Porter answered, looking at his pocket watch. "It's just over five and half hours from Madras. It's almost two now. So after we top off with water and get going again we should be in The Dalles by three-thirty, four at the latest."

"Thanks." Wapiti answered, rolling back over, trying to get comfortable and hopefully fall back asleep.

"Any idea as to when the west bound train usually get to The Dalles?" Shawn asked

"Not for sure, but I believe it usually comes in between six and eight in the morning, Marshal." The Porter said

"GOOD, that'll give me a couple hours to set up some kind of trap for them. Wake me when we get close to town please." Shawn said, pulling his self made pillow back in place, closed his eyes and shortly fell back asleep.

Before he knew it, the Porter was tapping him on the shoulder, handing him a large cup of hot coffee telling him they'd be in The Dalles within ten minutes. Then he walked over and did the same to Wapiti. Both men thanked him for the coffee. Then started getting all their gear back together waiting for the train to pull in to the Depot. Taking out his watch, Shawn could see it was about three thirty.

Within a couple more minutes all the light's inside the passenger cars came on and the announcer said they were pulling into The Dalles. Thanks to all the hanging lanterns at the Depot, they could see everything clear. There were two sets of tracks on the mountain side of the Depot and five or six on the Columbia River side with numerous cars lined up on the outside four track's. With the Depot and loading dock's in between them.

Shawn stood up and walked towards the door with Wapiti right behind him so they could be the first two off the car when they pulled in. When they had entered the curtain covered area between the two cars they were met by one of the Porter's who was waiting to unlock and open the door after it came to a complete stop and not until the train had come to a complete stop either. The Porter was explaining, holding the key in one hand and a step stool in the other. "It's a safety issue."

"I don't care if it is, unlock that door now or I'll do it myself." Shawn demanded while the train was still slowing down.

"But Marshal, I can get fired if that door opens before the train has come to a complete stop." the Porter kept explaining.

Shawn reached over and grabbed the key. "You tell them I took it from you, now get out of my way." Shawn said, pushing the man aside. Then unlocked the door and opened it up. The train only rolled about another hundred feet before it came to a stop on the outside track closest to the mountain. Jumping down, Shawn crossed the next set of tracks and headed towards the Depot.

Walking inside he took a quick look around till he saw the Ticketing Booth's. Walking over to one that had an Agent inside. "Now Listen Close Mister...I only want to say this one time. I'm U.S. Marshal Shawn Felton and this is my Deputy, Wapiti. I want you to get over to the local law office and tell the Deputy on duty to wake the Sheriff first, then wake up everyone in their Posse and tell them to be down here as soon as they can...Do You Understand Son?" Shawn said

"Yes Sir Marshal." The Youngman said, "The Sheriff's Office is over on second east, two blocks away, I'll get there and back as fast as I can Marshal." He said, pulling the curtain down in front of his window, running over to the entrance gate, he ran out the front door and out of sight.

"How long till they're supposed to be here?" Wapiti asked

"Couple hours if we're lucky." Shawn said, taking a pull off his flask, then looking at his pocket watch again, thinking out loud, looking at the trains schedules on the wall board "It's a quarter after four, that train's not due in until seven…It'll be daylight by then so we'll be able to see everyone's face coming off that train real easy…I wonder how big their Posse is…with enough men, we could place guards on both sides of the passenger cars so no matter what side they try to get off on we should be able to catch them without much gunplay." After a couple minutes of thinking out loud, Shawn looked over into one of the other Ticket Agent's Booths. "Where can a man get a cup of coffee at around here?"

"There's a small Café at the other end of the Depot Sir." The Youngman answered, pointing in the direction.

"Thank you, come on Wapiti, let's get a cup of coffee and wait for the troop's to arrive." Shawn said, walking towards the other end of the Depot..

"Sounds good to me." Wapiti said, following beside the Marshal. Looking around the over hundred feet long and thirty feet wide Depot. One side had a half dozen doors for the passengers to come and go from the station. At the far end was the little Café the Ticket Agent had told them about. The other side had five Ticket booth's with the other office's coming a third of the way down. Then there was four big freight doors for the worker's to load and unload the freight thru. There wasn't more than ten people total inside right now. But when daylight comes that would all change.

Walking up to the Café counter they both sat down on a stool, just as the Cook met them with a pot of coffee. They each turned their cup's over and the Cook filled them up. "Can I get you gentlemen anything to eat?" the Cook asked

"No Sir, we had a large Prime Rib Dinner just a few hours ago, but we appreciate the offer." Shawn answered, pouring a small shot of whiskey in his coffee. "AND YES WAPITI, I am thinking."

"I didn't say anything Marshal." Wapiti said, smiling, holding his hands up.

"Marshal, I have some fresh made cinnamon rolls, with a nice powdered sugar glaze topping." The Cook said

"That does sound good." Shawn said, taking a sip of coffee. "Can you heat one up just a little for me?"

"Don't have too Marshal ... Like I just said, I just took them out of the oven a couple minutes ago." The Cook answered. "You like a lot or a little sugar icing?"

"Thick please." Shawn answered.

"Light frosting on mine please." Wapiti said, looking over at the Cook.

The two had finished one cinnamon roll and Shawn was on his second when the Ticket Agent returned with a Deputy Sheriff. "Marshal, this is Deputy Brad Johnson."

"Thank you Youngman, Deputy Johnson, where's the Sheriff at?" Shawn asked, standing up and shaking his hand.

"I sent another Deputy to wake him, then told him to go wake all the other Deputy's and all members of the Posse up as well." Deputy Johnson smartly answered, shaking Shawn's hand. Then reaching for Wapiti's hand. "Deputy, it's a real pleasure to meet you...Marshal, does he really beat three, four men at a time, or are those News Reporter's stretching the truth like they do with everything else."

"Well now son, to tell you the truth, I haven't seen his last three or four battle's. I just hear what sounds like all hell breaking loose. But by the time I get inside the room, it's all over with and there's bodies laying all over the place waiting to be packed to the nearest Doctor's Office." Shawn said in a bragatory voice, smiling and puffing his chest up.

"You need to start your own Self Defense Fighting School for people who want to become Law Officer's." Deputy Johnson says, smiling. "I know I'd pay to go to a school that would teach me to fight three, four men at a time in hand-to-hand combat. Don't get me wrong, we practice taking people down to the floor or ground safely, in ways that make it hard for them to resist and fight back, all the time. But, taking on that many men at one time and coming out on top...!"

"I've fought that many in one fight before, but I usually get bruised up by the end of the fight too...But Wapiti here, let's just say, I've haven't seen anyone Draw Blood on him yet." Shawn said

"There was one time back in John Day, when I didn't get out of the way of one punch totally, he got me in the corner of my mouth and split my lip." Wapiti said

"How many were you up against then?" Deputy Johnson asked, looking over at the Cook. "Can I get a cup of coffee please, and these men need a refill."

"Right away, Deputy." The Cook answered, picking up the hot pot of coffee, walking over he turned over another cup. Filled it up, then asked the Marshal and Wapiti to please turn around so he could fill theirs back up.

"Thank you Cooky." Shawn said, holding out his cup for him to refill. Then taking out his pint, he poured a small shot in.

"You'd better not let Sheriff Ryder see you do that, he told us if he ever caught any of us drinking on the job, he'd fire us on the spot and put us in jail for a week for Public Intoxication." Deputy Johnson said, with a serious look on his face.

CHAPTER 5

"Well son, a U.S. Marshal out ranks a County Sheriff everyday of the week!" Shawn chuckled out as a half dozen plus men came walking in the front door with rifle's in their hands and their holsters tied down to their sides. Seeing the Marshal and Deputy Johnson, they headed towards them.

The first man to get to him, stuck out his hand. "I'm Sheriff Mark Ryder, how can me and my men assist you Marshal?"

"Looking up at the clock on the wall, Shawn could see it was just after five. "We have the Kostman Brothers coming in on the next westbound train." Shawn said "Cooky, you'd better fill your big coffee pot up, cause there's going to be a lot of sleepy men comin' in soon."

"It's already brewing Marshal." Cooky answered "If anyone needs anything to eat, the grill is hot and ready to go as well."

"The Kostman Brothers, The only Kostman's I know live over in Biggs Junction. Jim Kostman is the Sheriff of Sherman County." Mark said, taking a large hot cup of coffee from the Cook. "Thanks John."

Shawn took the three posters out of his saddle bags and laid them out on the counter top. "These are the Kostman men we're looking for." Shawn said, looking briefly at the wanted posters, then back to the Sheriff. "You recognize 'em?"

"YEAH,, That's Sheriff Jim Kostman and his two younger brothers Mike and Kevin." Mark said, pointing at each picture. "What is it they've supposedly done?"

"Four Bank jobs, one group of Train passengers, and one lucrative Stagecoach. All toll, over eighty thousand dollars." Shawn said, with a serious look on his face and in his voice.

"You're Joking Right!" Sheriff Ryder said, "I've known them for over twenty years, since we were kids...How'd anyone see their faces, if like most robber's, they cover their faces with something?"

"They stopped and ate at the little Café in Kamela." Shawn said "The youngest one Kevin, paid a young Lady with a Diamond and Saphire ring for her pleasurable companionship...Turns out, that ring belonged to her mother who runs the restaurant in Meachum. So she knew it was stolen, so she told the other two that the ring was enough to pay for them too. So of course they joined in on the fun. This gave her time to see each man's face clearly. Turn's out, she has aspirations of being an Artist, after they left, she sat down and drew these picture's."

"Leave it to Kevin to pull a stupid stunt like that." Mark said, taking a cinnamon roll from the plate full on the counter. "How do you know they're on this particular train Marshal?"

"The Ticket Agent in Huntington identified them when they bought tickets there thru to Portland yesterday morning." Shawn answered

"That would be a good spot to load up at. Small town, not likely to be noticed by anyone." Sheriff Ryder said

They had been talking for just over an hour when a train of about ten empty cattle cars pulled up alongside the station, not stopping till the last two cars were at the station. One was a box car, the other the Caboose. When the train came to a stop, the side door slid open and a man jumped out and ran over to one of the outhouse's, while the other jumped down and faced the train and started peeing on it hoping no-one would bother him. Then after a couple minutes a man with two armed guards with him, exchanged two Bank bags. Then the other man came running back from the outhouse, jumped back aboard, closed the door, and the train was heading back down the track.

"What's up with only one freight car being on that train of empty cattle cars?" Shawn asked, looking up at the clock. Seeing it was about ten after six. Then looking around at the fifty plus men standing around waiting to be told what to do.

"No-One is supposed to know, But that box car is full new money from the San Francisco Mint. Every couple months they ship money up to Portland, then the train stops and every bank manager's in every town from here to Salt Lake City Utah exchanging old money with new." Sheriff Ryder answered, in a low voice.

"What do they do with the old money, and if no-one is supposed to know about it, then how Do You Know About It?" Shawn asked

"They wire all the Banker's offices the week before with the day and approximate time of their expected arrival time." Sheriff Ryder answered.

"Still don't explain why you or anyone else would know which train they're using." Shawn said.

"They always use an empty bull wagons, most people would think they'd use a standard Freight Train. But those take too long to stop and get moving again. A small train with no weight on board, can start and stop a hell of a lot faster. The Banker's always tell their local Law Office's so we can have a few extra men in the area in case someone might try to rob them." Sheriff Ryder answered

"How long has it been going on?" Shawn asked

"Couple years that I know of." Sheriff Ryder answered

"If it was me, I'd use mixed cars, that single box car with all those cattle cars sticks out like a Sore Thumb!" Shawn said, shaking his head. "ALRIGHT, EVERYONE LISTEN UP...! The train is due in within the hour, We don't know how many passenger cars are on this particular train. So I want you to divide up into two equal size groups, one group will be on one side of the train and the other half on the other side, Any Question's?"

Deputy Johnson started dividing everyone up into the two groups. Picking out four men in particular, telling them to take their sniper rifles and get over on top of the box cars so you'll be able to look directly into each window on every car. Find a good high enough place that they could see both sides of the train if possible."

Four men took off at a slow run towards the other end of the Station and outside. "The rest of you men, I Want A Show Of Force!" Shawn yelled out. Half of you take the riverside of the track, and the other half take the City side. Stand about ten, fifteen feet apart. That should more than cover a couple hundred feet of track till we know how many passenger cars there are...I DON'T WANT ANY GUN PLAY! If anyone is going to have to shoot, I'll Say Who Takes That Shot And When...! Now we have a whole lot of innocent people on this train that we don't want to get hurt. So keep your rifle barrels pointed into the air...I don't want an itchy finger pulling the trigger and shooting anyone by mistake."

"We Really Looking For Sheriff Kostman?" one of the men yelled out.

"Yes We Are!" Sheriff Ryder answered "Here's their poster to look at for those of you who DON'T know what they look like." Handing the poster's to the closest man. "Pass these around."

After all the instruction had been given out and the poster's being passed around, Shawn started looking the Posse over. They were all excited and talking about catching some Outlaw's with the famous U.S. Marshal Shawn Felton. But, even more exciting, with Deputy Wapiti, most of them couldn't take their eyes off him. That Buck Indian had only been a U.S. Deputy Marshal for just over four months and he'd already bested over thirty five men in fair fights. ALL, three to five men at one time and nobody has been able to draw blood on him. In other words, not one man had even hit him with a decent punch. There he was, only a few feet away from them. How long would he be in town for, even more exciting, would any of them get to see him in a fight while he was in town?

Shawn was starting on a third cinnamon roll when they could hear the sounds of an explosion echoing thru the Columbia River Gorge. Everyone shut up and started looking around at each other wondering what had just gotten blown up. Looking up at the clock on the wall, Shawn could see it was six-thirty five. Grabbing his saddle bags, he took out his binoculars and headed towards the dock doors with Sheriff Ryder and Wapiti right behind him. Once outside, he saw a ladder nailed to the wall heading up to the roof. They all three climbed it as fast as they could. By the time they got up on top they could see a small black cloud floating up into the sky a few miles up river.

Looking thru his telescope towards the cloud rising above from above the sheer cliff's that lined the river's Gorge. "Are there any mines in that direction, Sheriff?" Shawn asked

"NO Marshal!" Sheriff Ryder answered "The only thing it could be is a River Boat or Barge coming down river."

"Something defiantly blew up." Shawn said, taking the scope down, handing it to Wapiti "How fare to the next town up river?"

"It's twenty miles from here to Biggs Junction." Sheriff Ryder said

"We wouldn't even be able hear the echo from anything blowing up that far away." Wapiti said, looking thru the telescope. "How far down river to a train trestle?"

"The only one is where Deschutes River flows in about twelve miles further up the canyon. With all the wetlands on both sides of the river it's a couple hundred feet long." Sheriff Ryder answered

"Here comes our train." Wapiti said, still looking through the binoculars. "Marshal, what did you say about a sore thumb…All that debris is pitch black like tar soaked RailRoad timber's." Handing the binoculars back to him.

Shawn took the binoculars back and told the Sheriff to get everyone in place. Then he started looking back through the binoculars. First, seeing their train was only a couple more miles down the track from them. Then looking back at what was left of the black cloud. "You really think, what I think you're thinking of, are you Wapiti?"

"Thinking of what Marshal?" Sheriff Ryder asked. After he ordered his men to line the track, the train was coming in.

"Wapiti's thinking someone just blew that train trestle and is in the process of robbing that money train." Shawn said

"How would they know when to blow it?" Sheriff Ryder asked

"A Crooked Sheriff Would Know When!" Shawn answered, walking towards the ladder. "Come on Wapiti, let's get down below."

Climbing down the ladder he walked towards the top end of the Depot. "I bet our men aren't on this train anymore." Shawn said, looking at the men lining both sides of the tracks. "Does this train stop in Biggs Junction?"

"Yeah, a short stop. Long enough to let passenger's on and off. But they wouldn't have had enough time to ride up to the trestle and blow it before got there…? It just left here what, ten, fifteen minutes ago?" Sheriff Ryder asked, as the train came in slowing to a stop.

"Give me those poster's." Shawn said, taking them and walking towards the first passenger car. Which happened to be the dining car as well.

"What's Going On." The Engineer yelled out in passing, continuing to bring the train to a complete stop. Just as soon as it stopped.

Shawn opened the door and walked inside, grabbing the first Porter he came to by the shirt and showed him the pictures. "Are these men on board?"

"Not any more," the Porter answered " Why, What's up Marshal?"

"Where and when did they get off?" Shawn asked

"Hey, what was that explosion. did you guys hear it too" the Porter asked

"Where and When Did These Men Get Off At?' Shawn demanded to know.

"Oh, Sheriff Kostman, Why Biggs Junction of course. Where else would he get off at?" the Porter ask "Hey, what was that explosion, did a River Boat blow up?"

"I Don't Know!" Shawn said, walking back off the train. "They're not on board any more. Where the hell can we get some horses at?"

"Down at this end of First Street is the Stock Yard. You and Wapiti should be able to get a couple horses and tack there." Sheriff Ryder said, turning towards the men on his side of the train. "Everyone get your horses rounded up and ready to ride as soon as the Marshal's ready."

"Yes Sir." They all shouted out running back towards the Depot.

When they got to the town side of the tracks, the men on that side of the train asked what was up. Some of the running men said they had gotten away so mount up.

Shawn, Wapiti, and the Sheriff walked over to where all the Posse's horses were tied up at. While everyone else ran and quickly started climbing on their horses and ready to ride. Shawn caught one man who was just about to climb aboard, grabbing him by his belt. He quickly pulled the man back down. "Sorry son, but I need your horse. Wapiti, you take that one." He said, pointing at the horse next to him. "Get off mister."

"Yes Sir Marshal." The man answered, climbing off and handing Wapiti his reins. "Here ya go Deputy, he's still a little green."

"Thanks." Wapiti said, grabbing the reins and looking into the excited and nervous eyes of the horse. Then around at everyone else, most of which were riding their horses in circle's just waiting for the word to go. He quickly put his foot in the saddle and climbed aboard and that damned horse went sky high. But Wapiti had gotten his foot in the other stirrup just before he took flight. Dropping his rifle to the ground, he followed the big horse up and around to his right, crashing back to the ground driving his head down between his front legs. Wapiti had a rein in each hand as the big horse continued bucking across the parking area. He was purposely trying to buck into or over any nearby horse trying to get Wapiti off his back.

Wapiti couldn't hear anything anybody was saying. He was just trying to show this horse who the boss was. He kept it up for a good dozen high flying crow hopes and Wapiti was staying right on top of him. After a couple more half hearted buck's the horse came to a stand still, still holding his head up high and nervously side stepping around.

Everyone was cheering through the entire ride. At one point someone blew the eight second whistle, but that horse kept it up for a good five plus seconds more before he called it quits and came to a sudden stand still.

When the ride was over, those close to him congratulated him on such a good ride. They didn't know Indian's were that good at riding bucking horses.

"We have to train our horses to ride too." Wapiti answered, reaching for his rifle

"Are you thru playing around Wapiti, can we go now?" Shawn jokingly asked

'Here Deputy." The owner of the horse said, handing him his rifle and saddle bags back. "I'd have bet money you weren't going to ride this horse."

"You'd have lost, just like everyone else who's bet against me so far." Wapiti said, with a big smile on his face. Thanking the man for picking up his gear and for lending him his High Spirited Horse. Then he turned the horse and followed the Marshal down the road with everyone else behind them.

In no time at all they were almost at a full out run. Sheriff Ryder pulled up alongside Shawn, hollering over. "I can only follow you to the Deschutes River, then you enter Sherman County and out of my jurisdiction."

"That's alright Sheriff, we can go on without you and your men if need be." Shawn said.

The road for most part was following the Columbia River. At the pace they were traveling at it only took them an hour and they could see the train backing up towards them. When one of the engineer's saw them, he started slowing the train up. Within a couple minutes they could see the side door on the box car had mostly been blown off.

"Anyone Hurt?' Shawn asked, riding up to the box car.

"No Sir." One of the three men standing in the doorway said.

"So what happened?' Shawn asked

"Whoever they were, they blew out this side of the train trestle. Then since we wouldn't open the door, they blew it open with a couple sticks of dynamite."

"How much money did they get away with and which direction did they go when they left?" Shawn asked

"No idea on exactly how much money Marshal. We start out with ten four by four pallets stacked four feet high on one end of the car. The other end we have four by four wood boxes that we put together to put all the old money in as we empty the pallets." One of the men was explaining.

"They took off back upstream on the Deschutes River." Another man spoke up.

"Shut up Tim, I'll get to that part." The first man spoke up. "Now, we have no clue as to exactly how much they stole yet. They had three of those large duffle bags like you get to put all your clothes in that the Cavalry Trooper's use."

"Those are pretty big bags, they could carry a lot of money in one of those." Shawn said

"They only took money out of our hundred dollar bill pallet, but they got well over half the pallet. So they probably got well over five hundred thousand dollars." The man said

"A minute ago you had no idea, now you're saying they got away with over a half million. Just how the hell you figure they got away with that much money MISTER?" Shawn snapped back.

The entire Posse started talking about just how big that reward was going to be for them to get to split between them. Shawn didn't like the sounds of it, but right now there wasn't anything he wanted to do about it. He was thinking, while looking around at all the men. "So Now, just how you figure they got away with that much money?" Shawn asked, glaring into all three men's faces.

"Like I said, they only took off the hundred dollar bill pallet. That pallet had one million dollars in it when we leave Portland, and like I said again. They got well over half the pallet inside those three military style duffle bags." The main man said

"How long ago did they leave?" Shawn asked

"A good forty five minutes ago." The Engineer said, walking up to them. When they blew the trestle, one of the rails bent backwards and got caught up in the cattle guard before we could get totally shut down.

"So when they left they went back up the river instead of following the main road." Shawn asked

"Yes, they did." All three men inside the car and Engineer said at the same time.

"Thanks," Shawn said, kicking his horse in the side, taking off down the road towards the river. Which was only a couple more miles down the road. Shawn ordered everyone to stay aboard their horse and stay on the road till Wapiti had time to identify their tracks.

Wapiti quickly jumped off his horse and started walking up the side of the train tracks towards the blown trestle. Walking out on the part of the tracks that were diked up to support the train before the trestle actually started.

He was only a few feet from the beginning when he saw where they all three had stopped and blew part of the door off the box car. Stopping, he slowly started looking the area over. The trestle had been blown up about a third of the way across the trestle. He could see the boot prints of two men who had gotten off their horses. He could see where they had obviously stood when they placed the dynamite on the door. He could see where the one that stayed on his horse, led the other horses away from the door riding closer to the trestle. He could also see where the other two men had obviously stood between two cars to protect themselves from flying debris.

Then back to the door area where he could tell by the twist in the foot print in the dirt that this was probably where they climbed up into the car at. Then over closer to the back side of the door, he could see where their tracks had slid just a little. Which meant, it was probable where they had landed when they jumped out at.

Starting to look at the hoof prints over where they had mounted back up at, he could see one was missing a shoe and another one had at least a third of one shoe had broken off. After following them back up the track, he quickly figured the one with the broken shoe was the back right hoof. The one missing the shoe, was a front right hoof print, and there were four sets of hoof prints.

Stopping, Wapiti looked back up the tracks. He could see the Marshal was having a hard time keeping that Posse under control, they were quickly turning into a wild mob. They wanted to know why they had to wait on Wapiti. The men on the train already told them that when they left, they all went up river. It's obvious that they're heading for Grass Valley.

"You men settle down, I'll shoot the first horse out from under any man who leaves here before me and Wapiti are ready. Do I make myself Clear Gentlemen!" Shawn demanded "Now just shut up so I can hear if Wapiti needs to ask me anything."

"Marshal, that river is my county line. Afraid me and my Deputy's are going to have to turn back." Sheriff Ryder said. "I'm sorry, I thought I had better men in my Posse than these men are turning out to be."

"Money can change a man's mind real fast, and with Banks paying fifteen percent reward on all cash returned from a robbery. These guys we're after are worth a hell of a lot of money." Shawn said, quickly looking the bunch of men back over. Then back out towards Wapiti, he could see he was tracking them back down alongside the tracks and looking up the river bank at the same time.

"Before ya leave Sheriff, you agree with those men and think they're heading for Grass Valley?" Shawn asked

"NO! I don't. Stop and think about it, why go out across that god forsaken desert. Especially, if it is the Kostman Brother's. Hell, Biggs Junction is only five, six miles back up the road." Sheriff Ryder said in a low voice. Hoping the men weren't paying him much attention, knowing all they had to do was cross the river and they would be out of his County

"You say you know this Jim Kostman fellow?" Shawn asks

"Yes Sir I do, I've had many meals over at house, and him at mine. But since his wife ran off with a gambler a couple months back. I could see a change in him, it's hard to explain." Sheriff Ryder was saying.

"Let me guess, his demeanor changed. The sparkle in his eyes went away, and a dark, emptiness look has replaced it." Shawn said

"That's about the best way to explain it, yeah. Like he don't care anymore." Sheriff Ryder said, watching Shawn take yet another pull off his flask of whiskey.

"I've seen that happen to a lot of good men, sometimes it can take them a year or two to pull their heads out of their ass's and come back to reality." Shawn said, taking a drink off his flask of whiskey.

"How much of that do you drink in a day, Marshal?" Sheriff Ryder asked

"All I CAN!" Shawn answered, with a big smile on his face. Thinking back to what Deputy Johnson had told him earlier. So he took one more big pull off the flask before offering him a drink.

"I don't believe a man should drink when he's on duty, he should wait till his shift is over with and has returned home for the night." Sheriff Ryder stated.

"Well Sheriff, I'm on the job twenty four seven, everyday of the year. My home is about a hundred and ten miles due south as the Crow flies. So I'll have a drink anytime I want one." Shawn stated, putting the flask back in his jacket pocket.

"Sorry Marshal, I didn't mean to piss you off." Sheriff Ryder said, appaulajetickly.

"It's alright." Shawn answered. "I do agree with you about drinking when you know you shouldn't be. This ain't one of those times and I find it helps me think."

"I'm not going to argue with you Marshal." Sheriff Ryder said

"You say you know where this Kostman man lives?" Shawn asked quietly. "How would I get there?"

"Stay on the road, just this side of the main town area there's a road that takes off to the south, it's called Welk Road. Go down that road about a half mile, you'll see his big two story blue ranch house from the road." Sheriff Ryder said "Marshal, other than a couple trees in his yard, there's not much cover out there. Least wise, not enough to hide a Posse this big behind."

"I'm hoping most of them might agree to go back with you. Then after a couple miles down the road they'll tell you they're going after that reward after all. They'll head towards Grass Valley and be out of my hair." Shawn said, looking the group of men over one more time as Wapiti came walking up.

"It's about damned time, let's get going." A couple men started shouting out.

"Remember my rule about leaving ahead of me." Shawn said

"GO TO HELL OLD MAN." A couple men started shouting. "That reward goes to whomever finds those men first."

"You want to stick around and see where your Indian guide thinks which way they're going. We already know the way to Grass Valley." Another man yelled out. "We don't need NO INDIAN to show us the way."

"You can't stop us all OF USE OLD MAN! A couple more men started yelling out.

"COME ON MEN, LET'S RIDE!" A man shouted out, waving his hand in the air. Kicking his horse in the side, he took off running towards the trail that followed the river upstream. Within thirty second all but the Sheriff and his Deputy were gone. Leaving a cloud of dust behind themselves heading up the narrow trail as fast as their horses could carry them.

Shawn started chuckling. "Those boys in the back are going to be needing a bath soon with the dust those men are kicking up."

"You just got through saying you wanted them out of your hair. Well, they're out of it." Sheriff Ryder said, smiling.

"So where do the other two brothers live at?" Shawn asked

"With Jim, I think that was the main reason his wife left him." Sheriff Ryder answered

"What did you find out?" Shawn asked Wapiti who was climbing aboard his horse.

"They're leading a packhorse and they started to go up river alright." Wapiti said, looking up the river's bank and started pointing. "From down there you can see where they rode through the cattails and grass going up this side of the river. But those Rail Road guys must not have been paying them much attention, cause you can see where their horses broke through the willows and cattails just a couple hundred yards further upstream. I'd say that's where they swam across the river at."

"Any distinguishing signs in their tracks?" Shawn asked, watching the Posse disappear around the hill side out of sight from them. But he could still see their cloud of dust off in the distance. "Sheriff, you and any of your men want to come along with us?"

"We'd better not Marshal." Sheriff Ryder said. "They could argue with the Judge and say we were out of our jurisdiction and had no right to arrest them."

"I agree it sounds stupid, but you're probably right." Shawn said, holding his hand out. "Sheriff, it's been a pleasure to meet you, but we need to get going."

"I understand Marshal," Sheriff Ryder said, shaking his hand. Then shaking Wapiti's hand, he wished the two good luck and he and his Deputy's headed back towards The Dalles.

Shawn and Wapiti started up the road towards Biggs Junction at a fast trot. Shawn looked down at his pocket watch, it was almost nine o-clock.

They kept the pace up till they could see the road turning off just ahead of them. Shawn slowed them down to a walk and took his pocket watch back out. It was only nine-twenty, they had made good time.

Just a few feet up from Welk Road was another street that went to the north side of the road. There was a couple house on each corner and a few more on the main road leading into the main business district of town which was only a couple hundred yards further away.

Stopping his horse, Shawn looked at his pocket watch again, shaking his head. "I don't think those boys went home just yet. Stop and think about it, they've been up all morning riding out there in time to blow the trestle right after the Westbound train went through, stopping the Eastbound train so they could steal all that money. With one of them being the local Sheriff, no-one in this town is even going to give them a second look over to see why they need a pack horse…They've been in town for at least an hour…I bet they rode into town for breakfast before going home to count their money."

"You really think they'd take a loaded pack horse into town instead of taking him home first and unload everything?" Wapiti asked, looking up the road towards their house.

"Why not, they don't think anyone is onto them." Shawn said, looking up the road and seeing the new bridge that crossed the Columbia River over to the Washington State side. "Let's go see if

I'm right… If I'm not, then we'll ride back here and hopefully catch them sleeping."

They both started walking their horses up the street towards the main part of the little town. When they got close to the main intersection where the two roads crossed. One continuing on down the river and the other towards the new bridge over the river.

Riding closer to the business, they could see three men coming out of a Café across the main intersection in the middle of town. When the three men saw them, they froze for a couple seconds making sure who they really were. But just as soon as they could tell it was Marshal Felton and Deputy Wapiti. They quickly climbed aboard their horses and headed in the direction of the bridge.

"Come On!" Shawn yelled out kicking his horse in the side, taking off at a full run after the three men. They had only gotten started when one of the Kostman Brothers threw a stick of dynamite at them. Exploding only fifty feet most from them. But it scared their horses into bucking, while the Kostman brothers kept riding towards the bridge.

After a long thirty seconds, they regained control of their horses and started back after the Kostman brothers who were almost at the Bridge. Kicking their horse back into a full run, they took back in after the Outlaw's.

It only took them a couple more minutes and they were coming up on the bridge. They could see the Kostman brothers had stopped about halfway across. They were all off their horses, one was holding the horses, blocking the view while the other two appeared to be holding sticks of dynamite in their hands.

"Hold Up." Shawn yelled out, pulling back on his reins.

"What Up Marshal?" Wapiti asked, bringing his horse to a stop.

"Looks like they're going to try and blow part of the bridge." Shawn said, looking at him. "You Men Don't Want To Do That."

He yelled out, jumping off his horse with both his rifle and saddle bags he headed for one of the support tower's to hide behind. Wapiti ran to the tower on the other side of the bridge for protection.

"Yes We Do." One of the Kostman Brothers yelled back, firing a couple pistol shot's towards them. While the other two were quickly putting fuses into each end of each stick making one long stick.

"If you have to shoot, make sure you don't hit any of that dynamite." Shawn said, looking over at Wapiti. Taking a cautious look back in their direction, Shawn could see one of them grabbing more dynamite off the pack horse. "You men don't want to come in over the saddle…come on man, give up!" he yelled back at them.

"We Told You To Go To Hell Marshal!" one of the Kostman Brothers yelled back, firing a couple more pistol shots at them from behind their horses. While the other two continued making their dynamite rope. It only took them a couple minutes and they had two ropes with twenty plus sticks in each rope.

"Can you get a shot?" Shawn asked, looking over at Wapiti.

"NO, they're staying out of sight behind their horses." Wapiti answered

"If they blow this bridge, we'll never be able to catch them." Shawn said, looking back and forth between Wapiti and the Kofstman Brothers.

"It would take a lot of dynamite to blow those steel beam's apart, Marshal." Wapiti said, looking over at him, then back towards the Kostman brothers a couple hundred feet further over the bridge.

"They don't have to blow the steel beams up, all they need to do is blow these six by twelve wood flooring beams apart." Shawn said, just as the Kostman Brothers slowly started leading their horses further away.

Both Shawn and Wapiti saw them light the fuse at the same time. "TAKE COVER!" Shawn yelled out, ducking down closer to the bottom of the support tower. Looking back towards the Kostman Brothers, he could see them mount up and took off at a full run just a couple seconds before the dynamite blew up. Sending wood flying in all directions, causing both Shawn and Wapiti to cover their heads from the falling debris. Which only took a couple very long seconds before most of the larger pieces had all fallen out into the middle of the Columbia River.

Shawn and Wapiti stood up and walked over to where the bridge wood started missing at. They had blown up at least twenty feet of the thick timber's that made the bridge passable. They both looked down into the fast flowing and very wide Columbia River below. Looking towards the other side, they could see the Kostman Brothers heading East down the main road that shortly turned north on the Washington side of the river.

"How are we suppose to get across now Marshal…SWIM!" Wapiti asked, looking at the large hole in the bridge decking, then back at the Marshal.

"NOPE, it's up to the Washington State Marshal now." Shawn said, watching the Kostman Brothers ride over the ridge and out of sight. "That's two groups of Outlaw's you've let get away Wapiti!" Shawn said, turning back towards the Oregon side.

"MMEE…! Wapiti shouted out, following behind.

THE END

Felton 9

CHAPTER 1

It was just after ten A.M. when both the Stagecoaches from Madras finally pulled into the Stage Stop in Prineville. Shawn quickly opened the door and held it open, for a Young Lady carrying sleeping twins and one of the other two men was carrying a third sleeping child into the Stage Stop. Looking over at the second Coach, he could see only Wapiti and two men get out. Just by looking at them laughing, joking attitude, they had had a much more peaceful, quiet, enjoyable ride than he had had.

"Here's your gear Marshal." Shawn heard a voice say, looking up just in time to catch his duffle bag before it hit him in the face. "HEY…Watch out where you're throwing thing!" He yelled out, just as a large chest crash landed on the ground next to him.

"Sorry Marshal." The Shot Gunner said, apologetically. "Because of that broken down Coach in Madras last night, I'm doing a back-to-back trip. Right now, I've been working fifteen plus hours with no rest."

"I understand, son, but if you're not careful and you break one of those big fancy chest like that one. The owner might want the Stage Company to pay for the Damages…If they have to pay, then it will be coming out of your wages." Shawn said, with a big smile on his face.

"So did those screaming babies ever quit crying?" Wapiti asked, walking up to Shawn

"YEAH, about ten minutes out." Shawn said looking at his pocket watch, it was just past ten. "I sure hope the Judge isn't holding Court. Cause if I go home and lay down, there's no-way I'm waking up by one to meet with him. So let's go see if he's in." He said, walking up the street towards the Courthouse.

"What if he's holding court?" Wapiti asked, following him.

"Then I hope he'll grant us a quick hour of his time, or, maybe he'll say we can meet at one o-clock tomorrow afternoon instead." Shawn said, nodding his hat to three Young Lady's crossing the street. They were all smiling, giggling, and looking directly at Wapiti.

"I think those Young Lady's like you Wapiti." Shawn said, smiling and stepping up on the boardwalk.

"I'm still waiting for Cathey to come over." Wapiti said, turning sideways to walk between the Marshal and two men. "Excuse me gentlemen." He quickly said to them,

"That's alright Deputy, we're the ones not paying attention." One of the men quickly and apologetically answered

It was only two and a half blocks from the Stage Stop to the Courthouse. But they had to say Hello, or Good Morning to more than half the people they passed. Personally, Shawn couldn't remember ever saying good morning to this many people in this Town before. So he was glad when they finally got to the Courthouse.

Walking inside, he walked over to the Courtroom door and looked inside. Seeing it empty, he quickly closed it and walked up stairs to the Judge's office. Walking into the first office, he asked Ruth if the Judge was in.

"Yes he is Marshal, but right now he's in a meeting with the Public Defender." Ruth said, standing up. "Can I get you gentlemen anything to drink?"

"Personally, I'd like a cold beer Miss. Twidwell." Wapiti said, looking at her. "But I guess it's going to have to be coffee."

"Not at all, Deputy." Ruth said, walking over to the cold cabinet, opening it up. "Marshal, would you like a cold beer too?" she asked, handing Wapiti one.

"Yes please." Shawn said, with a big smile on his face, reaching for the beer. "This should really piss the Judge off…Both of us drinking this early in the morning."

Ruth was about to knock on the door, when it opened up and the Public Defender Chris Warner came walking out shaking his head and grumbling to himself about something. "Your Honor, Marshal Felton and Deputy Wapiti are here to see you."

Judge Monson looked at the clock on the wall, then at all the paperwork on his desk. "Alright, send them in." he said, looking back at the paperwork on his desk. "Good morning gentlemen, I hear you let another Gang of Outlaws get away."

"Just how the hell do you think we could have gotten across the river?" Shawn asked, just as the Judge looked up and saw Wapiti taking a drink off his beer.

"WHAT THE HELL IS THIS… Now you're both drinking before noon!" Judge Monson shouted out.

"I'm sorry Your Honor. But after a long huntin' trip a cold beer relaxes me and helps me sleep." Wapiti answered, taking a small drink just for the hell of it.

"I don't care, you could have waited till this meeting was over with." Judge Monson snapped out at both of them. "NOW, what happened, how'd you lose them this time?"

"What, you didn't hear? They blew the wood decking out of the middle of that fancy new bridge they just built over the Columbia River at Biggs Junction." Shawn said, taking another long drink off his beer. "The last time we saw them, they were riding over the ridge and out of sight on the Washington State side. I figured since they were on the Washington State side, their Marshal could chase after them, I wired him in Olympia, then I put their pictures on the next train out of town so they'd know what they look like if they ever came across them." He was explaining, as he started to chuckle." "There's a needle in the haystack for you, three men out of tens of thousands, HELL, hundreds of thousands if you take in Idaho and Montana in four months so I don't think they'll get caught and they have more than enough money to buy a nice ranch up in Montana. Least, that's where I'd go, somewhere around that Yelloestone country. Now there's some beautiful mountains and mountain valleys to raise cattle, horses, or any other kind of ranch you desired to have.

"Where'd you wire them from to let them know they were on their side of the River?" Judge Monson asked

"Biggs Junction Of Course … NOW, if there's nothing more of real importance, we'd like to go get something to eat and then get some much needed sleep."

"REST, why didn't you sleep on the train up from The Dallse?" Judge Monson asked

"WE Couldn't!" they both answered

"There was a Young Lady on board that had one child about a year and a half old, and a set of twin's only a couple months old. If One Wasn't Crying, They all Were!" Shawn said.

"Why didn't you just move to another passenger car?" Judge Monson asked

"They Didn't Have One!" Shawn snapped back.

"So didn't you sleep on the Stage coming in from Madras?" Judge Monson asked

"NO, cause that lady and her three children got in my Coach!" Shawn said

"You try sleeping inside that bouncing Coach!" Wapiti said "We leave here today I'm sleeping till tomorrow morning, and I'll shoot the first person that trys to wake me, CLEAR!"

"Your beginning to sound and act more like the Marshal every-day Youngman." Judge Monson said, staring into each man's face.

"Sorry again, Your Honor, But we're both hunger and tired." Wapiti said

"So when did Oregon Trust and Loan finally open up that Fancy new supposedly Robbery Proof Bank?" Shawn asked, looking at it thru the window. Then looking over at Ruth. "Ruth, is there another beer in that cold box?"

"That's my beer for when I finish my day's work at the end of the day. Go get your own beer!" Judge Monson demanded

"I'll send Jose over to replace everything we drink in here this morning...Ruth, if you don't mind please." Shawn asked

"Right away Marshal, Wapiti, would you like one too?" Ruth asked

"Yes please Miss. Twidwell." Wapiti said.

"So when did they open that fancy new bank up?" Shawn asked again.

"About two weeks ago." Judge Monson answered, looking out the window at the part of the bank he could see two blocks away. "I saw the plans, the back third has twelve inches of cement all around the basement, that's where the main vault room is caged in at."

"Why'd they build it in between two buildings when they could have built it three blocks further down the street in that empty lot?" Shawn said, pointing back and forth between the two locations. "Don't both of those two businesses on either side of it have full basements too?"

"YYEEAAHH, but their just wood beams, now there's a cement wall in between them." Judge Monson said. "It's reinforced with one inch steel bars that run from top to bottom."

"That still doesn't make it robbery proof." Shawn said, thanking Ruth for the beer.

"They have two armed guards during all business hours." Judge Monson said

"That still doesn't make it robbery proof...But if they think so, we'll just have to wait and see how long it takes for someone to try and rob it." Shawn chuckled out, walking towards the door. "Like I said, I'll send Jose over with your four replacement beers, so they'll be cold this evening when you want your relaxing beer before going home and peacefully falling asleep."

Wapiti thanked the Judge for his beer and for his understanding as to why he was drinking so early in the morning. Then he followed the Marshal out the door, down the stairs and outside. They both took one quick look around, then headed up the street towards Carmen's restaurant.

Walking inside, they quickly found an empty table and set down. Just as a waitress walked up and set a beer down in front of the Marshal and an ice tea down in front of Wapiti. "Our lunch special is beef or chicken fajitas." She said, with a big smile on her face.

"I'll take one of each please, with the medium salsa and a beer please." Wapiti said. Smiling

"I'll have the same, only I'll have the hot Pico De Gallo salsa with a small cap full of OO-LA LA. "Shawn said, finishing his beer from the Judge.

"Right away gentlemen, I'll be right back with your order's." the Waitress said, walking away.

"I'm glad we at least got a hot shower at the Train Depot in Madras." Wapiti said, taking a drink of beer. "Now, we can eat and go get some sleep instead of fighting over who gets first bath here."

"Me Too." Shawn answered, looking around the room. Most of the people didn't seem to be paying them any attention, but he could still see most of them shyly looking their way. But trying not to make it too obvious that they were looking at them. The conversations slowly picked back up. Most of them were about, was someone going to be stupid enough to try and pick a fight with Wapiti, with the Marshal being there too.

It only took a couple more minutes and the waitress was setting their food and a beer for Wapiti down in front of them. "Is there anything else I can you gentlemen?" the Waitress asked

"No Darlin', I think this will just about do us." Shawn said, pouring a little OO LA, LA salsa on top of a fajita and taking a big bite.

Wapiti did the same, thanking her that is, watching Shawn pour that deep red sauce on top of his fajita. Then he started eating his.

Neither one said anything while they ate. They were too hungry and too tired to worry about anything or anyone. So it only took them about ten minutes and they were taking their last bites of food and washed it down with the last of their beers. Then each one put a dollar tip on the table and headed towards the back door.

Where Jose came running up to them. "You weren't gone for a very long time Marshal, Did You Catch The Outlaw's?"

"No son, they got away." Shawn said, walking out the door.

"Can we do some target practice today Marshal?" Jose asked, running along beside them.

"Not today son, but maybe tomorrow, it's Sunday, so maybe we can then." Shawn said "Jose, can you do us a favor, and make sure no-one wakes us up."

"What if it's important, Marshal?" Jose asked

"Only If It's Important." Shawn said, walking into the shake and over to his bunk. Neither him nor Wapiti either one remember anything within seconds of laying down. When all of a sudden there was the noise of two half sticks of dynamite blowing up within a couple seconds of each other.

Bringing them both up out of their beds as two more explosions went off. One in the downtown area and the other a few blocks away on the other side of town. "What the hell is going on?" Wapiti asked, just as another blew up on the other side of town.

Looking out the door, it was pitch black out, so Shawn lit a match and looked at his pocket watch. Just as two more blew up, again, one down town, and one a couple blocks further away yet in another direction from any of the other's. "Sounds like a couple of IDIOT'S decided to wake the town up." He said, still looking at his pocket watch, it was nine-thirty. "Since we're already awake, what say we go down to Moser's for a cold beer?" Shawn said, climbing out of bed.

"Sounds good to me too." Wapiti said, pulling his pants on, then he lit the lamp so they could see what they were doing.

Even though they were well over a half block away from the Saloon, they could hear men arguing inside Moser's Saloon. "Sure wish we had a couple cups of coffee first though." Shawn said, taking a drink off the warm water bag. Swishing it around in his mouth, he spit it out on the floor. "Looks like Griselda swept and mopped while we were gone."

"How do you know that?" Wapiti asked

"There's no dust inside the pooled up water or around it." Shawn said, standing up. "Make sure I have at least one five dollar bill on me before we leave the Saloon tonight please."

"Why's that Marshal?" Wapiti asked, putting his moccasins on.

"That's how much I pay her every time she cleans." Shawn said, getting dressed.

Wapiti stood up, took out his wallet and took out a five dollar bill. Then he stuck it between the salt and pepper shakers. "It'll be here for her in the morning when she brings us our morning coffee."

"Thanks." Shawn said, pulling his boots on. "Let's go."

Walking out the door, they heard two more explosion's go off. One a couple blocks down Northeast 3rd Street again, which was the main street through town, and another in a completely different area of town than any of the other's. "I wonder when they're going to run out of dynamite." Shawn said, walking towards the back of the buildings.

Walking up to the swinging double doors, Shawn took a quick look around the room as they walked in. The bar area was lined with some men and a few lady's. All ten tables were full, four had poker player's, some had a Young Lady setting on their laps. There were even a couple couples either going up or coming back down the stairs.

"It was Saturday Night and Everyone had come out to blow off steam." Shawn said, looking over at Wapiti. "Mark my words… there's going to be more than one fight in town tonight."

"That's alright." Wapiti answered, following him to the back where Dave usually sat.

"Beer Marshal, Deputy?" Dave asked

"You wouldn't happen to have a pot of coffee on would ya, we just woke up." Shawn answered

"You and the entire town just woke up…I always have coffee on the warmer." Dave said, filling up a cup. "How about you Deputy, what can I get you?"

"I'll have the same thing to start." Wapiti said, excusing himself up against the last cowboy so he'd have room to stand at the bar.

Instantly the Cowboy turned around to see who the hell it was pushing up against him. But just as soon as he saw it was Wapiti, he started apologizing to him and telling his buddy's to make room for Deputy Wapiti.

"Do you have any idea as to who might be playing with dynamite?" Shawn asked, taking a sip on the coffee.

"No I don't." Dave answered, but four of those little bangs were all within a couple blocks of here."

"Sounded to me like they came from the direction of that new bank." Charlie said "Marshal, would you like me to make a fresh pot of coffee.

"Maybe one more pot please." Wapiti said

"Yeah, I'd like a couple more cup's myself." Shawn said "So have you been inside that new big fancy bank yet?"

"YYEEAAHH, it's real nice inside…but ever since Oregon Trust and Loan opened up that new bank, they started charging me a dollar fifty for every transaction I do." Dave said in a disgusted voice. "On all my deposits and every check I write they charge me a dollar fifty. THEN, they charge whoever is cashing that check another dollar fifty to cash it if they don't have a bank account with them!

"How many deposits and checks do you do a month?" Shawn asked

"I used to do a deposit every day, but now I'm only going to do it one day a week." Dave said in a low voice, so no-one else could hear him. "I also used to pay all my employee's and Merchant's with check…Maybe thirty plus checks a month. But I think I'm going back to paying everyone in cash, it's cheaper that way."

"I agree with you, but I suppose they have to pay for that new bank somehow." Shawn said.

"Sure wish I'd been like you and stayed with Ole Yeller Savings and Loan." Dave said

"Why don't ya go back to them?" Shawn asked

"They're charging the same price on all new accounts. So I just as well stay where I am, at least their vault will be harder to get to." Dave answered

"I'm glad I didn't switch when the Oregon Trust first came to town." Shawn said "Charley, I think I'm ready for that beer now, please."

"Coming right up Marshal." Charley answered, filling a beer mug. "How about you, Deputy, you ready for a beer yet?"

"Yes please." Wapiti answered.

"I CAN'T BELIEVE ALL YOU COWARDS!" a man shouted out.

Everyone turned and looked at the table of five men. By the way they were dressed, you could tell they were loggers.

"You Believe these fool's allowing this wanna be Lawdog Indian to drink our beer." The man continued disgustedly saying "Look at that tin badge pinned to his chest. Is that supposed to scare us?" Another man sitting at the table shouted out.

"NO, but you are supposed to show him the respect DO of a man wearing that tin badge." Shawn said, standing up.

"Like hell I will!" the first man spoke up, chuckling.

"You men don't know what Deputy Wapiti has done to those who've tried to stop him from doing anything he's wanted to do." A man chuckled out in the crowd said, as everyone close to them started getting up and moving away from the table of five men.

"That's all we've been hearing for the last four plus months up at logging camp...BULLSHIT stories about him taking on and beating two and three men at a time." The logger disbelievingly said

"It's Your Doctor Bill." Another person in the crowd shouted out, while everyone within ten feet got out of the way.

"I still say they're all Bullshit stories, there's five of us." the first man said standing up. As his four friends all laid their cards on the table and stood up. Turning and facing the Marshal and Wapiti.

Wapiti stepped up off the bar stool and faced the men. While they all walked around to the front of the table within a couple feet of Shawn and Wapiti. Wapiti looked all the men over, everyone was six feet plus tall and at least one eighty plus in weight. "Those two are yours Marshal, I'll take these three!"

"You're Awful Cocky Boy!" The first man said. He was standing in the center of his three, and a couple feet further back.

"Sounds good to me." Shawn said, looking at the two men directly in front of him. Without hesitation, he took a step forward followed by winding up and throwing fist into the mouth of the man on his right, and his left into the man's mouth on his left. Sending both men stumbling backwards. Following the man to the right, he caught up to him just as he regained control of his legs. Shawn threw his right fist dead center of the man's face. Breaking his nose, blackening both eyes, sending him flying backwards into the wall and falling lifeless to the floor. Turning to face the second man, he felt something slide off his left cheek. Ducking under the second punch, he drove his right fist up under the man's chin, nearly ripping his head off its spine sending his body flying over and crashing down a table at least five feet behind him.

No sooner did the marshal start to take his first step forward and prepare to throw his right first punch, the closest two men to Wapiti came at him, each throwing a punch. Ducking under them and cutting between them, he brought his fist up into the biggest man's stomach. Picking him a good couple inches off the floor, taking ninety percent of his air away from him. Grabbing his head, he drove it down into his knee as he was bringing it up. Knocking one tooth out, breaking his nose, sending blood everywhere and knocking him out cold. Dropping his lifeless to the floor, Wapiti spun around on his left foot, bringing his right foot into the side of the head of the first man he came to. Sending him flying into and over the bar crashing down on the floor on the backside. Quickly, be brought his left elbow up under the chin of the man standing just behind himself, driving the man backwards. Continuing to turn, he followed after the man. Reaching out with his left he caught the man by the shirt and pulled him back towards himself, while throwing his right fist into the man's face at the same. Breaking his nose, blackening both eyes and knocking him out cold as well, so he dropped him on the floor.

"Shawn and Wapiti both looked at each other with big smiles on their faces. "You're still pretty good for an old man." Wapiti chuckled out

"OLD MAN!" Shawn said, picking up a pitcher of beer on the closest table. Then they both started pouring it into the men's faces slowly waking them up.

"Charley, you want to wake the one up on the backside of the bar for me please." Wapiti asked, watching all the men as they slowly came back awake.

Wapiti reached down and grabbed the biggest man by his hand. "Here let me help you back up." Pulling the man back up into groggy, wobbly legs, but still managing to stand up. "Remember me? I'm Deputy Wapiti...It's a pleasure to meet you gentlemen... Now then, Mister Moser, just how much money you figure these men owe you in damages.

"The chair is fifteen dollars, two table legs at ten dollars each, then about fifteen in broken dishes... So that fifteen plus twenty, that's thirty five, plus fifteen...call it fifty dollars." Dave said, watching the men slowly taking their wallet's out. "But for the entertainment, I'll buy each of you a double shot off my bottle. Charley, line 'em up."

All five men groggily stood back up, holding their aching, pounding, spinning heads. Trying to get their eyes back into focus. Slowly they started looking back and forth between themselves. Then out into the vast sea of spectator's. Slowly they could understand what was being said. Something about them owing fifty dollars in damages. After a couple more seconds everything was coming back into view and the memory as to what had just happened to them.

Reaching for their wallets, they each started looking each other over again. Then back over to the Marshal and Wapiti, neither one of them even had one mark on them. Slowly the four gave the biggest man ten dollars each. Walking up to the bar, he handed Dave the money. Then picking up the shot glasses, he started handing one to each of his friends. Picking up the last one, he turned back to Shawn and Wapiti, he held the shot glass in the air. "I Salute You Both." Then he drank the shot down. "Now, does anyone know where the nearest Doctor's office is…I need some serious pain relief pills."

"Me too." All the other men started saying still looking back and forth between the Marshal and Wapiti.

"Counting these three, don't that put you up to thirty eight scalps now?" Shawn said

"That's right!" Wapiti answered, with a big smile on his face. Still looking all five men over.

"The Doctor's office is out the front door to your right. Two doors down, up at the top of the stairs." Shawn said, taking a drink off his beer. "She usually stays open late on the week-ends waiting on late night costumers just like you five." He chuckled, watching the men walk towards the front door.

"Well now Marshal, since we've managed to unwind a little, how about we go finish that nap we started earlier today." Wapiti said, filling up two shot glasses on the bar and handing him one.

"Sounds good to me." Shawn said, holding the shot glass up in the air with a big smile on his face. "Here's to your health." Then they both drank then down, thanked Dave for the drinks, then they headed towards the door.

The word had gotten out about the fight and people were coming from Buxton's Saloon and the two Cat House's to see what everybody looked like for themselves. First, they watched the five wounded men slowly walk out. Staggering as they tried to walk. Then looking over at Wapiti, they could see yet again, No-One had laid a hand on that Buck Indian.

The people on the boardwalk were packed in like Sardines in a can. But everyone stepped aside and made enough room for the Marshal and Wapiti to walk side-by-side thru.

When they cleared the crowd of people, they started walking between the two closest buildings. Shawn started talking about how much fun that little fight had been. But yet again, he hadn't gotten to see Wapiti fight, cause he had his hands full too.

When they cleared the back of the stores they could see a lantern on inside their shack. "Who would have turned the lantern on and why?" Wapiti asked

"Carmen," Shawn answered "Bless her heart."

"What are you talkin' about?" Wapiti asked

"Carmen, sometimes when she knows I went to the Saloon, she leaves me a big piece of apple pie to eat before I go to bed." Shawn answered, walking into the shack and seeing two big slices of apple pie on the table. "She turns the lantern on so I'm sure to see it."

"How'd she know we went over to the Saloon?" Wapiti asked

"Those dynamite explosions earlier tonight must have woken her up too. She would know that it would have woken us up, so she probably came out to see if we needed anything before she went back to bed." Shawn said, picking up a plate and fork and started eating.

"That sure is nice of her." Wapiti said, picking up the other plate and started eating.

"She's always doing little things like this." Shawn said, in between bites.

"Only thing it's missing is a big scoop of ice cream." Wapiti said, in between bites

"It usually melt's before I get back, so she quit putting it on the plate." Shawn said with a mouth full of pie.

It only took them a couple more minutes to finish eating, then they both laid back down and fell fast asleep.

The next thing either one could remember was someone yelling. "THE BANKS BEEN ROBBED, THE BANKS BEEN ROBBED, over and over as he ran towards the marshal's shack."

Rolling over they both tried to wake up and figure out what was going on. When a man was beating on the Marshal's door. Yelling, "MARSHAL, The Bank Has Been Robbed, The Banks Been Robbed!"

"COME IN." Shawn yelled out, setting up in bed.

The door came flying open and the man ran in still yelling. "THE BANKS BEEN ROBBED!"

"We Heard You," Shawn said, holding his hands up, hoping to calm the man down. "Now which bank has been robbed?" Shawn asked, standing up. "Wapiti, would you please go get us a pot of coffee?"

CHAPTER 2

"Sure thing Marshal." Wapiti answered, slowly climbing out of bed.

"COFFEE…Didn't you hear me, the bank has been robbed." The man screamed out again.

"I said I heard you, but I need time to wake up and look everything over before I can just take off down the road." Shawn said, just as Griselda brought in a large hot plate and pot of coffee in.

"Mom thought you might want this Marshal." Griselda said, setting them on the table.

"Thank you darlin', here's your five dollars for cleaning the shack while we were gone." Shawn said, handing her the money with one hand and filling two cups up with the other hand.

"Are you going to hurry it up and get after those Robber's?" the Banker demanded, pointing back towards the bank.

"There's a lot to be looked at before I can go chasing after anyone. Like, which bank did they rob and which way they might have gone?" Shawn said, taking a drink off his coffee.

"The Oregon Trust and Loan Bank!" the Banker yelled out. Watching Shawn and Wapiti pull their pants on over their long handles.

"The Oregon Trust and Loan…I thought that place was Robbery proof, least that's what the banner across the front of that new bank brags about! 'ROBBERY PROOF VAULT ROOM'. Shawn chuckled out before repeating. "Robbery Proof my ass."

"It Is During The Day!" the Banker yelled out.

"Would You Please Calm Down, you don't need to scream at us." Shawn said, pouring a shot of whiskey in his coffee and took a couple big swallows. "Now, how'd they rob the bank?"

"They blew a hole through the cement wall." The Banker started explaining.

"That's what all those little explosions were last night." Shawn said, refilling his and Wapiti's coffee. "Come on Wapiti, let's go look at this and see how they did it?"

"Told Ya, They Blew Thru the cement Wall." The Banker said, following beside Shawn and Wapiti.

"How were they able to dig a hole that big without being seen?" Shawn asked, looking at the Banker.

"They built the bank fifteen feet shorter than it was supposed to be. So I bought fifteen feet from both businesses on either side. Then I hired three men to build a wall out of railroad ties from top to bottom. Then fill the empty space back up with dirt." The Banker was explaining.

"Who was doing the work?" Shawn asked, walking into the street.

"I don't remember their names." The Banker said "They were three men out of work when the job came up, so I hired them."

"That was pretty stupid of you. For a job like that you should have used a local contractor to do the job." Shawn said, walking up on the boardwalk in front of the bank. "Well, show us how they did it."

"This way Marshal." The Banker said, walking up to the front door and opening it.

They all walked towards the back of the bank to a set of stairs that went down a locked cage door. They could see the vault on the inside, both doors were blown open and it was empty. Looking over at the backside of the room they could see a large hole in the cement revealing the eight foot tall, one inch diameter bar's about a foot apart that went from the floor to the ceiling, the two in the center had been bent wide enough so any man could easily step sideways through.

"How long did those three work for you?" Shawn asked

"About a week and a half, they did the other store first. The fill in ramp on this side was supposed to be on the other side, so the Bank's wall would get covered first. But they already had the wall up and this wide ramp was left Friday night." The Banker was explaining, as he unlocked the cage door and everyone walked inside. "They got so much work done in the last week, that I gave them all a hundred dollar bonus."

"Looks like they wanted a Bigger Bonus!" Wapiti chuckled out, with a small smile on his face.

"How much money did they get away with?" Shawn asked, walking inside the caged room and over to the back hole.

"Little over thirty five thousand in cash…and two hundred and thirty troy pounds of gold." the Banker answered.

Shawn and Wapiti walked through the hole to the other side. They could see the wood railroad ties stacked and tied together from the floor to the ceiling. Seeing how the men had filled the dugout ramp that led up and out behind the bank's wall to the Alleyway behind the buildings. Where they could see two wagon's loaded up with dirt, along with three wheel barrows and three shovels.

"I'd like to know How we're supposed to go chasing after three men with No Name's and No Description of them to Know WHO we're looking for?" Shawn asked

"I can tell you how to find them, Marshal." A voice from behind them said.

Shawn stopped and looked in the direction of the voice. "Who said that, and how are we supposed to know who's who?"

"Me Marshal," a man said, walking towards him. "I have an eye for horse flesh…One's riding a big black with a white star in the center of his head and one front left white sock. One rides a big Red Medicine Hat mare and the third, rides a big Buckskin with a Calvary 76 counting brand number on his right hip. Plus they all have their U dot S dot brand X'd over. All three horses are a good seventeen plus hands tall.

"Why'd he have a number brand on him horse? AND, How would someone even get an X Calvary horse?" Wapiti asked

"When the Calvary rounds up herds of Mustangs, they brand them with the number they are going through the counting chute. That way there's no misunderstanding as to how many are in the herd." Shawn said, looking around. "After you've done your time in the Calvary, if you have served Honorably, with the exception of a couple fist fights. The Calvary will give you up to two months vacation pay and a good horse of your choice to start over with."

"That's nice of them." Wapiti said, following the boot prints back to where they had their horses tied up at. Kneeling down, he started looking their tracks over.

The description of the horses the bank Robbers were riding was being re-told over and over again through the crowd of spectators. Everyone in the crowd started talking about them not needing the Marshal to find them. Most of them remember seeing that big red Medicine Hat Mare themselves. Fact, a couple had tried to buy her for themselves, but her owner wouldn't even take two hundred dollars plus his pick of what one big horse rancher had in his corral that wanted her too.

"By the looks of these tracks, all three horses have recently been shid." Wapiti said, standing up. "But there's no-way of knowing which way they went."

"They said they were from northern California!" the Banker yelled out.

"Will you please calm down Sir, we're trying to figure this out as fast as we can." Shawn said.

"I wish you'd hurry up and get going after them!" The Banker demanded again.

"Well Sir, just where the hell do you think we should start looking for them at?" Shawn asked, sarcastically.

"I told you, they said they were from Northern Cal, somewhere close to the South Klamath Lake area." The Banker yelled out. "I bet they didn't go any further than Bend before they stopped off at a Brothel. Thinking no-one will even know about the robbery before Monday."

"He does have a good point Wapiti, what do ya say we take a quick ride over to Bend and see if we can find 'em, or find someone who's seen their horses. That big red Medicine Hat will stick out like a sore thumb." Shawn said, looking at Wapiti, then back over to the Banker.

"Will You Please Stop Talking About It and Go Get My Money Back!" the Banker shouted out.

"Are we ever going to get a full day off?" Wapiti asked, walking back to the Marshal.

"Maybe someday we will, but for right now, let's get back to the shack and get our gear." Shawn said "Mr. Banker, can you go over to the Livery and asked Gordy to get our horses ready to ride please."

"Yes I can, but would you please hurry up and get in gear. Every minute you stand around talking, they're getting further away." The Banker yelled back, walking down the Alleyway to the closest street then over to the Livery as fast as he could.

By the time Shawn and Wapiti got back to the main street that went through town. They were just in time to see a mob of forty plus men take off at a full run heading out of town towards Powell Butte. "Maybe they'll catch them before we can get to Bend." Wapiti said, watching them ride away.

"I doubt it." Shawn said, crossing the street. "Those wild mob's usually come back empty because they don't have a clue as to what it is they're looking for."

"They'll get to Bend ahead of us and warn the Robber's if they're not careful." Wapiti said, stepping up on the boardwalk in front of Carmen's restaurant.

Shawn stopped and looked around the street, he could see another wild Posse forming and fixing to head out of town.

"Why not just let those men chase them down and we go get some breakfast." Wapiti said

"Most of the men in those wild Posse's can't even find their way to the Out House in the dark. Yet alone find a Bank Robber." Shawn said, walking into the restaurant where a waitress met them.

"Would you men like a table Marshal?" the Waitress asked

"Not today, could you please have Carmen send one of the kid's out to the livery with something we can eat on the run please?" Shawn asked

"Yes Sir Marshal, right away." The Waitress answered, heading for the kitchen.

Shawn and Wapiti walked out the back door towards the shack. "You going after more Outlaw's Marshal?" Jose asked, running along beside them.

"Yes we are son." Shawn answered

They quickly walked over to the shack and inside, picking up their gear they headed towards the Livery Stables. No sooner had they stepped up on the boardwalk and the Banker met them yelling. Wanting to know what was taking them so long to get chasing after those Bank Robber's.

"Why you worried about how long it's taking me to get going, you already have two Wild Mob Posse's of at least fifty men riding towards Bend already." Shawn said walking across the street.

"If one of those Wild Mob Posse's catch up to them, they'll probably split all the money up amongst themselves and say they didn't find them." The Banker yelled out.

Shawn stopped and looked down at the Banker. "I never thought of anyone doing that...I mean think about it, no-one has seen the Robber's faces and no-one was killed...So let the Robber's go This Time, BUT Warning them about what would happen to them if they ever returned. Those Robber's would scram out of there as fast as their horses could carry them. Then, the Mob, with no true Lawman amongst them...They split the money equally up amongst themselves and tell you that the Robber's had gotten away ... Sure the hell beats splitting only fifteen percent."

"So Will You Please Get Moving!" The Banker yelled at them again.

"Yes Sir, right away." Shawn said, chuckling. With a, I wonder look on his face. Had any of those Wild Mob Posse's in the past had ever done that...Let the Robber's go and split all the Bank's money up amongst themselves. He was thinking to himself as he walked into the Livery.

With a quick glance, he could see Gordy had both horses saddled and was just finishing loading the pack horse. "Thanks Gordy." Shawn said, as he and Wapiti tied their gear down on their horses.

Then leading the horses outside, where a large group of spectator's, men, women, and children had all gathered to see them off.

Which only took a couple more seconds and they were mounting up and slowly riding through the crowd of people. They could hear the Banker yelling for everyone to get out of their way.

Shawn started to chuckle just as they got through all the people, then he kicked his horse in the side and they took off at a medium trot down Northwest Third Street. When they started up the small hill going out of town, Shawn looked at his pocket watch, it was just past two. "It's only eleven miles from here to Powell Butt"

"Sounds good to me." Wapiti yelled back, just as they started riding past and around a wagon and people walking down the road in both directions.

Neither one was saying much, they both had hoped on a couple days off before they'd have to ride out again. But they weren't quite so lucky, only one night's sleep on a soft mattress. Tonight would be on that hard ground, but at least unlike four of the last five days, they'll be able to stretch out. Instead of being cooped up on a bench seat on the train, or inside a bouncing, cramped Stagecoach.

It took them just over an hour before they rode into Powell Butte. Not much there, Livery Stables, small Mercantile store, couple cafes, one Cat House, the town's school, and a couple dozen house's. Riding over to the water trough at the Livery, they both dismounted and started stretching their leg's out while the horses drank.

The Blacksmith saw them ride in, so he walked out to talk to them. "You're runnin' a little late aren't ya Marshal?" the Blacksmith said "Two Wild Posse's came thru here over an hour ago."

"Those men don't have a clue as to what the hell it is they're looking for." Shawn said, dumping his warm water bag out, walking towards the hand pump to refill it.

"They're looking for a big Red Medicine Hat Mare!" the Gordy said, handing Shawn a pint of whiskey.

"Thanks," Shawn said, taking the bottle and taking a small drink off it and giving it back. "So which way did those two Posse's go?"

"One went on to Redmond and one went over the mountain…which way you going Marshal?" the Gordy asked

"We're going over the mountain too." Shawn said, pumping on the handle and holding his water bag under the flowing water till it was filled back up.

Wapiti quickly did the same, and they were heading out of town within five minutes. Riding at a fast trot, in no time at all they were riding through the timber lined road. It wasn't as wide or as well traveled as the main road was. If two wagon's meet on this road, they might have a hard time getting past each other in more spot's than not.

They were lucky in one way, Wapiti was thinking to himself. Because of the tall Ponderosa Pine and Douglas Fir trees they were riding in the shade ninety percent of the time. So they could keep the faster pass up for a couple extra miles before they'd have to slow them down to a walk and let the horses rest for a couple miles. Then Shawn kicked them back into a slow trot.

They had been traveling for a good two plus hours when Shawn slowed them back down to a walk. "I figure we're just a couple miles out, the only thing we have to go on…is the same thing those Mobs are looking for. That Red Medicine Hat Mare." He said, looking over at Wapiti.

"Those Robbers are going to know that, that Mare is going to stick out, so they need to get rid of her." Wapiti said

"Your right…Fact, they're all going to have to get rid of their horses. That's the only description the telegraph wire can send, is a description of their horses." Shawn said "So we need to find out who they might have traded horses with.

"Sounds to me like we're back to looking for a needle in the haystack…You have any idea how many people would jump at the chance to trade their horses for the kind of horses we're looking for." Wapiti said, looking around and seeing a couple houses on the outskirts of town.

"You're right..! We'll be looking for someone who has good stock to trade out with." Shawn said, seeing and hearing the kids playing around them. He could also see a couple Lady's outside removing clothes off the cloth's line. Riding up to the first lady they came to. "Excuse me Ma'am, I'm looking for someone who might have some good horses to sell or trade?" Shawn asked

"Yes Sir Marshal, just go up one more block and take a left on 8th Street. It only goes down about a block and a half. At the end you'll see a big ranch house, it's on the edge of town. Chris Hensley has a big Registered Quarter Horse Ranch…if your lookin' for a good horse, everyone in town will tell ya to go to him. But his prices are high." The Lady said, dropping an arm load of clothes into a laundry basket.

"We can afford his prices, thanks for the information Ma'am." Shawn said, turning his horse down the street.

"At least we're close to a good horse ranch, but you sure that's where they'd go. What would a horse rancher like that want with a couple mixed breed horses?" Wapiti asked, as they turned the corner on 8th Street.

"They're not selling, they're buying horses." Shawn said "So they lose a little money on their horses…they're getting themselves a tested strong horse in exchange for theirs." Shawn said "They have over thirty five thousand in cash, I'm bettin' they'll even agree to give him a couple extra thousand more if he tells all them Mob

Posse's they went in the other direction." He said, riding up to the hitching rail with a water trough on the back side. Dismounting, tying their horses up, they looked the place over.

They had just stepped up on the front porch, the front door came open. "What can I do for you gentlemen?' a Young Lady asked

"I'm U. S. Marshal Shawn Felton and this is my Deputy Wapiti. We're looking for Mr. Chris Hensley?" Shawn said

"What can I do for you Marshal?" they heard a voice say, coming from inside the house.

"Please come in Marshal, Deputy." The young Lady said, stepping back and holding the door open.

Walking inside the house Shawn re-introduced himself and Wapiti.

Shaking both men's hands, Chris asked them again. "How could he help them?"

"We're looking for three men that might have been in the market for some new horses." Shawn said, with a serious look on his face.

"You talkin about a big black, a Buckskin, and a red Medicine Hat Mare that I traded for this morning?" Chris asked.

"That sounds like the three we're looking for. How'd you know we were looking for those three specifically?" Shawn asked

"I've had two large Posse's come just over an hour or so ago." Chris said, getting three beers out of the cold cabinet and offering each of them one. "It is ok for Deputy Wapiti to have a beer too, isn't it Marshal?"

"Of course it is." Shawn said, taking two beers and giving one to Wapiti. "What'd you tell those other two Posse's about the horses?"

"Well, I couldn't lie to them or you, not with them being out there in one of my corrals." Chris said, pointing and walking towards the back door. "Come on, I'll show 'em to you."

"How much did you give them for them?" Shawn asked, walking across the barnyard towards three corrals over half full of horses.

"I have over a hundred brood Mare's and two Stallion's, all Registered Quarter Horses. They gave me their horses plus one hundred dollars each to buy one of mine. They were all three year olds." Chris was explaining.

"That's a lot of money to pay for a horse." Shawn said

"Mine horses are all trained for cuttin' and ropin'." Chris said "I sold a six month old Stallion for thirty-five hundred last fall."

"That's good money...what are you going to do with these three?" Shawn asked

"I'll easily get fifty bucks each for the Black and the Buckskin... But I ain't getting rid of the Medicine Hat Mare for nothing." Chris said, pointing her out in a corral of about twenty additional horses.

Looking on the back side of the corral they could see a larger arena. Then on the backside of it was a couple corrals full of cattle. "These are all year and a half to three year olds. I don't keep any replacement Mare's under sixteen and three-quarters hands."

"Why not sell the Medicine Hat?' Shawn asked, looking the horses over. They were all sixteen to seventeen hands plus in height. All muscular built, with a good disposition. First look he could see right off that they could easily go for as few hundred dollars plus. Especially with them already trained to work cattle. "Why not sell that Medicine Hat Mare, sure she's a big beautiful horse, but you raise Quarter Horses."

"What are you kidding...Those horses are special and rare to find. Ask Deputy Wapiti, he'll tell ya." Chris said with excitement in his voice. "I'd like to find a Medicine Hat Stud to breed her too ... Isn't that big Black Medicine Hat of yours a Stud?" he asked

"Yes, he is." Wapiti answered "But with the way we're always on the trail, I don't know where we'll be next time she comes back in heat."

"I'll lend ya any horse you want if you leave him here with me for a couple months." Chris said

"What's in it for me?" Wapiti asked

"Why you so hung up on raising Medicine Hat's for?" Shawn asked

"A few years back, there was a horse race that started somewhere in Texas, Houston or Dallas and it went all the way up into one of the northern New England States, Boston or Portland Maine. Something like four thousand mile long. Anyhow, a man from Wyoming area entered his Medicine Hat Stallion and bet five hundred dollars at forty to one odds that his horse could beat all the other hundred plus horses in the race...He not only won, but he beat the second place rider by teens of days. High teens, like, sixteen, seventeen plus...No Bullshit Marshal." Chris stated

"I do seem to remember hearing about that race. But I didn't realize the winning horse had been a Medicine Hat." Shawn said

"Wonder what he did waiting for the second place rider to come in?" Wapiti asked

"I heard he spent it in the Cat House's." Chris chuckling. "Figure it out, five hundred at forty to one odds... that's twenty thousand dollars he won, not to mention the ten thousand dollar purse. They said, not only did everyone buy him drinks while they were waiting on the second place rider to come in, and none of the women were charging him either because of how far ahead of everyone he was."

"Sounds to me like the horse deserved all the rewards." Shawn said, with a big smile on his face.

"How about it Deputy, I have a real nice four year old that I ride myself." Chris offered again.

"You still haven't told me what you're willing to do for me?" Wapiti asked again

"If it's a Stud foal, you get him, if it's a Philly, I get her. Regardless of who wins the first foal, the loser gets the second foal regardless of sex." Chris said

"Why you want the Philly, you can't breed them back together again." Wapiti said

"No, but by then maybe I'll be able to find another Medicine Hat Stud to breed both to them." Chris said, walking towards the barn. With Shawn and Wapiti following beside him.

"Where we going to?" Shawn asked

"To get Deputy Wapiti that horse I was tellin' him about." Chris said

"So you going to tell us the truth about which way those men really went?" Shawn asked, in a serious voice, walking inside the barn.

"Depends…You aren't going to take my bonus money away from me that they paid me to tell everyone what direction they didn't go in, are you?" Chris asked, walking up to a stable pen. "This is the horse I was tellin' you about, Deputy."

"I suppose we could swap out for a little while, but as soon as you know she's pregnant, you bring him back to me in Prineville." Wapiti said, taking the lead rope to the big Bay Gelding. Looking him over real quick, he agreed he was a fine looking horse, he was well over seventeen hand's tall.

"NO, I Will Not take your bonus money away, I'll say, they must have spent it in all the Brothel and Saloon they visited on their way back home." Shawn said "So what way did you tell to tell the Posse's they went in and what way did they really go?" Shawn asked, looking the big Bay over while they were walking back to their horses.

"I told the Posse's that they headed back north leading one of my mules, but they really headed south." Chris answered

"They should know those men wouldn't be turning back north. What if they ran back into one of those Posse's" Wapiti said

"They're not riding the same horses anymore. Now they're riding two Bay's and a Chestnut." Chris said "Right now, NO POSSE would even look twice at them today. They're all still looking for that Red Medicine Hat Mare. So now don't they only have to look for matching horses, but horses with my circle H brand on them."

"I know you're right about that." Shawn said, watching Wapiti unsaddle his Black Medicine Hat, wondering what the foal might look like. "So which way did they really go, and how much did they bribe you with to tell everyone they went the other way?"

"They went south Marshal, said they had a place just outside of South Klamath Falls in Northern Cal, and to answer your other question. They gave me a fifty pound bank bag just about a third of the way full of gold." Chris answered, with a big smile on his face.

"That would be more than enough to bribe me into telling EVERYONE they went in the opposite direction too." Shawn chuckled, tightening his cinch.

It only took Wapiti a couple more minutes to finish swapping out horses and they were ready to pull out. "So did they happen to mention any place they might be stopping for the evening?" Shawn asked, looking down at Chris.

Sunriver Stage Stop is the closest Brothel, it's about twelve miles up the road, give or take a mile." Chris answered

"We greatly appreciate your help Mr. Hensley." Shawn said, turning his horse back up the street.

"Glad to be of assistance to you Marshal." Chris said, watching them ride away.

Shawn took out his pocket watch and looked at it, it was just a little past seven. "If we push it, we can make Sunriver by night fall."

"Alright," Wapiti said, kicking his horse into a medium trot. Riding at that speed made it hard for either one to get a good drink without spilling it all over the front of themselves. Or in Shawn's case, alcohol abuse. He was spilling more than he was drinking, and Wapiti hollered over to him to quit thinking so hard or your shirt was going to be drunk before we get to Sunriver.

"Don't you worry about how much I do or don't drink!" Shawn snapped back. Trying to take another drink.

"What if they decide to go onto La Pine tonight?" Wapiti asked.

"That means we grab something to go to eat at the Stage Stop and push on for a couple more hours tonight." Shawn said "Not to change the subject, but what about Gordy. It's HIS horse you're breeding that Mare with."

"If it's a Stud Foal, I'll swap him out horse's. If we have to wait two more years, I'll still give him the Foal." Wapiti said "You think he'll go for that?"

"Yeah, I think he'd like that deal just fine." Shawn said. Just as a Stage Coach came flying around them, stirring up all kinds of dust from the road. Causing both of them to slow up on their horses and cover their mouths and noses till the thick cloud of dust settled and they could see where they were going. After a couple more minutes they could see the Stage Stop just ahead of them. So Shawn quickly turned off the road and headed into the timber for cover. Slowing up he rode around behind the store, they could see the Livery right next door.

Riding up behind the Livery they dismounted and tied their horses up. Walking up to the back door, Shawn slowly opened it and looked around. They could see four horses inside the Livery and the corral had at least three teams of six horses to replace the tired Stagecoach horses out with.

Fact, that's exactly what the Blacksmith and the Stagecoach Driver were doing…changing out the teams. Shawn walked over and looked at the brands on the horses. Two were the same, and two had different brands on them. Walking over to the edge of the door, Shawn looked out to see if there were any horses tied up in front of the Stage Stop. There were at least six so Shawn whistled over to the Blacksmith to get his attention.

The Blacksmith turned around in his direction, so he waved him over. He quickly told the Driver he'd be right back. Then he started leading two horses back inside the Livery. When he had both horses inside and out of sight, he stopped and asked the Marshal what he needed?"

"How'd you know I was a Lawman?" Shawn asked

"Outlaw's don't come in the back door. They usually come in the front door Hootin' and Hollerin'." The Blacksmith smiling. "Just like those three that came thru here about three maybe four hours ago."

"The men we're looking for are riding two big Bay's and a Chestnut. Their brands are a large circle with an H inside." Shawn said, looking at the Blacksmith, then back outside.

"That's them." The Blacksmith answered, assuredly. "When they came in I wasn't busy, so when they all went inside I went over and checked them over. Both Bays were at least seventeen hands and the Chestnut wasn't far from it either. They all had a real good disposition, if you get my meanin' Marshal."

"I do." Shawn said

"I noticed they all had the same brand, so I went inside to talk to them about where and who they bought them from. They were buying drinks for the house and paying with hundred dollar bills." The Blacksmith was saying.

"YEAH, Yeah…we know who and where they got those horses from." Shawn said, staring straight into the Blacksmiths face. "How long ago did they leave?" he asked, just as the Stagecoach Driver came leading the other four horses in.

CHAPTER 3

"What's taking you so long Dave?" He yelled out. Then he saw the Marshal and Wapiti. "You out lookin' for those Stagecoach Robbers that robbed two Coach's last week?"

"NO, we're chasing after three Bank Robber's." Shawn answered

"I heard about that, did you hear about it Dave...They say three men robbed that new robbery proof bank in Prineville Saturday night." The Coach Driver said in a serious voice. But started chuckling when he finished telling the story. "Robbery Proof my eye...It hasn't even been open two weeks."

"I did hear about that." Dave said, starting to chuckle. "You really think these three men are the ones that robbed the bank Marshal?" Dave asked

"No thinkin' about it!" Shawn said "Wapiti, go get the horses and water them, I'll go get us a couple Bacon Cheeseburger's and deep fried tators to go."

"Yes Sir Marshal." Wapiti said, walking back out the back door and over to the horses. Quickly untying them he led them back around to the water trough and started refilling their water bags with fresh water.

"Thanks for the info" Shawn said, walking towards the Stage Stop Café.

When he walked inside, with a quick look around, he figured there was close to a dozen people inside and they all went quiet, staring directly at him and watching him walk across the room. Walking up to the counter he ordered two Bacon Cheese Burgers with the works. OH, no onion's on one. Then give us two orders of deep fried tators and four beers to go..."I'll take two of those beers right now. Then bring the other two, along with our food over to the Livery please." Shawn asked, semi-sternly. Handing her a ten dollar bill. "Keep the change for your tip, Darlin'."

"Yes Sir Marshal!" the young Lady answered. Walking over to the cold cabinet, she took out two cold bottles of beer and handed them to him. "I'll make sure your order is cooked next...Then I'll bring it right over to you Marshal."

"Thank you darling." Shawn said, turning and walking back out the door. Taking a quick look around he walked back over to the Livery and gave Wapiti a cold beer.

"Thank You Marshal!" Wapiti said, opening it up and taking a big drink. "Now that hits the spot...So how far to La Pine?"

"Eighteen miles, give or take. But the last few summer's there's one of those Roving Brothel's camped out where Paulina Creek flows into the Little Deschutes about ten miles up the road from here." Shawn said

"But aren't those Roving Brothel's usually just a bunch of fat Lady's that couldn't make it in a bigger town?" Wapiti asked, taking another drink off his beer.

"Most are, But not this one...These Ladies are Independent Operator's and don't split their money with anyone. Beside, sex with a beautiful women out in the mountain's with the sounds of a flowing river going by...Something about it, just makes it more enjoyable." Shawn said, with a big smile on his face.

"Isn't that hard ground hard on the women's backs?" Wapiti asked

"They all have Cavalry officer's size tents, twenty by twenty, seven and a half feet tall in the center and six feet tall on the edges. They even have a small fir box in them if needed." Shawn said "They each have their own tent spread out up and down the two rivers."

The two had been talking for about ten minutes when the waitress brought their food and four more beers to them. "Your tip was too much Marshal, so I brought you both an extra beer." The waitress said, handing him two bags. One with the food in it and one with the four beers.

"Thank you Young Lady." Shawn said, taking the two bags. Setting the beer bag down on the back of a wagon, he handed Wapiti his Burger and tators. Then took his out and started eating. Just as the Blacksmith walk over with a big bucket of grain and dumped a good size pile in front of each horse.

"Sorry it took me so long to get to your horse's Marshal." Dave said, setting the bucket down, he started walking around all the horse's and checking their hoof's over, making sure none of their shoes fallen off or were loose. Then looking at the circle H brand on Wapiti's horse. "I thought they said you rode a big Black Medicine Hat?"

"He's going to be having some fun for a couple weeks." Shawn said, smiling.

"How's that?" Dave asked

"He's playing with a Mare." Shawn said, finishing off his second beer and opening his last.

Looking out over the mountains to the east, Shawn could see the near full moon rising up over them. With very few clouds and the light from the moon, he figured they could make Paulina Creek by ten if they were lucky.

Looking at his pocket watch, it was just past eight forty. "Come on Wapiti, let's get riding." Shawn said, taking his last bite of hamburger.

"Alright," Wapiti said, standing up and stretching out. Then walking over they tightened their cinch straps up, climbed aboard and headed down the road. Just as the sun was setting over the mountains to their west. Kicking their horses in the side, they took off down the road at a medium trot. They had only gone a couple miles when they came to the first group of wagon's camping together for the night.

They could smell the food cooking, sure they had just finished eating, but that food sure did smell good and made them hungry again.

They had been traveling at a good pace for just over another hour when they came upon another group of wagons. With the moon light, it was almost daylight out. Shawn pulled back on the reins. "How about we see what these folks have for dessert?"

"Sounds good to me." Wapiti said, riding over to the group of wagons.

"How you folks doing tonight?" Shawn yelled out, riding in between the wagons and dismounted. "I'd pay five dollars for a piece of pie and a cup of coffee."

The light from the fire made it easy to see who was riding into camp. Everyone could see the fire flickering off their badges. Right off everyone could tell by the size of the man leading the way he was none other than U. S. Marshal Shawn Felton himself. But then everyone saw Wapiti ride into view and they went totally quiet watching them tie their horses up.

"Over Here Marshal." They heard a voice call out. So they headed towards a Lady filling up two cups of coffee and handed it to them.

"Thank you Ma'am." They both said, taking a couple sips.

"You men stopping for the night Marshal?" someone yelled out.

"NOPE, just in need of a cup of coffee and something sweet to eat." Shawn answered

"Do you want Apple, Peach, or Cherry pie gentlemen?" the Lady asked

"How about a slice and a half of Apple Ma'am, I'm willing to pay extra." Wapiti said, taking a drink off his coffee.

"NON-SINCE Deputy. There's plenty to go around." The Lady said, handing him a plate with a large piece of pie on it and a fork. "You want a piece the same size, or bigger Marshal?"

"That size is more than big enough for me Ma'am. If I eat too much, it'll make me sleepy." Shawn said, handing the Lady a ten dollar bill.

"No Thank You Marshal, obviously you men are in a hurry to catch up to someone." The Lady said, holding her hands up.

"Yes Ma'am we are. But we have an expense account, so we get re-unburst on all money we spend on any supplies we need." Shawn said, making her take the money.

The two slowly ate their pie, then each had one more cup of coffee then it was time to go. Thanking everyone for their hospitality, they quickly tightened their cinch straps and headed back down the road at a medium trot.

As the night got later, the camps they were riding by had gone from noisy conversation into quiet camps as everyone went to sleep while their fires slowly burned out. By the time they came to the fifth camp, they were riding past the wagons before they realized there was even a camp close to them.

After another hour, they could smell smoke in the air again. Shawn slowed them down to a walk. "We must be getting close to Paulina Creek."

"How you figure that?" Wapiti asked

"I figure that smoke we're smelling is coming from one of those Young Lady's tents." Shawn answered

After about ten more minutes of walking their horses, they could hear the river flowing up ahead of them. So Shawn rode over to the side of the road, dismounted and started tying his horse up to the bows of a fir tree, while Wapiti did the same thing.

"The river flows east west up here, last time I was through here there was something like six to eight Lady's. On your side, a couple hundred feet downstream Paulina flows into the Little Deschutes." Shawn started explaining. "They have their tents set up on both sides of the rivers. So, you take that side of Paulina creek and I'll take this side. Here's some stick match's you can use to see the brands on their horses without putting out to much light and draw attention to yourself."

"Alright Marshal." Wapiti said, taking the matches, then headed out into the darkness of the timber. The road had been easy to see, but being down under the boughs of all the trees, made it hard to see all the brush they had to walk around.

After a couple minutes Wapiti could smell smoke again. Stopping, he slowly started looking around, seeing a couple tent's just up from the river, he could also see a horse tied up out front of each one. Slowly and cautiously he walked over to each horse and checked each horse's brand over. But neither of them had the right brand. Walking back up into the timber line, he slowly started walking back down the river till he saw another tent. So again, he slowly and quietly worked his way down to the white tent and checked out the brand on the horse. But with just the moonlight itself, he again found it wasn't the brand they were looking for.

Looking down the river, he could see a small foot bridge that crossed over the Little Deschutes. He could see a couple tents on the other side. So he quickly crossed over the river to the other side. Walking closer to the two tent's, he noticed there were no horses tied up anywhere around them. Which took him by surprise, cause he could hear someone snoring inside the closest tent to him.

Continuing up stream, he quickly came to two more tents. One on each side of the river. He thought the Marshal said there were only six to eight Lady's working here. He'd already come across that many tents himself. But just like the last two, they didn't have a horse tied up out front of the tent, but he could hear voices coming from inside two. Whoever they were, they weren't thru playing yet.

Shawn quickly worked his way through the timber and brush till he came to Paulina Creek. He could smell smoke in the air but couldn't see where it might be coming from. Sticking his finger in his mouth, he held it up in the air. The breeze was coming from downstream, so he slowly crossed over the river to the other side. Then started working his way back downstream towards the Little Deschutes River. He'd only gone a couple hundred yards when he looked across the river and could see Wapiti checking out a couple horses in front of a couple tents.

He hadn't gone even fifty feet and he could see the white canvas tent in front of himself. Looking the camp over, he could see a horse tied up to a tree. Working his way over to it, he struck a match and looked at the brand. It wasn't the one they were looking for, so he continued on downstream. He'd only gone another fifty feet when he came to two more tents out in the open. With a foot bridge back across Paulina Creek to the other side. Seeing both horses tied up to the trees behind the tents, he slowly and quietly worked his way over to them and checked them out. Again, neither one had the brand they were looking for. Walking downstream another hundred yards or so, he could see where the two rivers came together. With the help from the light of the moon, he could see the foot bridge that crossed over the Little Deschutes a couple hundred feet down river.

Continuing down to the Little Deschutes, he waded across to the other side. Walking back towards the foot bridge he could all of a sudden smell perfume and a dark colored tent appeared only ten feet away from him. It wasn't white like all the others, it was dark green in color like the soldier boy's they call Marines sleep in. The Calvary's tents were all white and their uniforms were blue with two yellow stripes down the sides of the pants to fight in. But the Marine's had green uniforms so they'd blend into the background better, so they wouldn't be easily seen.

Stopping, he slowly took a couple steps back away looking at the tent the entire time. When he was about fifteen feet away, he started working his way around it, looking for a horse. But there wasn't one, which made no sense…Maybe she was alone in there tonight, he was thinking to himself.

Wapiti could hear the Young Lady inside telling the man it was past bed time, if he wanted to play longer it was going to cost him another hundred.

He agreed to pay her, but she could wait till morning for him to give her the money. She told him if he didn't pay up right away, he could spend the rest of the night outside.

"Alright," the man agreed. Turning the lamp up so he could see inside his wallet.

Wapiti could see the silhouette of them inside. He was handing her the money and she was taking it from him. Then they turned the lamp back down low, so he couldn't see them anymore.

That just didn't make any sense, WHERE, was that man's horse?" If he had a hundred dollars to spend on a Lady, he defiantly had money for a horse…But where was it?" Wapiti was thinking to himself as a big Screech Owl screamed out, causing a couple horses to whinny out somewhere further up the ridge.

Wapiti slowly and quietly started working his way in the direction of the whinny. Looking for the horses and anyone that might be watching over them as well. After he went a good couple hundred feet, he could smell fresh horse manure. Stopping, he slowly started looking around. After about thirty seconds he could see four horses tied up to a rope between two trees.

Wapiti slowly worked his way closer to the horses, making sure there was no-one sleeping under a tree nearby. When he had worked his way around the horses and was sure there was no-one hiding out, he worked his way down to the horses. Lighting a match, he looked at the right hip of the closest horse as the match flared up. Right away he saw the circle H brand, so he quickly put the match out and started looking around the area.

He quickly found all three saddles, the packsaddle for the mule and all their supplies were laying just on the other side of the rope. Digging under their gear he found the four large satchels that the gold was inside. Picking up two he quickly took them about forty, fifty feet further up the hill and laid them down behind a dead tree. Then went back and grabbed the last two bags, restacking the supplies back on top like nothing was missing. Then he quickly took both bags to the same area.

He knew the Marshal would cross over the river to this side when he got to it. So Wapiti slowly started working his way back towards the river. Which only took him a couple minutes. When he was within seeing distance of the river, he turned and started walking up stream.

After a couple minutes he heard a branch break. Stopping, he started looking and listening the area over. After a couple more seconds he could see someone slowly and quietly walking through the trees. Seeing it was the Marshal, he called him over.

"I didn't find 'em." Shawn whispered, as he started walking over to Wapiti.

"I didn't find them all, but I think I know which tent one is in, and I found all their horses and a mule a couple hundred feet further up the hillside." Wapiti said

Shawn took his pocket watch out and lit a match, it was just after midnight. "Let's get back to our horses and get back here as soon as we can." Shawn said, walking back towards the river, with Wapiti following.

It only took them a couple minutes and they were wading back across the Deschutes River. "There's two tents down at the mouth of the river on this side of the Paulina, then one more a little further up in the timber well out of sight. I think it might have one of our men in it." Shawn said, in a low voice.

It took them a long five minutes of stumbling over and through the brush till they found the road. Quickly and quietly they started walking back in the direction of their horses. "I wonder how long they'll sleep in?" Shawn asked

"Well, at least one of our men is still playing with the Lady he's with." Wapiti said, smiling.

"They better get it while they can, cause they're going to be spending three to five years over in Pendleton." Shawn chuckled out.

It only took them a couple more minutes to get back to their horse. Quickly untying them, they lead them back up the road. "Where do you want to tie these back up at?" Wapiti asked

"I'd like to be as close to their horses as possible." Shawn said, walking back across the bridge.

"I don't think we can lead these horses through all that brush without waking someone up." Wapiti said "I think we'd be better off if we tied them off just off the main road and went back to their horses and waited for them to come to get them and their gear."

"You might be right." Shawn said, walking back into the timber and out of sight from the road. When they had gone a good hundred feet off the road, they quickly tied their horses back up and started working their way back through the timber.

"We're going to have to stay close together tonight so one of us will be awake when they come out for the horses and gear." Shawn said, quietly.

"No we don't." Wapiti said "Trust me, we'll know when they come out and start to load up their gear."

"How do you figure that?" Shawn asked

"I hid all four bags of gold on them, so as soon as they see they're gone, you can count on them getting upset." Wapiti answered, as they got back to the Little Deschutes River.

"That was pretty smart." Shawn said, wading back across the river.

It only took them another ten slow minutes to get back to where the three horses and mule were tied up at. "I hid the gold about forty feet or so further up behind a large log." Wapiti said, in a low voice pointing.

"Alright…their horses are tied facing away from the tents. So you go hide behind a bush with that ten gauge about thirty or so feet in front of them. I'll hide back here about the same distance… They'll have their backs to me, that's when I'll make my play." Shawn said, whispering and pointing. "You don't come out of the brush till their pistols are on the ground clear."

"Yes Sir." Wapiti answered, as they both went to go find a big brush pile to hide behind and wait for the Outlaw's to come to them.

Neither one was even setting down for a couple minutes when they both fell sound asleep.

It only seemed like they had been dozing off for a couple minutes when they awoke to the voices of people talking. They both anxiously woke up and started looking around trying to see if they could see who was talking. They could both hear men and women talking, one lady was yelling at one man to pay up the additional eighty dollars he still owed her for last night's nightly games they'd played till well after two o-clock this morning."

"I said I'd pay you after I got back up to my gear and got the rest of my money." A man yelled back.

"Then Go Get It!" a woman yelled back.

"I'll go after breakfast." The man's voice said "Now, who's making coffee and who's cookin' the food?"

"We'll be more than glad to make you gentlemen coffee… But I'll Be Damned If We're Doing Any Cookin'!" one of the Lady's yelled out.

"Alright" They heard a man yell out. "I'll go up to our horses and get our grub and will be right back."

Both Shawn and Wapiti started looking around for each other. After a couple seconds Shawn could see Wapiti waving at him from inside the fir boughs of a stand of young Douglas Fir trees all about eight to twelve feet tall. Holding his hand up, he signaled for Wapiti to lay low.

"NO SHIT!" Wapiti was thinking to himself. Watching one of the three men walking up towards them. They didn't even want that man to know they were anywhere around. They needed all three men together or none at all.

It only took the man a couple minutes to walk over to the pile of gear to get their food. What if he noticed the four bags of gold were missing, they weren't all together yet. But luckily the grub bag was on top, so he just grabbed it and ran back down to the fire pit out in front of a couple tents.

It wasn't long and the smell of coffee was waking everyone else in the other tents up too. It only took a couple more minutes and everyone was coming out of the other tents, bringing their grub bags. They too headed over to the large fire pit to cook themselves breakfast.

It was hard enough on both Shawn and Wapiti, smelling that coffee and not being able to have a cup. But when the smell of bacon, sausage, and fried tators started filling the air, their stomachs started growling. Shawn reached into his pocket and took out a couple corn biscuit's to nibble on. While Wapiti took out a piece of jerky and started eating it.

They both could see most of the going on's down below. It was a nice area the Lady's had built their Roving Brothel in, an area where the two river's came together. The ground was semi-flat for a good hundred feet on all three sides of the rivers. Wapiti counted twelve tents altogether, and could count at least nine men standing around the fire drinking coffee.

One of the lady's was still yelling at one of the men to go get that eighty dollars he still owed her. But he assured her, he'd get it right after breakfast was over with.

"WHY DIDN'T YOU GET IT WHEN YOU WENT UP AFTER YOUR FOOD!" She yelled out.

"Sorry Darlin', I wasn't thinking about that when I went to get our food." The man chuckled out "I was to damn hungry…How about a refill on coffee."

"NOT UNTIL YOU GO GET ME MY MONEY!" she yelled out again.

"We're almost ready darlin', just give me another half hour and we'll be ready to go. Then you can follow me up to our supply's and I'll give it to you." He calmly tried to tell her.

"You better not be lying to me or I'm keeping your horse." She yelled out.

"We'll all make sure if you don't pay her the eighty dollar, she gets your horse!" they heard all the other Lady demandingly stated.

"I HAVE IT, I PROMISE!" the man yelled out.

It may have only taken them an hour to eat, but it was one of the longest hours Wapiti could ever remember setting thru. Finally, their three men followed by two lady's, one with a double barrel shotgun just in case he didn't have the eighty dollars, came walking towards the horses.

All three men were laughing and joking, assuring the Lady's he had more than eighty dollars, so don't worry about it.

Just as soon as the three men and two lady's started walking in their direction, Wapiti signaled over to Shawn that they were coming.

Shawn tried to look around the bush he was hiding behind to try and see them. But for the first thirty or so seconds he couldn't see them, till they started walking up through the timber in his direction. Pulling his lever back on his rifle, he double checked to make sure there was a bullet in the chamber, there was.

When he saw the one lady with the double barrel shotgun, he started quietly chuckling. She wasn't foolin' when she said she'd take his horse if he didn't have the money. It only took them a couple more minutes and they were all up at the horses. Lucky, the two women were holding back a good twenty plus feet.

Shawn couldn't make a move, the horses were in the way. Setting anxiously watching over the men, waiting for them to find out the gold was gone. Which didn't take very long, no sooner had the man that owed the Young Lady the money, he took a wad of cash out of his saddlebags and started to pay her when one of the other men shouted out "THE GOLD IS GONE!"

"WHAT!" the other two yelled out. Digging through their supply's again and not finding the four bags of gold.

"FREEZE GENTLEMEN!" Wapiti spoke out, holding that big double barrel ten gauge at them. Right off, they all three could see both hammers were pulled back. "YOU TWO LADY'S, step back out of the way please."

"You've only got two barrel's with that gun boy!" one of the men said, sliding his hand down towards his pistol. "You can't get all three of us."

"NO, But I Can Take Out Two Of You, So Which One Of You Wants To Die With Your Buddy There…!" Wapiti firmly stated. "MISTER, you move your right hand one more inch and I'll blow it off."

That brought all three men to a sudden stop, and they started looking around at each other, then at Wapiti, and wondering where the Marshal was.

"ALL THREE OF YOU, put your hands over your heads and stand full up!" Wapiti ordered, raising the barrel of the shotgun up and down. Which all three did. "NOW, one at a time from my right, your left. Using your left hand, reach down and throw your pistols over here to me."

Slowly, one at a time they each did as they were told, but kept looking up at Wapiti and wondering where the Marshal was hiding at.

"YOU IN THE CENTER, AND THE ONE TO HIS RIGHT. THROW THOSE TWO SNUB NOSED .38's OUT WITH THE OTHER'S." Shawn spoke out. "Just like the last time, use your left hand, and move real slow. I don't like shootin' a man, and I really don't like shootin' him in the back. It's even harder to explain to the Judge why I had to shoot you in the back."

Slowly they both tossed their second pistols on the ground in front of them.

"He still hasn't paid me the money he owes me Marshal!" one of the Lady's yelled out.

"Marshal, if you'll let me move, I'll get her money out of my saddle bags." A man said, looking behind himself, watching Shawn walk towards them.

"Sorry son, but that money belongs to the Bank. All three of you men pull out your wallets and toss them over towards the Lady's." Shawn demanded

All the men quickly did as Shawn told them to and the Young Lady quickly opened them up. "They only have hundred dollar bills, Marshal?" she said, looking over at him.

"Looks like you get a bonus for last night's work, Young Lady." Shawn said, walking up behind the men. "NOW, you three start saddling up."

"Yes Sir." They all answered, watching Wapiti walking closer to them with that ten gauge and both hammers were still pulled back ready to fire. "You can drop the hammers on that ten gauge." Two of the men said, picking up their saddles.

"NOT UNTIL WE GET HOME...! Just so you know, this things loaded with ball bearings, NOT bee-bees, so I can blow your head off from fifty yards away. So I don't want any trouble from any of you all the way home...UNDERSTOOD!" Wapiti demanded

"Yes Sir." All three men said, slowly saddling their horses up.

Marshal, Deputy, would you men like a cup of coffee and something to eat?" the Lady with the double barrel twelve gauge in hands asked.

"Yes Ma'am, that would be very hospitable of you, thank you. But make that breakfast to go please." Shawn said

"MARY JO, BRING MARSHAL FELTON AND DEPUTY WAPITI UP A LARGE CUP OF COFFEE." The Young Lady with the hundred dollar bill in her hand yelled out. "How's a couple toasted ham and egg or sausage and egg sandwich's sound Marshal?"

"That would be real nice Miss. I'll take one of each" Shawn answered, briefly looking over at her, then back over to the Outlaw's as they saddled their horses.

"Me too." Wapiti said, looking over at the two very beautiful and sexy Young Lady's. They were wearing extra short cutoff jeans and you couldn't, and he could almost see through the cutoff half T-shirts and see her nipples pointing out and the darker brown section shown thru her white shirt. Then her bare slender waist and long sexy legs and very little clothing on would make any man's might go wild with lustful thoughts. He was thinking to himself watch the two walk away and a third coming up the trail with the morning coffee. Believe it or not, he could smell it when she was still a good twenty feet away.

Walking up to them a beautiful brunette with big brown eyes handed them each a cup of coffee. "Deputy, why don't you leave the Marshal here to watch over the prisoner's and me and you go back to my tent for a couple hours." Mary Jo said, with a big beautiful smiling face and eyes.

"Sorry Ma'am, but I'm going to have to pass, we need to get these men back to Prineville today." Wapiti said, taking a sip of coffee, trying not to blush too much.

"The Marshal can start out and you can catch up with him later. I promise, we'll have lots of fun." Mary Jo said, rubbing her hip's up against him.

"I'm Truly Sorry Ma'am, I truly am...But like I said, we need to get these prisoner's back to Prineville." Wapiti said, feeling a little hot under the collar and blushing at the same time.

"WELL THEN, if you ever get back up this way you be sure to stop in." Mary Jo said, giving him a small kiss on the cheek.

"Why not tell him about the Cat House we're building in Terrebonne." Another Young Lady said.

Looking over at her they could see more than a dozen men and women standing by watching them arrest these three Outlaw's. "What did they do?" another Lady asked

"They Robbed the Oregon Trust and Loan Bank in Prineville a couple days ago." Shawn answered, taking a drink of coffee.

Seeing they all had their horse's saddle and the pack on the mule, Shawn ordered them to follow Wapiti up to where he'd stashed the gold and get it loaded up.

"Yes Sir Marshal, but would you please ask him to drop those hammers on that big ass ten gauge, what if he trip's." All the Outlaw's started saying.

"All four bags are just on the other side of the dead tree." Wapiti said, waving the shotgun back and forth walking about twenty feet apart from them up the small draw.

By the time they got the gold loaded two more Young Lady came walking up the path with their breakfast and handed each lawman a sandwich and handed Wapiti a paper sack, while the other Lady refilled their coffee.

"There's two more sandwiches inside the bag, so you can eat them later." The Young Lady answered, smiling and winking at Wapiti.

"We sure do appreciate this Lady's." Shawn said, taking a bite off his sandwich

"Wapiti, get down here with that shotgun." Shawn said, putting his sandwich next to his coffee on a small downed dead tree. Tucking his rifle up under his arm, he took three pairs of handcuffs out of his saddle bags. "You three men get over here so I can cuff you, if any of you try anything stupid, Wapiti will kill at least two of you, WE CLEAR GENTLEMEN!"

"Yes Sir Marshal, we won't give you any trouble." All three men said, while Shawn put their handcuffs on. "Now head on down the main trail towards the road and we'll get our horses."

Within a couple minutes they were heading down the small trail towards the center of camp on the other side of the river. "You be sure and stop in our new Cathouse in Terrebonne this fall, Deputy." A couple of the Lady's were saying as they walked through camp then up the trail back towards the road.

It only took them a couple minutes to get back to their horses, Shawn quickly saddled both horses while Wapiti watched over the Outlaw's with the ten gauge.

When he finished, he recuffed all three men with one cuff around their saddle horn's. "Alright, everyone get aboard and let's get out of here." Shawn ordered out.

CHAPTER 4

I n no time at all they were on the main road and heading north at a medium trot. Shawn took out his pocket watch and looked at it, it was ten minutes before eight, if he pushed them they should easily be back in town before nightfall.

It only took them just over an hour and a half to get back to Sunriver and Shawn ordered everyone over to the Livery to water their horses. So everyone followed his orders and rode up to the long water trough and their horses all started drinking.

"Can I get you anything Marshal?" Dave asked, walking over to them. "See you got your men again, where'd you catch up to 'em at?"

"No, we're good to go." Shawn said, looking at Dave. "We caught up with them at that roving Cat House camp on Paulina Creek where it flows into the Little Deschutes."

Dave slowly looked around making sure no-one could hear him. "Tell ya the truth Marshal, I take me a couple trips down there every week. They may be expensive, but they're all more than worth it. A lot of people are going to be upset when their fancy new Cat house they're building in Terrebonne gets finished."

"Those Lady's made enough money to build their own Cat House?" Shawn asked

"Took them three years to save the money, I've seen the plan's." Dave said, handing Shawn his pint. "It three stories with something something like sixteen rooms per floor full bar and poker tables downstairs along with ten bathing room's you start out in, sometimes you end up losing it in there before you'll even get to go upstairs."

"I image you're right Sir." Shawn said, taking a drink off the pint and handing it back to him. "But we need to get moving… Gentlemen, let's get moving at a slow trot." He ordered out, turning his horse down the road and out of Town.

They only rode for a short distance out of town and Shawn ordered them to walk the horses. As usual every wagon or rider that passed them looked them over at Wapiti, out front with that big Ten Gauge in the ready position followed by three rider's, one with the pack mule tied off to his horse, and the Marshal bringing up the rear with his rifle in the ready position.

Everyone knew they had to be the men that had robbed the new braggingly, supposedly unrobbable Oregon Trust and Loan Bank in Prineville. But where was the red Medicine Hat Mare that one of the men was known to be riding.

After a good two and a half to three mile walk and over a dozen plus dusty wagons going both ways had passed them, Shawn ordered them back up into a medium trot.

In no time at all they were catching back up to the last wagon that had dusted them out, because he had slowed his team down to a walk. "Sorry about that Marshal, I didn't know it was you till after I passed YA." The man yelled out as they rode by.

"It happens a lot." Shawn said, tipping his hat towards the man riding past him.

As they slowly caught up to and passed other wagons, the ones with kids inside them, the kid's would always shoot at the Outlaw's with their hand pistols. After a half dozen wagon load of children pulling and firing their hand pistols and continually shooting them with their hand pistols, it started making all the Outlaw's feel just a little uneasy inside. What if the Marshal and Wapiti had come in with guns blazin', they could all be dead right now...and they knew it.

Each one at different times would look over at the others then back at the Marshal. He was known for bringing most his captured criminals in over the saddle, NOT setting up. They were all setting up and were very grateful for that. They had gone and done something stupid and would be spending a few years in prison. But if one of those wild mob Posse's had caught up to them, they more than likely would be dead right now. Those kind of Posse's were all well known for shooting first and talking later.

After about an hour of riding they came up to the edge of Burn's, so Shawn slowed them down to a walk and told them not to stop till they got to the Livery to water our horse. Everyone did what Shawn had ordered, they weren't even two blocks into town when the people started coming out of the woodwork to see Marshal Felton and Deputy Wapiti bringing in more Outlaw's.

"Are those the men that robbed the Bank in Prineville." Some of the people started yelling out.

None of them said a word, they just rode up to the Livery to the water trough to let their horses drink. Shawn took out his pocket watch and looked at it, it was just past a quarter after eleven and his stomach started rumbling from hunger.

Looking into the crowd of people that had gathered around them, he called a young teenage boy over handing him thirty dollars. "Son, I want you to run into that Café and order me five Bacon Cheese Burgers with the works along with deep fried tators, then run next door to the Saloon and get me seven bottles of beer. Pay for our meals with the twenty and our beer with the ten, bring our beers back out to us and go back and get are food after it's cooked, OH

YEAH, give the waitress that takes this order a dollar tip from each of me and Deputy Wapiti, then one for the other three. I figure it's three orders in one ?" Shawn said, handing him the money.

"YES SIR MARSHAL." The boy said, taking off running across the street.

"Everyone dismount and stretch your legs out the best you can. Wapiti, you want to change out the water in our water bags please." Shawn said

"Yes Sir Marshal." Wapiti said, handing him the ten gauge and walking around to all the horses he grabbed everyone's water bag and started dumping them out.

"We'll Help You, Deputy." Two boy's cheerfully shouted out, as one of them started to pump on the pump handle.

"Thanks." Wapiti said, handing the first empty bag to them. One pumped and the other held each bag under the flowing water refilling them, then handing them back to Wapiti. They were just finishing up when the boy came running back across the street with their beer.

None of the Outlaws could believe the Marshal had bought them a cold beer, no other Lawman would do that and they knew it. So they all thanked him a couple times, when he handed the bottles to them and again after finishing their first big drink, they 'thanked' him again.

"You men didn't give us any trouble, we didn't have to fire one shot so it's the least I can do." Shawn said, taking a drink off his beer.

"Are these the men that robbed the Oregon Trust and Loan Bank?" people kept asking, over and over.

"Yes we are." The three Outlaw's started answering, as the boy brought their lunch out to them. Each hamburger and deep fried tators were each in their own paper bag.

"Here's your change Marshal." The boy said, handing it to him.

Shawn took out a dollar bill and gave it to him. "This is for your help young man."

"THANKS MARSHAL." The boy said, running back into the crowd.

Shawn told them to hurry up and eat, he wanted to be out of there as soon as possible.

All the spectator's stood around watching every move they made and the fact that the Marshal was once again bringing the Outlaw's in alive and not dead, and none of them looked beat up either. So they must not have put up too much of a fight when the Marshal and Deputy Wapiti caught up to them. "Where'd You Catch Them At?" someone yelled out.

But Shawn, Wapiti, and the Outlaw's didn't answer any more of their questions, they just quickly ate their lunch and Shawn had them riding out of town within twenty minutes at most. But they were all glad for the chance to stretch out their legs even if for only twenty minutes. The Marshal was pushing them hard and they were all tired of sitting in the saddle.

Shawn kept them at a walk for the first couple miles so the horses could continue to rest. The back road over the mountain to Powell Butte wasn't as wide as the main roads were. But it had been hot and dry with no rain for weeks and the dust on the road was a good couple inches deep. So when any wagons did pass them they all had to cover their faces so as not to get dust in their eyes. mouths, and up their noses.

After Shawn figured the horses had rested for well over an hour counting the twenty plus minutes in Bend, he kicked them all back into a medium trot. It was getting on to past early afternoon and the sun was directly over the top of them. So the shade from all the tall Ponderosa Pine and Douglas Fir trees didn't help much to cool them down.

Shawn couldn't believe the amount of traffic that was beginning to take this road when going to Burns from Prineville. It was originally a logging road just a couple years ago, now, the County has Judge Monson assigning community service hours to men to come up here and fall and remove as many of the smaller trees twenty feet wider on both sides of the road. All trees one feet in diameter and bigger at butt-cut would be bid out to a logging company to remove within a year. Why not, it cuts off the additional eight, nine mile further to Redmond before turning back north towards Bend, which is sixteen plus miles away.

When they were about half way to Powell Butte they started coming across some of those men doing community service. They were cutting down and limbing everything under one foot in diameter. There would be five to six men at each job site. They had a couple four foot one man saw's to fall and buck up the trees into shorter lengths and hand loaded on to a flatbed trailer with a set of four horses for each wagon. The branches, they threw out into the timber outside the twenty foot clear cut area.

"What are they going to do with all the wood from all those trees?" Wapiti yelled back at the Marshal.

"The County prisoner's will cut it all up into fire box size and split it all, then they're going to sell it for five dollars a cord. The money they raise goes to the school for a wood working class where the kids can learn how to make cabinets or whatever they want to build out of wood."

Shawn slowed them back down to a walk when he saw the small lite smoke plum from the Café in Powell Butte. Taking out his pocket watch, he saw it was almost two-forty. They were making real good time, he thought to himself.

Nobody was doing much talking, the Marshal and Wapiti wanted the ride to be over with so they could get a good night's sleep. But the Outlaw's didn't want the trip to be over with, because when it was, they were all going to be staring out of steel bars for a couple years.

It only took five more minutes and they were riding up to the intersection with the main road between Prineville and Redmond. Shawn seen two young teenage girls walking down the street as they rode by, slowing up Shawn looked down at them. "Girl's, would you please run into the Merc and get me seven beers please?"

"Marshal, they won't sell us any beer!" both girls said, chuckling

"Sure they will, you just tell them it's for me, then bring them across the street to the Livery please." Shawn said, handing then a five dollar bill.

"Yes Sir Marshal." Both girl's said, taking off running ahead of them.

Shawn continued following the others up the road into town and across the road to the water trough in front of the Livery Stable.

"Everyone give me your water bags." Wapiti said, getting off his horse.

"I thought I just heard the Marshal order us all a beer?" one of the Outlaw's yelled out. Grabbing his water bag and getting off his horse to stretch his legs and body, with one hand still cuffed around their saddle horn.

"I did, it's still eleven miles to Prineville and I'd rather have something fresher and colder to drink than this warm water we have now." Shawn said, getting off his horse. Giving his bag to Wapiti and taking the ten gauge from him to detour any thoughts of escaping by the prisoners.

Which they had no intentions of doing and asked if he'd please drop that hammer on the one barrel. But like Wapiti had told them earlier, Shawn told them that that hammer will only be dropped when they all got back safely to the Courthouse.

It only took the girls a couple more minutes and they came running up with the beer and change for the Marshal. "Thank you girls, you can keep the change for your tip for running for me."

"Thanks Marshal." Both girls said, keeping the money and giving everyone else a beer.

"Who gets these last two bottles Marshal?" one of the girls asked, holding them up.

"Me and Wapiti darlin'." Shawn said, taking one from her and putting it in his saddle bags. "Go give that other one to Deputy Wapiti please."

"Yes Sir Marshal." The girl said, running over to Wapiti.

"Here Deputy Wapiti." The girl said, with a big smile on her face.

"Thank you Young Lady." Wapiti said, setting it on the ground next to the refilled water bags.

"Would you like me to take a couple of these back over to the horses. I can see your two have a large U dot S dot brand on them, so I know which water bag to hook over your two horses?" the girl asked, picking a bag up in each hand.

"Thank you again Young Lady." Wapiti said, picking up the other three with one hand and his two beers with the other he followed behind her over to Shawn.

"Here ya go Marshal." Wapiti said, handing him his water bag.

"Everyone tighten your cinch straps back up, I want to get out of here." Shawn ordered out, looking at the three Outlaw's, then around at the crowd of people that had gathered around them. There had to be close to a hundred plus men, women, and children. He didn't think that many people lived in Powell Butte. There were also well over a dozen wagons that had stopped to check them out as well.

Within a couple minutes they were heading out of town at a walk so Shawn and Wapiti could drink their second beer. After a good ten minutes Shawn finished his beer and put the empty bottle in his saddlebag and kicked them back into a medium trot.

For the first thirty minutes the only traffic they saw was going west when they caught up to their first eastbound wagon. Which had three young boys in the back of it all pulling out the hand pistols and started shooting the Outlaw's over and over and over again.

Shawn rode up alongside the three men "You men all see how gun happy people are, I bet each one of those kids shot each one of you over twenty times. You're Damn Lucky I'm Not Gun Happy Like They Say I Am … Understand Gentlemen."

"Yes Sir we know and we appreciate it Marshal." All three men started saying

It was just only twelve minutes after four when they came riding into town on Northwest Third Street and the people were coming out of the woodwork to see the Marshal and Wapiti bring three more Outlaw's in. all alive again. Shawn was leading, followed by the three Outlaws and their loaded down mule, Wapiti was bringing up the rear with that big ten gauge in the ready position. Even those on the far side of the streets could see the one hammer pulled fully back. They all hoped that the new horse he was riding didn't trip. By the way…where was the red Medicine Hat? As well, as where is your big black Medicine Hat, had it broken a leg and needed to be put down? Everyone one could also see that each man had one hand, cuffed to his saddle horn, leaving them one hand free to control their horse.

Judge Monson looked out his window and saw the Marshal and Wapiti bringing in three more prisoner's. "I'll be damned, he brought them in alive again." He said, standing up. "Miss Twidwell, will you please get me two beers."

151

"Yes Sir, Your Honor." Ruth answered, walking over to the cold cabinet, opened it up and grabbed two bottles and handed them to the Judge just as he walked out the door, down the stairs and out onto the boardwalk.

"I see you brought them in alive again." Judge Monson said, handing him a beer. "Wapiti seems to have slowed your shooting and killing of Outlaw's down."

Wapiti got off his horse and started uncuffing the cuffs around the saddle horn so they could all get off their horses. When he finished uncuffing the third man, Judge Monson was handing him a beer. "Thank You, Your Honor." He said, opening it up.

"How about us, Your Honor, we're hot and thirsty too." All three Outlaw's yelled out.

"There's a water bucket inside each jail cell." Judge Monson informed them.

The Banker came running up the street towards them. "Thank You Marshal, thank you, thank you, thank you." He kept repeating till he got up to them. Running over to the pack horse, he started counting the Bank satchels of gold. "There's one missing!" He shouted out.

"They must have spent it on all the wild women they've been playing with since they robbed your Bank." Shawn said "Wapiti, please take those men downstairs to the jail cell area."

"Yes Sir Marshal." Wapiti said, pointing the way as the door came open.

"Judge, I do believe this is the first beer you've ever bought me." Shawn said, taking a drink. Watching the Judge walk over and give Wapiti a beer.

"You keep bringing them in alive and I just might buy you a couple more." Judge Monson said, with a big smile on his face. "So did these men give you any trouble on the way in?"

"NOOO…I told them if they tried to run on me, I'd shoot their horse and then they would be walking back in. But with Wapiti bringing up the rear with that ten gauge, that detoured their thought's the fastest." Shawn said, just as Wapiti came walking back up to them.

"You ready Marshal, I'm hungry, Thirsty, and tired." Wapiti said, looking over at the Judge. "Are you going to give us a couple days off yet?"

"There's been a lot of cattle rustling from north of Madras south towards Redmond over the last week and a half." Judge Monson said, looking back and forth between the two.

"Didn't they just open a new stockyard in Redmond, they'll probably take them there." Shawn said, taking a drink off his beer."

"Not yet they haven't." Judge Monson said "Most of the brands have been turned into all stockyards within fifty miles…They haven't shown up anywhere yet and they have well over a hundred cows with calves."

"A hundred head of cows and calves." Shawn yelled out. "Sounds to me like someone wants to start their own herd in another state…I bet they're making their own Bill of Sales when they rebrand them."

"Could be, but how would you hide a herd that big going around town's without being seen" Wapiti asked.

"How about you let us rest up today and we'll head out of town around eight-thirty, nine." Shawn suggested

"That sounds good to me Marshal, Wapiti…You two go get some rest and I'll see you tomorrow." Judge Monson said, shaking both their hands.

Shawn and Wapiti led all the horses and mule over to the Livery where Gordy met them handing Shawn a pint of whiskey and asking Wapiti where was the Medicine Hat at?"

"Remember that red Medicine Hat mare that one of those three men was riding?" Wapiti asked

"YEEAAHH, she was a nice looking mare." Gordy said, following them inside.

"The man they traded horses out with wants to breed the Black to her." Wapiti said "If the first foal is a Stud, you get it, if it's a Philly we have to wait for the second foal."

"That's alright." Gordy said, starting to unsaddle the Outlaw's horses. That sounds like a pretty good deal. I was hoping to find a nice Mare to breed him with...Medicine Hat to Medicine Hat, that's going to be a special foal."

"So you're not upset I agreed to wait the extra two years if you have to?" Wapiti asked.

"Not at all Wapiti. Fact, if she has a Stud foal, I'll trade out with YA." Gordy said, starting to look the horses over. "These three look nice and strong, I wonder where they got them?"

"From Chris Hensley over in Bend." Shawn said "Their Registered Quarter Horses...Chris is the one that came up with the idea of breeding your Black Stud to that Red Mare."

It didn't take long and the only thing left to do was unload the pack horse, so Gordy told them to take off and he'd take care of feeding them.

"Thanks" They both said, walking towards the door. Taking a quick look around the street, they both headed towards Carmen's restaurant and a good hot meal.

It was almost four-thirty, so most of the patrons were back at work. Just like every other time Wapiti walked into the room, everyone started looking in his direction. They quickly walked over to an empty table and set down. Just as the waitress met them with a pitcher of beer and two mugs. "I figured you'd like a cool beer instead of tea Deputy."

"Yes Ma'am, thank you very much," Wapiti said, filling both mugs

"I Can't Believe You People Allow This Buck Indian To Openly Drink!" A man setting a couple tables away with two other men, all were wearing nice three piece suits.

"Mister, as far as we all are concerned, that Buck Indian can drink anything, anywhere his heart desires." A man sitting at the table next to them said, in a serious voice looking at three men.

"YEEAAHH, we've all heard stories about all the fight's he's been in against three and four men at the same time." The Man braggingly and loudly started saying. "We're all members of a Professional Wrestling League that goes from Seattle to Los Angeles...I bet he can't beat us!"

Wapiti started looking the men over while he took a drink off his beer. He could tell they all were very muscular under those suits.

"We have over four hundred members." the man in the middle started explaining as he pointed out each man. "That's Sam Oliver Bass, or better known by his initials, No Good S. O. B...he was the Pacific West Coast Champion last year, pointing at the man to his right. Dutch Savage here, The Flying Dutchman beat him and he became the HeavyWeight Champion. Then two months ago, I... Rip Off their heads and shit down their windpipes, Rip Oliver, I beat Dutch, so now I'm the Reigning Pacific Coast Heavy Weight Champion...! I have five hundred dollars that says we'll kick your ass up between your shoulder blade and you'll have to take your shirt off to shit."

"But this little brawl is just between us three and Deputy Wapiti, ok Marshal." S. O. B. said "We have five hundred dollars saying he can't take the three of us at the same time...We promise we won't hurt him to bad Marshal."

"No guns and knives, I'll stay out of it." Shawn proudly said, looking the three men over. "Don't they have some kind big fancy Championship Belt that the Champion gets to wear?" He asked, looking at Wapiti with a big smile on his face.

"Yes they do." Rip proudly said

"You thinkin' what I'm thinkin' Marshal?" Wapiti said, smiling back at Shawn, then back over to the three men. "You wouldn't happen to have that belt on you, would you?"

"It's Right There In That Briefcase." Rip said pointing.

"How about we take this out into the street so we don't destroy the furnishings in here." Shawn suggested.

Wapiti continued to just sit there slowly drinking his beer, looking the three men over while they took their suit jackets and tie's off. Both X-Champs were six, two plus tall and two twenty in weight. Rip, was a good three inches taller and a good thirty pounds heavier, obviously all muscle.

"You Comin Deputy." Rip spat out "Or You Two Big Of A Chicken Shit To Take Us On.?"

Wapiti looked over at the three men and slowly started to rise, looking over at the waitress. "Darlin', tell Carmen I'd like a T-bone Steak, medium, baked potato…and whatever else comes with it." Standing full up, watching the three men walk past him towards the door. "Tell her, I'll be back before she can finish cookin' it."

"He sure is full of himself." Dutch says, chuckling at Wapiti and holding the door open for him. "Deputy, are you going to join us?"

"You say you have that Championship Belt on you?" Wapiti asked, walking towards the door.

All the customer's went out the side door as fast as they could. They all wanted to get outside and get a good spot to watch the fight from.

"Like I said, it's right over there in that briefcase." Rip said, pointing back into the restaurant.

"How about you put that on the line instead of five hundred dollars. But If I Lose, I still have to pay you men five hundred dollars." Wapiti said, walking toward the center of the street.

People that were already on the street were asking those coming out of the restaurant, "What was going on?"

Everyone started telling them Wapiti was going to fight those three giants of men, but this time out in the street where there's more room.

Wapiti and Shawn were looking at all the people coming out of every business running towards them and surrounded the five in the middle of the street.

"You, Against The Three Of Us For The Championship Belt." Rib said, laughing. Looking around at the crowd of people that were still coming from everywhere to see the fight. "HELL YEAH...I'll Put The Belt On The Line." By now all four were getting closer to the center of the street inside a twenty foot circle of people. Both S. O. B. and Dutch were laughing at him too while they unbuttoned their shirts and rolled up their sleeves.

Wapiti removed his pistol and knife, winking at Shawn when he handed them to him. Of course, Shawn just smiled back.

"ALRIGHT, here is the ONLY rule...! Rip said loud enough for everyone to hear. "If a man gets knocked down and semi-out, he has a ten second count to regather his thoughts or he's out of the fight...in other words...he's the loser!"

"Sounds fair to me." Wapiti said, looking at all the men standing only a couple feet away from him. They all three towered over him and were all laughing at him and bragging on how much fun it was going to be, to be the first men to kick this Wanna Be Indian Lawman's Ass!

Just before he finished speaking, Wapiti smashed his right fist into the man on his left's face with everything he had, sending Dutch stumbling backwards. Spinning on his left foot, he brought his left elbow up under Rip's chin into his throat, collapsing his Adam's Apple, sending him backwards stumbling to the ground, grabbing his throat, gagging and trying to breath. Spinning on around, he brought his right fist into S. O. B.'s face, sending him stumbling backwards. But Wapiti followed after him, reaching out with his left, he pulled S. O. B. back towards himself. Bringing his right fist up under his rib cage, picking him up a good foot off the ground, taking all the air out of his body while doubling him over in severe pain. Grabbing him by the back of the head, he drove it down into his rising right knee, breaking his nose, blackening one eye an knocking him out cold.

Seeing Dutch starting to rise, Wapiti spun back around on his left foot, catching the man on the side of his head with his right foot sending him backwards into the crowd of people, who just pushed him back towards Wapiti. Who met him with a powerful right fist dead center of Dutch's face. Breaking his nose, blackening both eyes and knocking him out cold all at the same time as his lifeless body fell to the ground.

Seeing Rip coming up behind him, Wapiti spun back the opposite direction on his left foot. Catching him in the side of his rib cage, breaking the three in the center and cracking one more on both sides Continuing around, he grabbed Rip with his left hand, pulling him back towards himself, driving his right fist dead center of his face. Again, breaking his nose, blackening both eyes, and knocking him out cold as his lifeless body hit the ground.

Wapiti started looking down at all three men lying knocked out on the street. "Here's a pitcher of water to wake them up with Deputy." One of the by-standers said, handing it to him.

"Thank you Sir." Wapiti said, taking it and slowly started pouring into their open mouths and up their noses, gagging them back into waking up. "Good Morning Gentlemen."

All three men slowly set up, holding their aching, pounding, ringing heads. Trying to get their eyes to focus, but everything was blurry and there were little white star's floating in the air, wiping the blood out of their eyes and spitting it out of their mouths full too. They could see all the people standing around them cheering, but for a good thirty seconds none of them could even remember what had happened to them.

Wapiti slowly turned around looking at everyone that came to watch the fight. The street's and boardwalk's were full of people, some had even climbed up the rooftops to get a better view. Reaching over to another man who had a full pitcher of beer, Wapiti took it and again slowly started pouring some more over the three men's heads. Helping them to wake up and remember what had happened to them. "You remember who I am?" He asked, helping Rip to his feet.

"UUUHHH…YEAH, I Do." Rip said, holding his ribs and taking slow, shallow breaths.

"How about you two?" Wapiti asked, extending his hand and helping each man back to their feet.

"Yes Sir, Deputy. We Remember…and we're sorry we didn't show you the respect of a man wearing that U. S. Deputy Marshal's Badge is due, we're truly sorry." S. O. B. said, apologetically.

"Apology accepted." Wapiti said, shaking the men's hands and listening to all the cheering going on from the crowd of people standing all around them.

"THAT MAKES FORTY-ONE SCALPS NOW." Shawn shouted out, patting Wapiti on the shoulder and handing him a beer. "Gentlemen, where's that Championship Belt at that Deputy Wapiti just won?"

"I have it inside my lock briefcase inside the restaurant." Rip said, pointing. "But, how about we leave all our gear in the restaurant while we go find a Doctor…When we get back, we'll leave it with the owner of the restaurant."

"You men going to be here tonight?" Shawn asked

"We are now!" all three men answered, as the floating star's started going away and they could see what each other looked like. They had NEVER been beaten that fast in a fight before, and they were all saying so.

"How about tomorrow morning around nine o-clock you hand over that Championship Belt to Wapiti and the front steps of the Courthouse." Shawn said, pointing down the street. "The Doctor's office is two blocks that way…A couple of you by-standers want to help them please, I don't think these two can even see who I am yet."

"I'd be honored to hand the Belt over to him then." Rip said, spitting out some more blood.

"Sure Thing Marshal." A couple men said, grabbing the three men by the arms and leading them up the street.

Everyone in the crowd was talking about how much bigger those men were in size compared to Wapiti. They all were a good half foot taller and fifty plus pounds heavier. Yet Once Again. No-One had laid a hand on that Buck Indian.

Shawn and Wapiti walked back towards the restaurant, everyone was still hollering and cheering. Those close enough were trying to reach out and pat Wapiti on the back.

Shawn and Wapiti just pushed their way through the crowd back into the restaurant, sitting down at the table just as the Waitress was setting their food down on the table. "Did you work up a bigger appetite, Deputy?" She asked, with a big smile on her face.

"Yes Ma'am I did… I told you I'd be back before she finished cooking it." Wapiti said, with a big smile on his face, cutting into his steak.

Felton 10

THE GREEDY ELDER BROTHER'S

CHAPTER 1

They had just started to cut into the steaks when Jose came running up to the table. "That Was Cool Deputy Wapiti, I was watching from the upstairs window. You kicked those three guy's asses before they knew what hit them." He shouted out, excitedly. "Could you teach me to fight like that?"

"SURE, I'd be glad to Jose." Wapiti answered, taking a bite of steak.

"Can You Teach Me Today?" Griselda asked, all starry eyed.

"Not today," Wapiti answered "Right now I just want to eat, take a bath, and go get some sleep. But next time we're in town longer than a day, then I'll be glad to teach you some moves."

"Thanks Wapiti…Marshal, did you get to see Wapiti's fight too?" Jose asked, still overly excited.

"Yes I did." Shawn said, in between bites. "You're right, it was fun to watch. Jose, grab those three men's coats and brief cases and take them back to your Mom please. Let her know, they'll be back in a couple hours to reclaim them. ALSO, tell her to remind them about handing that Championship Belt over at nine o-clock tomorrow morning."

"Yes Sir Marshal." Jose said, looking over at the table with everything on it. "Where did they go?"

"They're over at the Doctor's office." Shawn answered

"Are they getting pain pills like you do when you get shot?" Jose asked

"I imagine so." Shawn said "I imagine that they all have real bad headache's…Plus one is having a hard time breathing"

"I Hope I Get To See Your Next Fight Too!" Jose said, jumping down out of the chair. "I'll take their stuff back to Mom." He said, walking over to the table.

"I'll let you have first bath." Shawn said, taking a drink off his beer.

"Thanks," Wapiti said, continuing to eat.

The waitress brought them another small pitcher of beer and asked if they needed anything else.

They both thanked her, and said they were just fine. It only took them ten minutes most to eat and head towards the shack to get a clean pair of clothes.

But Griselda met them in the back room and told them she hadn't taken their clean laundry back out to the shack yet. So everything they needed was over there in a laundry basket.

"Thanking her, Wapiti walked over and grabbed a clean set of clothes and Shawn walked back into the dining area and sat back down to wait his turn. Where the waitress came back over and asked him if he'd like anything while he waited.

"Coffee, actually sounds better to me than another beer please?" Shawn answered, setting his near empty mug down on the table.

"You want me to just bring you a small pot and hot plate Marshal?" the Waitress asked

"Yes please." Shawn answered, looking around the room at the dozen plus customers, then out the window. Looking up and down the street while he passionately waited for Wapiti to finish up with his bath.

The waitress startled him just a little when she set the hot plate down and started filling him a cup. "What are you thinking about Marshal?" she asked

"Nothing important." Shawn answered, pulling out his flask and spiking the coffee. "Just tired Darlin'."

"Is there anything else I can get you Marshal?" the Waitress asked

"Nothin' now, but could you ask Carmen to bring out a couple slices of pie and a small pitcher of beer for later please?" Shawn asked

"What Flavor…Cherry, Apple, Pumpkin, or Banana Cream?" the Waitress asked

"Two large slices of Banana Cream tonight, instead of apple tonight." Shawn answered, with a big smile on his face.

"You think Deputy Wapiti might like a glass of ice tea instead of beer with his pie?" the Waitress asked

"You might be right…Why don't you ask her to bring a small pitcher of each." Shawn answered

"Ok Marshal." The Waitress said, walking back towards the kitchen.

Shawn was just sitting there staring out the window at nothing in particular for a good ten minutes when Wapiti finally came out and told him it was his turn. "Thanks," he said, looking at his pocket watch, it was almost five. Standing up, he drank down the last of his coffee cup, then headed into a nice hot bath.

Even though he felt like he'd taken a nice long relaxing bath, it actually only took ten minutes, another five to get dressed, and even though it was only a few hundred feet to the shack, he needed to strap his holster belt on and firmly tie his holster down before stepping outside. Briefly stopping, he glanced inside the dining area, before heading out the back door, and walking across the open area at the bank diagonally across the street, right off he looked to see if the lantern was burning, which meant the banker was still inside, not seeing one he quickly walk back to and into the shack, looking down at his pocket watch, he could see it had only taken fifteen minutes. Wapiti briefly rolled over and saw who it was, then rolled back over. Shawn quickly walked over and laid down on his bunk and fell fast asleep.

The sun was just setting behind the mountains and it soon would be dark when Carmen and Griselda quietly opened the door to the shack. Trying not to wake them, but it did and they both could smell the coffee.

"Thank you so much Lady's." Shawn said, setting up in bed.

"Yes, thank you Lady's." Wapiti said, too. Climbing out of bed and walking over towards the table.

"Sorry, I brought coffee instead of ice tea." Carmen said, setting everything on the table.

"That's alright, I'd rather have a couple cups of coffee after I first wake up." Wapiti said, walking towards the table. "What kind of treat did you bring us tonight?"

"Marshal said to bring Banana Cream pie tonight." Carmen answered, filling up two coffee cups. "Is that okay, or would you like something else?"

"Yes Ma'am, Banana Cream is just fine." Wapiti said, reaching for the cup of coffee she was handing him.

"You men going over to the Saloon tonight?" Carmen asked, setting the coffee pot on the hot plate.

"I might go down for a couple cold beers." Shawn said, taking a bite of pie.

"Not Me!" Wapiti said "I just wanted to lay down and relax on a nice soft bed. Knowing the Judge, he'll want us to go after those Rustler's tomorrow." Wapiti answered

"I ain't going chasing no Rustler's without a plan." Shawn said, taking another bite of pie.

"I made some cinnamon rolls today, would you each want a roll too before I go to bed?" Carmen asked

"I don't mean to sound like a pig, but yes Ma'am, I would like one." Wapiti answered

"Me too please Carmen." Shawn said, taking a drink of coffee. "It will go better with a cold beer to wash it down with."

"I'll bring them right back out." Griselda said "Do you each want just one, or two each?"

"One will be more than enough for me." Wapiti answered, refilling their coffee.

"Bring a couple each with our morning coffee instead of bacon and eggs." Shawn said, taking another bite.

"Alright," Carmen said "Come on Gris, let's get going and let these two relax."

"Okay Mom, Marshal I'll be right back." Griselda said, walking out the door behind Carmen.

"Thanks sweetheart." Shawn said

They were just finishing up their pie when Griselda came running back in with the cinnamon rolls. "What's ya runnin' for?" Shawn asked

"Mom's been reading us a story about a pig and a spider, it's a fun story and I don't want to miss any of it." Griselda answered, running back out the door.

"You think the Judge will make us go after those Rustler's tomorrow afternoon?" Wapiti asked, filling his coffee cup up with the last of the coffee.

"I don't have a clue, but I hope not." Shawn said, filling a beer. Then taking a bite off the cinnamon roll. "You want to go down for a beer?"

"Not tonight, I just want to lay down and relax tonight. Besides, I had enough beer today…You goin' down?" Wapiti asked, taking a bite of his cinnamon roll.

"After the pie and this cinnamon roll, I'm getting tired again." Shawn answered, taking a drink off his beer. "I think I'll join you and catch up on some much needed rest."

It only took them a slow enjoyable ten minutes to finish eating and they both laid back down and fell fast asleep

They both woke to the smell of hot coffee and warm cinnamon rolls as Carmen set them on the table. "Good morning." She said to both of them.

Rolling over, they could see it was barley dusk outside, which meant it was just before six. Thanking her, they both climbed out of bed and walked over to the table. Shawn filled both cups, then asked Wapiti to grab the rolls and hot plate so they could go out on the porch this morning.

Picking them up, Wapiti followed behind Shawn out to the table and set everything down. Picking up a cup of coffee he sat down and picked up a big warm cinnamon roll covered in powdered sugar.

"Yeah know, that Deputy Johnson down in Hood River had a good point." Shawn said, taking a small sip of hot coffee.

"What did he say?" Wapiti asked

"Said you should teach a self-defense course for young wannabe Lawmen." Shawn chuckled "I think you could make a hell of a lot more money than being a Lawman."

"You really think so?" Wapiti asked

"Sure, most lawmen nowadays have served in the military, either the Cavalry or the Navy's new Marine Corp soldier's. They go thru a three month bootcamp where they're taught in hand-to-hand mortal combat using the bayonets that mounts on the end of their rifle barrels" Shawn answered, taking a bite of cinnamon roll

"It takes a long time to show and teach someone to fight." Wapiti answered "My Dad said he started teaching me as soon as I could walk. … I notice you haven't spiked your coffee yet this morning Marshal." Wapiti said, with a big smile on his face.

"Not chasing after any Outlaw's, so I don't need to think as hard." Shawn answered, taking his flask out. "But now I have to think about our new school."

"Our New School, I thought I was going to be the one to teach them how to fight." Wapiti said, refilling both their coffee cups.

"Someone has to teach them how to shoot." Shawn said, pouring a small shot in his coffee.

"How much could we charge and how many people in a class?" Wapiti asked

"The Military does something like sixty to eighty in each group of new Soldier's. But they have more men to help teach them with, figure we could do something like, twenty to thirty at a time." Shawn answered

"How much you figure we could charge each man?" Wapiti asked

"Not sure, you'd have to figure in room and board, plus ammunition." Shawn questionably answered. "That could run into more than a few hundred per man. "SHOOT, figure each man is going to cost you at least one hundred dollars a month to feed, cloth, and wash their clothing, plus we'd have to build a barracks for them to live inside, but that's just one big open bay area, you remember the barracks we slept in in Pendleton, They made room for us in RP berthing, which stood for Ranked Personnel, Corporeal or higher. But the under ranked troopers claimed it was because they 'Stunk To High Heaven', that's what Ranked stood for.

They had been talking for almost thirty minutes, when Griselda brought them out another pot of coffee and one more cinnamon roll each. "Mom figured you were out of hot coffee and said you each might want a third cinnamon roll for breakfast."

"Thank you Griselda." Shawn said, dumping his semi-warm cup of coffee out and refilled it with fresh new coffee. "Tell your Mom we said thanks too." He said, reaching for the third roll.

"Don't know that I can eat another whole one, but I sure will try." Wapiti said, reaching for the last cinnamon roll. Then taking a silver dollar out of his pocket, he gave it to Griselda.

"Thanks Wapiti, is there anything else I can get for you?" Griselda asked

"I'm fine, how about you Marshal?' Wapiti asked

"No, I'm more than good." Shawn answered "But thank you sweetheart."

"Are you going to practice shooting again today Marshal?" Griselda asked

"If we do, I'll make sure to have Jose come and get you sweetheart." Shawn said, with a big smile on his face.

"OKAY, I'll get my chores done early then." Griselda said, with excitement in her voice, then she took off running back towards the restaurant.

"Those two are the politest, nicest, and smartest children I've met in a long time." Wapiti said, smiling, watching her run away. "The way they speak English and Spanish both, granted, I can't understand a thing them and Carmen are talking about...But they do whatever it is she asks them to in her homeland, or Spanish language."

"She's used that language on me a couple times running me out of her kitchen. Don't know what she's sayin', but I get the hell out of her way when she does." Shawn chuckled with a big smile on his face. Pouring another small shot into his fresh cup of coffee.

"So what are you are thinking about now?" Wapiti asked, nodding his head towards the cup of coffee.

"Our Wannabe Lawman Academy." Shawn answered, with a serious look on his face. "Hell, instead of chasing these Outlaw's around the countryside. You teach 'em to Fight, and I'll teach 'em to shoot."

"You're Serious, Aren't You?" Wapiti says, chuckling just a little.

"SURE, Why Not. Then the next time Cathey comes over, We Might Be Here." Shawn said

"That's true, in her letter's she's told me she's been here two times now." Wapiti sorrowfully answered

The two had been talking for a just over an hour when Twick came walking through the open area leading through the view of the Bank across the street. "I hear there's an award ceremony for Deputy Wapiti at nine o-clock." Sheriff Shaver said, smiling. "How old is that coffee?"

"OLD…!" Shawn said "How you doing, Sheriff?"

"Sorry I was out of town yesterday when you had your last fight Wapiti. I heard it was something to see." Twick said, shaking both their hands.

"Have a seat Sheriff, I'll whistle for one of the kids and have them bring us out another pot of coffee." Shawn said.

"That's alright Marshal, I've been up since five coming back from settling a grazing dispute over sheep grazing a few miles up the Ochoco since yesterday" Twick said, setting down.

"Some of those can turn deadly real quick!" Shawn said, with a serious look on his face.

"I got there just short of them hanging that sheep rancher." Twick said

"How'd you talk them out of it, not hanging him that is?" Shawn asked, whistling real loud towards the restaurant.

"Told them I'd shoot the man holding the reins and as many others as I could, then you specifically would deal with the rest of them after they kill me." Twick said with a big smile on his face. "That changed most of their minds real quick…So where are these three men at you beat in your last fight? I want to see if they're as big as everyone says they are. I've heard they were all as big or bigger than you were at their age, right about thirty years old."

"I imagine they're still over at the Doctor's office taking pain pills to get rid of their serious headaches." Shawn said, with a big smile on his face.

"So what's the Award they're giving him?" Twick asked

"One of them is the Reigning Heavyweight West Coast Wrestling Champion." Shawn started explaining.

"Heavyweight Champion…I heard he took on three men." Twick said, looking back and forth between the two. Just as Griselda came up with a fresh pot of coffee and three more cinnamon rolls.

"Mom saw you had company, so she sent out some more cinnamon rolls." Griselda said, setting everything on the table.

"Thanks," everyone said, as Shawn started filling everyone's coffee cups up.

Twick reached for a cinnamon roll. "Aren't you guys going to have one of these?"

"We each already had three." Wapiti said, reaching for his coffee cup

"So what's this Award they're giving you Wapiti?" Twick asked, again.

"He's getting the Heavyweight Championship Belt." Shawn stated

"NO SHIT! Who were the other two?" Twick asked, taking a bite of the cinnamon roll.

"The Two Previous Heavyweight Champions." Shawn said, braggingly.

"NO SHIT, that must have been something to see." Twick said

"It was," Shawn said, pouring another small shot in his coffee.

"How come you can drink this early and no other Lawman can?" Twick asked, with a small chuckle

"Cause, I'm a U.S. Marshal, so I can drink anytime my heart desires." Shawn firmly answered

The three had been talking for a good twenty minutes when Jose came running up to them. "Marshal, the Judge wants to know when you and Wapiti are coming over to the Courthouse."

Shawn took out his pocket watch and looked at it, it was just about five minutes to nine. "Oh Shoot, we're almost late." Shawn said, standing up. "Come on Wapiti, I want to see what those men look like today."

All three men started walking towards the back of the building's to make it a shorter walk to the Courthouse. When they came out between the two of the buildings and stepped up on the boardwalk they could see the streets were crowded with people, all heading towards the Courthouse. When they saw Wapiti walking towards them, they all started cheering for him and stepping aside so he and the Marshal could get to the Courthouse.

They were half way across the street when they saw the Judge and the three men from yesterday come walking out on the top steps of the Courthouse. It only took a couple more minutes and the three Lawmen were walking up the steps and the entire crowd of people started shouting out Wapiti's name.

"WAPITI, WAPITI, WAPITI…" They kept yelling till Wapiti held his hands up to quiet them down. Which only made them cheer louder. "WAPITI, WAPITI, WAPITI,"

"Settle down Please." Judge Monson said, holding his hands up. After a long minute everyone finally shut up and started listing. "A little over five months ago, Marshal Felton hired Wapiti on as a U.S. Deputy Marshal…Like all of you, I thought he'd lost his mind. But Deputy Wapiti has proved time and time again he can more than handle the job…I can't begin to say how proud of him we all are."

"Then shut up and let the Champion give him his belt already." Someone in the crowd yelled out.

"Alright, Alright…!" Judge Monson said, looking over at the three large men standing behind him. He looked at them, then over to Wapiti standing beside them. All three towered over Wapiti and out weighted him by fifty pounds, the current Champion was the tallest. Yet all three looked like they were lucky if they could see through all the swelling. Not to mention, being able to breathe thru their noses "I remember when Marshal Felton came here over twenty four years ago, he was almost as big as these two." He says pointing at Dutch and S.O.B.

"WAPITI, WAPITI, WAPITI," the crowd started yelling again.

"Please settle down, we'll get to Deputy Wapiti in a minute… But first, let's let the Champion speak." Judge Monson said, extending his hand towards Rip.

Slowly Rip looked at the other two men, then at Wapiti and the Marshal.

"WHO ARE YOU, WHAT'S YOUR NAME'S?" someone yelled out

The Champion started looking out into the vast crowd of people still filling the street. "Speaking with a sore, hoarse throat.

"That's Dutch Savage…The Flying Dutchman. That's Sam Oliver Bass…He's known for being a dirty fighter, so he goes by his initials, S. O. B., and you all know what those initials stand for… I'm Rip Off, Rip Oliver…I like Ripping My Opponents Heads off, Then Shit Down There Wind Pipes. Usually we wrestle for five, three minute rounds, throwing each other around a fifteen-by-fifteen foot ring. Sometimes we even throw each other out of the ring in the first two rounds…to get the crowds excited. Then we get serious in the third round to see who will be the real ultimate winner." Then he looked back at Wapiti and his two friends. Shaking his head, he couldn't believe just how beat up they were. "As you can plainly see, U.S. Deputy Marshal Wapiti DON'T play around when he fight's. Everyone of his blows are precise and deadly."

"WAPITI, WAPITI, WAPITI…!" the crowd started cheering again.

"We'll get to him in just a minute, but first I'd like to say, I honestly don't believe ANY of us have ever been beat this bad and knock out cold in such a short time. Like Deputy Wapiti did to all three of us yesterday. Our hats go off to you Sir." He said, extending his hand towards Wapiti, and the crowd all started cheering again. "Deputy, if you will please come forward Sir."

Wapiti looked over at the Marshal, then the Judge, then at all three men as he walked up to the podium with the Champion.

Holding the Championship Belt over his head so everyone could see it. They all started cheering again. "I truly figured I'd be able to hang on to this for a couple years before anyone would be able to beat me and take it away from me…But as you all can plainly see, Deputy Wapiti is the TRUE West Coast HeavyWeight Champion. We wrestle two men at a time, one-on-one. Deputy Wapiti took the three of us out before we knew what hit us. Every punch he throws sets up his next punch…It's my Great Honor To Hand Over My

Championship Belt to U. S. Deputy Marshal Wapiti." Then walking behind Wapiti, he put the belt around his waist and buckled it off in the back. "Ladies and Gentlemen, I give you the New, West Coast HeavyWeight Wrestling Champion…Wapiti!"

Everybody started cheering, Wapiti looked down at the belt. It covered most of his midsection, then he stared out into the crowd of cheering people. "I Don't Know What To Say." Wapiti said, looking down at the belt again, then over at the three men. "I hope I didn't hurt you guys too bad…Back home in the village, we were all tested in taking on three, four other Brave's at the same time. Your right Mr. Rip Oliver, it is more fun to make the fight's last longer so you can put more bruises on their body's before you knock them out…But With Men Your Sizes, You Get It Over With As Fast As Possible."

"YOU DID THAT!" people in the crowd started shouting out.

"You took them out so fast that not one of them even laid a hand on you." Another couple of men yelled out.

Shawn stepped up to the podium, raising his hands to quiet everyone down. "Three Months Ago, after we left the Fort over in Pendleton, we went back up to Wapiti's village at Wallowa Lake. They had an Award Ceremony for him, for every man he's taken out in battle he gets one feather…Chief Joseph placed a headdress on him with twenty four feathers on it. One, when he was tested and became a Warrior, and twenty three more for each man he's taken out in battle…Since Then, he's taken out seventeen more. But I think he deserves an extra feather for these three gentlemen. So I need to get ahold of Chief Joseph and get these all added to that headdress of feathers …"

"You Better Tell Him To Send An Extra Dozen Marshal." Someone yelled out "He's going to earn them shortly." With that comment everyone started laughing.

"I WANT TO SEE THIS HEAD DRESS." Another man yelled out.

"YEAH, Where Is It, we'd all like to see it too." Other people started yelling

"It's kept back in the village for protection in the Medicine Lodge, So The Great Spirit Can Watch Over Me!" Wapiti said, looking around the street. The people were all packed in tight for a couple hundred feet in each direction and some had climbed up on the awning over the boardwalk on the other side of the street to get a better view. He could remember walking these streets when a NO good for nothing Redskin wasn't welcome in their town…Now look at them, cheering him on. Most important however, was he had won THEIR RESPECT!

"GO GET IT!" some yelled out

"YEAH, GO GET IT!" Everyone started yelling. "WE WANT TO SEE IT."

"It's only worn for special occasions, like going into battle, wedding ceremonies, peace talking ceremonies, and the like" Wapiti started saying

"I'LL MARRY YOU WAPITI." Women started yelling out.

"I'M not Looking For A Wife." Wapiti chuckled back at them.

"You Go Into Battle Almost Every Other Day Chief, So Bring It Over Here To A Smoke Lodge." Another man yelled out.

"It Stays With My Tribe!" Wapiti stated

"I told the Judge when I hired Deputy Wapiti on, that everyone would know who he was before he came into any town in a couple months…and now, THEY DO…!FACT, now when the kid's play Sheriff's and Outlaw's, they fight over 'WHO' gets to be Deputy Wapiti…! Shawn started saying, looking around at the massive crowd of people while he was talking. They had all gone quiet and were anxiously listing to all battle's Wapiti had won since becoming a Lawman. "He's Brought All His Outlaw's In Setting Up To…W-E-L-L, he did tie two over the saddle, just so they'd know what it really felt like…He out drew Tom Skerritt, TWICE… he brought him in alive too."

"ALRIGHT, I Think We've Talked About Me Enough." Wapiti yelled out. Looking around at the crowd, then back at the three Wrestler's. "I know it's early gentlemen, but how about we go over to the Saloon and I'll buy you all a shot of Bourbon with a beer chaser."

"Sounds good to us." All three men said. Looking at each other, then over to the Marshal and Judge. "If you'll lead the way, Deputy, we'll gladly follow you." Rip said, waving his hand in the Saloon's direction.

All seven walked off the steps and into the crowd of people. Those close were trying to reach out and pat Wapiti on the shoulder as he passed. Judge Monson was trying to follow behind Wapiti and the Marshal. Shawn was trying to push people back so they could get through. It must have taken them a good five minutes before they all walked into Moser's Saloon and Brothel. But it was already filled up from the people who were already on that side of the street.

Shawn was thirsty and tired of pushing his way through, so he pulled out his pistol and fired it into the roof of the boardwalk. This made everyone stop, shut up, and wonder who was firing their pistol and WHY!

"Now everyone, just get the hell out of the way or I'll start bustin' some heads myself." Shawn shouted out, as everyone started backing up and giving them the room they needed to walk through. However, those close did quietly try to reach out and pat Wapiti as he walked past.

Working their way to the back where Dave sat, Wapiti told Charley to line up six double shot's and six beers please.

"Right away, Deputy." Charley said, reaching for the glasses. He started filling them up and setting them down in front of everyone. "Isn't it a bit early for you to start drinking Your Honor?"

"On account of the celebration I'll have a drink with Deputy Wapiti and these three men." Judge Monson said, looking up at all three men. "Can you three even breathe thru your noses?"

"No we can't Your Honor." All three men answered. "If it wasn't for them opium based pain pills from the Doc, we wouldn't be up and walking. Our heads feel like they got knocked off."

"How long do those pain pills work?" Shawn asked, holding up his shot glass.

"Not Long Enough!" Dutch said. Trying to smile, he held his shot glass over his head. "Here's to you Deputy Wapiti, God Bless Any Man That Comes Up Against You In Battle." Then they all drank the shot of whiskey down and followed it up with a drink of beer.

Then everyone in the place wanted to buy Wapiti a drink too. Holding his hands up, he started looking around at the crowded Saloon. "I appreciate it, but I'm a one drink man this early in the morning. So the next time I, or me and the Marshal come back in, you can buy me a drink then."

Dave looked over at the three Professional Wrestler's, then back at Wapiti. He had gone up to one of the bedrooms above and got to watch the fight. These men looked big from up there, but bigger standing this close to them. Then he started talking about all the fight's he'd seen Wapiti in, they were all over too soon, but fun as hell to watch.

"Mr. Moser, when Wapiti comes in next time, put a double shot on my bill." Judge Monson said, taking another drink off his beer, then set the half full mug on the bar counter top. "Keep up the good work Deputy. Now if you men will excuse me, I have work to do…Marshal, you still plan on coming over at one?"

"Yes Sir, Your Honor." Shawn answered, taking a drink off his beer.

"Very good, Deputy Wapiti, I'll see you later too." Judge Monson said, walking into the crowd of people he pushed his way through.

CHAPTER 2

Shawn and Wapiti finished their beers, then said good-bye to everyone and walked towards the door and outside. But walking back up the boardwalk wasn't that easy. Because everyone they passed wanted to shake Wapiti's hand and tell him what a good job he was doing and to keep up the good work.

Wapiti was glad when they finally started walking between the buildings and out of sight from everyone. When they came out the other end, he took off the Championship belt as they walked towards the shack.

"Where you going to hang that up at?" Shawn asked, reaching for it. "Here, let me look at that thing." Grabbing it, he started looking it over. "This thing's heavier than it looks."

"Where do you think I should hang it up at?" Wapiti said, as they walked into the shack.

Jose came running in right behind them. "CAN I SEE THE BELT?" he yelled out, reaching for it.

"Here," Shawn said, handing it to him.

"This things big and heavy." Jose said, looking it over. "So Now You're the HeavyWeight Champion of the West Coast it says"

"Looks like," Wapiti answered, walking over to his bunk. "Could you wake us around twelve-thirty Jose?"

"Sure, can I go show this to Mom and Griselda?" Jose asked, with excitement in his voice.

"Yeah, just don't come back till twelve-thirty." Wapiti said, as he and Shawn both laid down for a short nap.

Which for them was too short before Jose was waking them up. At least Griselda brought them out a pot of coffee. Which they both needed to help wake themselves back up with.

After a quick couple cups, Shawn looked at his pocket watch and saw it was just about ten minutes till. "We'd better get going, if we're late Judge Monson will be mad." He said, standing up and walking towards the door.

"What do you want me to do with this Championship Belt Wapiti?" Jose yelled at him.

"Throw it on my bed, I'll put it away later." Wapiti said, following Shawn out the door. They quickly crossed down the open AlleyWay to the backs of the store's, then walked in between them out to the boardwalk. No sooner had they stepped up on the boardwalk and everyone stopped and looked in their direction. They were better than halfway across the street before all people continued on to wherever it was they were going to.

It only took them another couple more minutes and they were walking thru the door of the Courthouse. Then upstairs to the Judge's office.

Walking inside, they could see Ruth sitting at her desk, the Judge's door was open and they could see him sitting at his desk. "Afternoon Ruth, Judge ready to see us?" Shawn asked, slowing down just long enough to ask the question.

"Come on in gentlemen, Miss Twidwell, would you please get us all a large glass of cold tea and your note pad please?" Judge Monson asked

"Yes Sir, Your Honor, right away." Ruth said, standing up and walking over to the cold cabinet.

"So tell me more about these Rustler's." Shawn said, walking over to the map on the wall. Just as Ruth returned with a try with four full glasses and set them on the desk and handed a glass to everyone.

"They've only been taking eight to ten cows and calves at a time. So sometimes it takes longer for some of the larger herds to realize their short. But they've been cutting the wire fences around some of the smaller rancher's too." Judge Monson was explaining.

"They're only stealing eight to ten at a time, and they're stealing this year's calves…They have to stay close to water." Shawn said, pouring a large shot of whiskey in his cold tea.

"FELTON…DAMN YOU…! NOOO, I'm not going to get mad, if I do, you'll just pour more in." Judge Monson was saying, walking in a circle. Trying hard not to get mad.

"You're learning Your Honor." Wapiti chuckled out, looking around at everyone.

"So how long have they been at it, and which direction are they heading in?" Shawn asked, taking a long drink off his glass of tea.

"With the report's that have come in lately, show's they started north of Madras to just south of Redmond a couple days ago…All toll they've stolen from at least thirteen rancher's we know of on both sides of the main road." Judge Monson was explaining, pointing at the pins pinned into the map showing each place missing livestock.

"Whether they steal from one side or the other don't really matter. Those calves can't travel too fast or too far in a day, plus, they need water." Shawn was explaining, running his finger across the map. "They probably followed Crooked Creek to the top of the ridge, then dropped over into the Little Deschutes River."

"Why they stealing calves if they slow them down that much?" Wapiti asked, looking the map over.

"Sounds like someone who wants to start a new ranch somewhere. They'll have a bill of sale register showing all brands with the owner's original brand, and the old owner's initials authorizing the new brand. So most of the people they'd run into might not know better." Shawn said "Most of those range hands have been out there all summer, only coming in for more grub once a month. So if someone's stealing livestock, they might not know about it for awhile."

Just then a Ticket Agent from the tele-graph office brought a tele-graph in for the Judge. Thanking him, Judge Monson read it. "This says P.O. Nicely lost four Black Angus Bull's yesterday."

"They know good breeding stock." Shawn said "They got their cows, now they got themselves a couple bulls to rebreed them with next summer...I just about bet they're thru stealing and will start heading that herd home."

"Where's home?" Wapiti asked

"That's anybody's guess." Shawn said, taking his last drink of tea. "Ruth, do you have some more cold tea?"

"Yes Sir Marshal, I'll be right back." Ruth said, standing up and walking out of the room. It only took her a couple minutes to return with a large pitcher and refill everyone's glass, then set back down with her notepad.

"No matter where they go they have to have water." Shawn said, pouring another shot of whiskey in his tea. He could tell Judge Monson wanted to blow his top, but he didn't. Smiling at him, he poured another small shot in, then took a drink off the flask before putting it away. "Anyhow, I bet they're thru stealing and are heading home. We know they can't go back north or they'd be found out... P.O.'s place is just south of Redmond. They need to get those cattle further off the main road. It's not too hard of a trail from Redmond over towards Sisters and Squaw Creek south."

"Then where to?" Judge Monson asked

"Your guess is as good as any Your Honor." Shawn said "That's a hell of a lot of country to go looking through on a hunch."

"We know they were in Redmond yesterday, if they're heading towards Sisters like you think…You and Wapiti can easily be in Sisters by nightfall. Then to Squaw Creek by early afternoon tomorrow." Judge Monson said, pointing at the map.

"We can go back to the shack, give Rodger and Gordy a chance to get everything ready for us and we can pull out at sun-up and still be in Sisters by late afternoon." Wapiti said.

"Yes, but if you make it to Redmond tonight, you can stay in a Hotel tonight, you'll be that much closer to them in the morning." Judge Monson said, looking at the clock on the wall. It's not even two o-clock yet, if you push it, you could probably make it to the stage stop halfway to Sisters tonight, hell, it's only forty miles, so about a six hour ride."

"YOU RIDE THEM SIX HOURS, YOUR HONOR." Wapiti firmly stated, not only does your "ASS" get sore." Wapiti said, using his finger to make quotation marks. "But your back hurts from all the bouncing up-n-down all those miles … Plus, they only have a hay loft at that Stage Stop." he finished saying as he stood up. "Come on Marshal, you'd better get me out of here while the getting is good. I just might throw something or someone out that window!" he said pointing, setting his glass down on the table.

"What's wrong with you Deputy?" Judge Monson asked

"Unlike you, Your Honor, we don't get to sleep in a nice soft bed every night like you do." Wapiti stated, walking towards the door.

"I'm sorry Wapiti, but that's what comes with the job." Judge Monson quietly said.

"You're just sending us off on a wild goose chase. No-one knows what way those Rustler's might be heading." Wapiti said, stopping and pointing back at the map. "You don't know if they'll be anywhere around where you want us to go look for them at."

"Marshal Felton's right, they have to move slow and need plenty of water for them calves." Judge Monson was explaining.

"Come on Marshal, if we don't get out of here soon, something is going out that window." Wapiti said, walking towards the door.

"I already asked Rodger to get your supplies ready and told Gordy to have your horses ready as well." Judge Monson said, looking at Wapiti walking out the door.

"Thanks Your Honor." Shawn said, following Wapiti to the door. "Like he said, YOU get to sleep in a nice soft bed every night while we're out there on the hard ground." He said, turning and walking out the door. Catching up to Wapiti on the front steps. They both looked around the street before they headed back towards their shack.

As they crossed the street and walked along the boardwalk, everyone was still congratulating Wapiti on him winning the Championship Belt.

After a couple more minutes they were back at the shack picking up their gear. Then heading back out the door towards the Livery Stables. Jose came running up with the Championship Belt and wanted to know what Wapiti wanted him to do with it.

"Just throw it on my bed, I'll put it away when we get back." Wapiti answered, walking between the buildings following Shawn.

Again, when they got out to the street, everyone wanted to congratulate Wapiti on his fight and winning the Championship Belt. Wapiti polity thanked them, but kept walking towards the Livery.

Walking inside, they could see Gordy already had ninety percent of everything loaded and ready for them to leave. "Why aren't you wearing that Championship Belt Wapiti, I was hoping to get to see it." He said

"It's over in the shack." Wapiti said, tying his bed roll down.

"Where you going to hang it up at?" Gordy asked, looking back and forth between them.

"Don't know that I will." Wapiti answered

"You need to hang it over at the Saloon, so whenever anybody get any idea about taking you on, they can look up and see the belt to remind them of your capability's." Gordy said, following them outside.

"I don't want them to remember." Wapiti said, climbing up in the saddle, lightly chuckling "I like showing people I'm not afraid of them or what they think they can do to me."

"I got to watch that fight from my loft. It was to short but sweet." Gordy said, watching them ride away.

"See you in a week or so." Shawn yelled back. Then they both kicked their horses in the side and took off at a medium trot heading back out of town.

Like every other trip they were passing Freight Wagon's, wagons, carriages, and people walking, packing everything they owned on their backs going in both directions. After just over an hour's ride they came into Powell Butte. Riding over to the Livery and water trough, they dismounted and started walking around stretching their legs while their horses drank.

It wasn't long and the Blacksmith came walking over asking the Marshal who he was looking for this time?

"Cattle Rustlers!" Shawn answered, taking a drink off his flask.

"I heard P.O. Nicely lost five young two year old Black Angus bulls he was planning on auctioning off in the spring." The Blacksmith said, taking a drink off his pint bottle. "He gets between four and five hundred dollars each for his two year old bulls."

"I know, he pays me a hundred and fifty bucks every year to escort him to the bank." Shawn answered, refilling his water bag. "He also auctions off twenty bred heifers that'll calve their first calve in the spring, usually around late April, early May, so they don't get caught in a freezing snowstorm, killing their newborn calves. Their buyer's are hoping on getting a bull calf of course, but then if it's a heifer, he can still breed his Black Angus, Herford's, and Charolai bulls to them and get a bigger calf.

"Why don't he just use a half dozen or so of his hired hands to guard him?" the Blacksmith asked

"Their cow hands, not gunfighters!" Shawn stated "Their usually slow on the draw, cause they don't want to die when they come face-to-face with a gun staring them in the face."

"I can see their point…No amount of money is worth dying for." The Blacksmith said, pointedly.

Shawn pulled out his pocket watch and looked at it, it was a quarter till four. They still had a good four hours of daylight left. "Well Sir, I'd love to be able to sit around and Bullshit with ya, but if we hurry we can make Sisters before it gets to dark out." He said, climbing back up in the saddle and he and Wapiti headed down the road at a slow trot.

"What if their follow the Little Deschutes instead of going all the way over to Squaw Creek?" Wapiti yelled over.

"Doubt it…They have to get that herd away from the main road so they're not easily seen." Shawn said, taking a small drink off his flask.

"Won't they be seen going through Sisters Too?' Wapiti asked

"They'll keep the herd well out of town, but one or two of them might go into town for supplies." Shawn said, slowing the horses to a walk.

"How long till we get to the Stage Stop?" I'm past being hungry." Wapiti said, taking a drink off his water jug.

"Carmen made us a couple beef burritos before we left. I have them right here in this grub bag." Shawn said, grabbing the canvas bag with a pull string cord to close it up tight, and the pull rope was wrapped around his saddlehorn.

"Will you please get me out one?" Wapiti asked, pulling on the reins to stop his horse.

"Sure, I'm getting hungry too." Shawn said, opening the canvas. "I don't know which is which." Shawn said, handing one to Wapiti. "So if it's too hot for you, then it's probably one of mine."

Wapiti quickly took the burrito, unwrapped the wax paper around it and took a big bite. Right off it set his mouth on fire, and his face showed it.

"I think this one is yours." Shawn said, handing it over to Wapiti.

"I agree with you. This one is way too hot for me." Wapiti said, switching burritos with Shawn. Then he quickly took another big bite. It wasn't as hot as the other one, but it still heated his mouth up after he chewed the bite. "These are good, but they're hotter than usual."

"She must think you're getting used to them by now, so she must have added a few more jalapenos." Shawn said, taking another bite. "I think she might have put too much OO-LA,-LA salsa on this one."

"So are we going to spend the night in Hotel in Sisters tonight?" Wapiti asked

"Yeah, we should get in there just before nightfall if we push it." Shawn said, taking a drink off his water bag.

The two rode and ate their large burritos, and didn't say anything till Wapiti took his last bite. "My mouth and lips feel like they're on fire, but damned if those don't taste good. I really like the flavor of her Pico De Gallo salsa, those five items together taste great." Starting to chuckle. "Seem's the jalapeno peppers add the best flavor, cause the hotter it is, it tastes better." chuckling disbelievingly. "But once you start eating, you better stop talking, cause if you breathe in with an open mouth, it's like pouring kerosine on an already lit fire."

"Give it a couple more months and you'll be putting more jalapenos on them, trust me." Shawn said, taking his last bite. Then kicking his horse in the side to pick up the pass just a little bit.

After a good hour more riding they could see some people pulling over to camp for the night. By the time they came to the second camp, they could smell the food and coffee cookin' and it smelt good. Making them both hungrier than they really were.

It only took them just over another hour before they were riding into town. Shawn looked down at his pocket watch, it was just past seven-thirty. "We made good time." He said, pulling into the Livery Stable.

"What can I do for you Marshal, Deputy?" Tom asked

"Could you take a quick look at our horses and make sure they don't have any loose shoe's so we can pull out in the morning." Shawn asked, climbing down out of the saddle.

"Sure thing Marshal…What happened to your big Medicine Hat Deputy?" Tom asked, walking around the horses and picking up each hoof and looking them over.

"He's been playing with a Mare for a couple day." Shawn said, handing him his reins. "We'll be staying across the street at the Hotel."

"Sure thing Marshal, these horses all look real good. I'll just feed and water them tonight." Tom said, leading all three horses inside the Livery.

Shawn and Wapiti walked across the street to the Hotel. Right off the man was reaching for two keys as Shawn signed the register. "You men need a hot bath tonight Marshal?" the man asked

"Yes please." Shawn answered, taking the two keys, handing one to Wapiti.

"The shower room is right down the hall there Marshal." The man said, pointing. "Dinner special is meat loaf, mashed potatoes, vegetable, salad, and dinner roll."

"How much longer are they open?" Shawn asked, looking over at the man. Remembering the last time they were here and he had to pull him over the counter before he'd allow Wapiti to stay in his Hotel.

"Usually till eight o-clock, but if you gentlemen are running late, I'll have them save you each a plate full." The man said, looking both men over, taking a step backwards. He remembered the last time they were here, about a month ago and what the Marshal had done to him when he refused to let Deputy Wapiti stay in his Hotel.

"Tell them to put an extra half slice of meat loaf on each plate, a couple extra biscuit's…Do they have brown gravy to cover everything with?" Shawn asked

"Yes Sir Marshal, I do believe they do." The man answered, as four Cowboys came walking into the lobby.

"Good, have them bring two dinners, a large pitcher of beer and two mugs to my room please." Shawn asked, hearing someone behind them start talking.

"Did you guys hear that bullshit story about Chief Wapiti beating three Professional Wrestlers in Prineville yesterday…I say that's the BIGGEST Bullshit story I've ever heard." One of the Cowboy's disbelievingly boasted, as the other three started laughing.

"Those Professional Wrestlers go well over six feet and two hundred and twenty plus pounds each, and they lift weights to build their muscles up bigger than the normal man." Another Cowboy started explaining. "Chief Wapiti' is lucky if he even goes one eighty...There's no-way in hell he could have taken three men that size out in what, didn't they say the fight didn't even last a couple minutes before He Beat Them All Up And Knocked All Out Cold!"

"I don't think it took him much over a minute, thirty." Shawn boasted back, looking the four Cowboy's over. They were all wearing pistols with their holsters tied down. Laughing and joking about Wapiti.

"Could you just really see him up against three men that size, why, they'd tear you up boy." The first Cowboy said again.

"You Men Don't Be Causing Any Trouble In Here Please." The Owner nervously said.

"Don't worry about us." All four men said, still laughing and pointing at Wapiti.

"I don't believe I've ever heard a Bigger Bullshit story so unbelievable in my life." Another one of the Cowboy's shouted out.

Wapiti set his gear on the floor and started walking towards the four men. Who all stepped a couple feet further away from each other, but keeping their eyes on Wapiti.

"You think you scare us Chief?" the first Cowboy boasted out.

"You Men Don't Be Starting Any Fight's In Here!" the Owner yelled out again.

"Don't worry about it." Shawn said, leaning up against the counter. "They'll pay for everything that gets broken."

"The only thing going to get broken in here is this Wannabe Indian Lawman!" the first Cowboy disgustedly chuckled out, looking at Wapiti, then over at his three buddy's.

Wapiti slowly looked all four men over and around the room. There was only about ten feet of open space around them before the furniture, the walls and the windows.

"You men throw those pistols over here on the floor!" Shawn said, with a big smile on his face.

"MARSHAL, You Can't Allow This To Happen In Here!" the Owner yelled out.

"No problem Marshal." All four men said, tossing their pistol's at the Marshal's feet.

"I Told You Not To Worry About It…! Now Just Sit There and keep your mouth shut!" Shawn said, demandingly pointing his finger into the Owner's chest.

"NOW MARSHAL!" the Owner started to say, looking into Shawn's serious mad face. He knew if he didn't shut up, the Marshal would shut him up. So he quickly stopped speaking and stepped a couple more feet back away from him and out of his reach.

The man with the biggest mouth was in the center to his right, they were all laughing and looking back and forth between themselves. When Wapiti reached out and grabbed the third man from his right with both hands by the shirt. Doing a quick one eight turn, he threw him into the man to his fare left, sending them both crashing to the floor. Continuing on around, he brought his right fist up under the big mouth's rib cage picking him up off the floor. Taking every ounce of air out of him, causing the man to lean forward and down in pain. Grabbing him by the back of his head, he picked his head up, then drove it down into his rising right knee, breaking his nose and knocking him out cold.

Feeling a breeze from a fist go past his left cheek. He quickly spun back to his right on his left foot, kicking the man in his shoulder with his right foot, sending him flying into and breaking a small table in the corner.

Quickly, Wapiti turned back to the other two men as they were coming up off the floor. First, the two started looking at each other, then over at their other two friends.

Wapiti quickly turned back around on his right foot, doing a one eight turn, bringing his left foot into the side of the man to his right's head. Sending him flying over a coach and crashing partly through the window. Hanging halfway in and halfway out, laying lifeless.

Continuing to spin backwards on his right foot, he brought his left elbow up under the chin of the Cowboy to his left, driving him backwards. Quickly, he followed after the man grabbing him with his left hand, he pulled him back towards himself, while throwing his right fist dead center of the man's face, breaking his nose, blackening both eyes, and knocking him out cold, so he dropped him to the floor, Wapiti turned to face the last man.

Wapiti saw him coming at him from only a couple feet away and throwing his right fist at him. Ducking under it, he brought his own right fist up under and into the man's stomach. Picking him a good six inches plus off the floor, taking all the air out of his body, causing him to bend over gasping for air. So once again, Wapiti grabbed the man by the back of his head, picking it up, then driving it down into his raising right knee, breaking his nose, blackening both eyes and knocking him out cold.

"That's Forty-two!" Shawn yelled out, looking around the room. Seeing one of the waitresses watching from the dining area's hallway. "Young Lady, would you please bring a couple large pitchers of water to help wake these men up with please."

Wapiti looked at the three men laying on the floor and the one hanging out the window, then turned back to the owner. "You figure up damages, if they can't pay, they'll get jail time for inciting a riot!" He had no longer finished speaking and the waitress was handing him two large pitchers of water. People had come from the dining room to see what all the commotion was. Some had gone out the door of the Café and watched the fight through the glass windows.

"Here Ya Go Deputy." She said, with a big smile on her face and winking at him. "Is there anything else I can get for you?"

"No thanks, least not right now" Wapiti said, starting to pour water on the four men's heads to wake them up. "The Marshal already placed our order with that man right over there...But then he only ordered one pitcher of beer for our dinner. How about you bring two small pitcher's to the bathing room please."

Wapiti only dumped water on the three laying on the floor, the fourth, he pulled that man back inside the window first. So he wouldn't get cut up any more than he already was.

"Right away, Deputy." The Waitress answered, walking fast back towards the dining room.

Everyone had filled the hallway and just about every inch of windows to see the four men slowly rolling around on the floor trying to set up and wake up. Their heads all had the worst headaches they'd ever had, with a loud ringing noise that made their heads hurt worse, everything was blurry, and what they could mostly see were the continually falling little white stars in a field of brite blue backing. After twenty or so seconds the blue field was going away and the image of everything was slowly coming back into view over the next minute plus. They weren't saying anything, first, they were trying to remember what had happened, as they looked at each other, then they started looking around the room until they saw Deputy Wapiti. That's where they eyes stayed and it hit them what their last thoughts and memories of picking and laughing about him and his abilities to fight. As the first man to start to stand up started chuckling in disbelief. "I guess we were wrong!" They couldn't seem to start to figure out what had happened to them for a good couple minutes.

"You Men Remember Who You Are Yet?" Shawn chuckled out, taking a drink off his flask as Wapiti emptied both pitchers over their heads waking them up and they first tried just sitting up with a dazed and confused look on their faces.

"Yes Sir Marshal." Their probable leader said, still slowly looking around at his friends. Who were all looking at each other, then around at everyone looking at them. Looking up at Wapiti, they could see that none of them had even laid a hand on that Buck Indian.

"Is there a Doctor in town?" one of the men groggily asked.

"NO, but I have some opium based pain pills over at the Mercantile." They all heard a voice say. "It's what most Doctors use on patient's after they operate on them for their pain."

"Would you please go get us as much as you have, we'll pay you double if we don't have to walk anywhere just yet…That's if you don't mind Sir." One of the Cowboy's said, looking up at the owner.

"WHO'S PAYING ME FOR ALL THIS DAMAGE?" the Owner yelled at them and the Marshal.

"I told you before the fight started these four men would be paying for all damages." Shawn said, still smiling. As the waitress brought him and Wapiti their beer and glasses. "Thank you Darlin'."

"He's right mister." All four men started saying. "We'll pay for the damages, you just figure up how much we owe you."

"You wouldn't happen to have any empty room for the night would ya?" one of the Cowboy's asked

"I've got two left, but they only have one double bed in each room." The Owner said.

"That's alright, we just need someplace soft to lay down for a couple hours." The Cowboy answered

CHAPTER 3

"Alright boys I'll go get you those pain pills. BUT, you can't take more than two in an eight hour period or you could overdose and die on them, especially if you mix them and alcohol together." The Mercantile owner said, looking at all four men sitting on the floor still holding their heads. "That's a total of four pill's each for tonight, at two fifty a pill. You come by the store in the morning and I'll sell you two more days worth each and no more."

"Why not sell them all to us tonight?" one of the Cowboy's asked, angrily.

"Like I said, if you took all those pills tonight you'd overdose and die." The mercantile store owner repeated. "This way, you come by in the morning and get the rest on your way out of town. That way if you overdose on them, it's not my fault and I won't lose my Medical Sales License…You men just go on up to your rooms and I'll be right back." He said, walking out the door, chuckling.

Shawn and Wapiti headed for the bathing room, while the other four men slowly stood up and signed into the Hotel registry. Then slowly walked up the stairs to a soft bed to lay down in hoping it would help their aching, pounding heads stop hurting.

It only took Shawn and Wapiti about fifteen minutes each to wash up and head out to the dining room to see if it was still open. It was, so they walked over and sat down at a table. The same waitress came walking over and set down their two meals Shawn had ordered earlier. "I'll be right back with your beer gentlemen." She said, smiling and winking at Wapiti again.

Neither one said much as they ate dinner, they were both hungry and tired. So as soon as they finished Shawn laid a ten dollar bill on the table and they went upstairs to bed.

It was barley dusk outside when Shawn woke up. Lighting a match he looked at his pocket watch, it was almost five-thirty. Setting up, he leaned back and knocked on the wall behind him to wake Wapiti up. It only took them five minutes to wash up a little and get dressed. Then he walked over and opened the door just as Wapiti was doing the same.

Saying "Good morning" to each other, they walked downstairs and over to the dining room. They could smell coffee and hear a couple voices back in the kitchen, as they walked in.

Shawn picked up the closest coffee pot and started filling two cups up. "You don't mind if we help ourselves do ya?"

"No Sir Marshal." The Cook said. "What would you gentlemen like for breakfast?"

"How about three eggs over easy, hash brown potatoes, four, no make it six slices of bacon, and two sausage patty's please." Shawn answered

"That sounds good to me too." Wapiti said, taking a drink off his coffee.

"You men go set down and I'll bring it right out as soon as she gets it cooked." The Waitress said

"Thank you Darlin', you wouldn't happen to have a hot plate for this would ya?" Shawn asked, holding the coffee pot up.

"Sorry, but no we don't, Marshal." The Waitress answered "But I'll make sure you don't run out, promise. Now, go ahead and sit down and I'll be right out with everything."

"Thank you." Shawn said, topping their coffee up. Then they both walked out and sat down at a table.

The waitress had just brought out their breakfast when two more men came walking into the dining area. Taking a quick look around they walked over and sat down close to the Marshal and Wapiti, saying 'good morning' to them as they sat down.

They both said "Good morning" back to them and continued eating breakfast. Which only took them maybe fifteen more minutes for them to finish. So then they sat there and drank one more cup of coffee before asking for their bill.

Which Shawn quickly paid and Wapiti left a two dollar tip, one for each of them. Then they headed out the door and across the street to the Livery Stables. Walking inside, they could see Tom already had their horses saddled and was loading up the pack horse.

"I remember you like to get an early start Marshal, so I had the Cook send someone over to wake me up whenever you came in for breakfast. That way I could have you ready to go before you were ready." Tom said "Sure did enjoy getting to watch you fight yesterday as opposed to just hearing or reading about it, Deputy Wapiti."

"He is fun to watch isn't he?" Shawn said, tightening his cinch strap.

"Where's that Championship Belt you won the other day?" Tom asked, with excitement in his voice.

"It's at home." Wapiti said, leading his horse towards the door.

"Why didn't you bring it with you to show everyone?" Tom asked

"It's fine right where it is." Wapiti said, climbing up in the saddle. Just as the Mercantile Owner came walking over to them.

"Marshal, I had a couple strange character's come in last night." The mercantile owner said

"What was so strange about them?" Shawn asked, looking down at him.

"They traded me a cow and calf for food supplies that would last them for another week on the trail before they would be back home." The Mercantile Store Owner said.

"Where do you have them at, I'd like to check their brands against these on this list we're looking for." Shawn said, reaching into his vest pocket and pulled out a piece of paper.

"Back behind my place in my corral." The man answered, walking back across the street towards the back of the Mercantile with Shawn and Wapiti following him.

"I just knew something was wrong, now I'm going to be out fifty dollars in stock." The man said under his breath.

"FIFTY BUCKS, why the hell would you pay fifty bucks for a single cow and calf?" Shawn asked, seeing the corral.

"It has her heifer calf, so now a full cow and already bred with next spring's calf. Figured I was getting three really, but then Tom told me you were looking for Rustler's and I knew I'd been taken." The mercantile owner said, in a discussed voice.

Shawn rode over to the side of the corral and looked the cow and calf over, seeing the double WW brand on their left hips. He started looking down the list of brands he had, and there it was. Almost at the bottom of the fourteen brands they were looking for.

"Afraid you're right Sir, those two belong to the Williams brother's just north of Terrebonne." Shawn said, looking down at the man, reaching into his pocket, he took out his wallet. "Now you get ahold of the Williams brother's by telegraph and let them know where to come and pick up that cow and calf up at. Here's the fifty bucks you're out, I'll put it in my expense book as being paid out for information on the Rustler's. They didn't by chance mention which way they were going did they?"

"No Sir, but they headed upriver when they left." The man said pointing.

"Can you show me about where they left the road and went back into the timber at?" Wapiti asked

"In between those two big Ponderosa Pine trees right there." The man said pointing.

Wapiti turned his horse and headed over to the two big Ponderosa Pine trees. Dismounting, he started looking the area over for fresh hoof prints. Which didn't take long before he found them leading into the grass, breaking all the stem's with every step. Walking back out towards the road, so he could find a better set of prints to look over. They were easy to find, cause most of the traffic had stayed closer to the middle of the road. Sure, there were hoof prints closer to the side of the road going to or coming from town. But theirs were the only three sets going west. In the soft dirt on the side of the road he could see where one shoe had broken partly off on the inside back third of one shoe.

"They went in over there," Wapiti said, pointing to the area. "Back tracking here, I can see three sets of hoof prints, one is missing part of the inside of one shoe."

"Anything on either of the other sets?" Shawn asked, taking a pull off his flask.

Wapiti looked over and saw him take the drink. Starting to chuckle and shake his head at the same time. It wasn't even seven o-clock in the morning and you're already trying to out think these Rustler's. He spoke out as he thought it.

"That Mercantile man said those boy's came through about an hour and a half ahead of us, that means they're close by." Shawn said, thinking out loud.

"By the wear on the other horse's shoes they're all worn down." Wapiti said, standing back up. He started leading his horse and walking back into the taller grass, following their tracks. After about thirty feet or so, he could see the tracks were dug deeper in the front and the clumps of dirt were thrown back further behind. "They took off at a trot right here Marshal."

"That means, if their true Cowboy's they'll all be re-shoding shortly." Shawn said, still thinking out loud. "UUUH, What… What did you say?" Shawn asked, looking back over to Wapiti.

"I said they took off at a trot right here." Wapiti said, pointing at the ground. Then walking back over to his horse and climbed back aboard his horse.

"With all this tall grass it's going to be harder to track them in." Shawn said, looking out across the hill side.

"Not really," Wapiti said, turning his horse down the trail. "If you look out at the taller grass you can see how the sun reflects off the bend over and broken stems. I can still follow them, just not as fast as they're going, but they won't get away from me."

"You're the tracker…lead the way, Deputy." Shawn chuckled, taking another small pull off his flask before putting it away.

The tracks quickly side hilled their way down the side off the ridge to Squaw Creek. Wapiti stopped his horse and started looking around on the ground for sign of a hoof print and not bent over grass. It didn't take long and he could see where all three horses had gone into the river. So Wapiti slowly followed behind them to the other side. Stopping again, he started looking at the river's edge to see where they came out at. After a long two minutes, he started heading his horse downstream. Still staring into the sandy, rocky shore line that lined the river all the way up and down for a good five plus feet up from the water's edge. After a long slow hundred plus feet, they came to a semi grass covered area. Stopping again, he started looking the area over. After just a couple seconds he saw their tracks. Riding over to the edge, he climbed off his horse and started looking the tracks over again. But he was specifically looking for the broken shoe track. Which he found easily, but looking at the others, he could see that one of their horses had lost two shoe's, which would make them easier to follow.

"They went back upstream thru here." Wapiti said, leading his horse and following their trail into the taller dead grass and the heavier, thicker timber being down low on the north side of the ridge. Climbing back aboard his horse he started up the trail. In no time at all Wapiti could see all the freshly broken off dead branches they were riding through.

After only a half mile or so, the tracks and broken branches headed back downhill towards the river. After twenty more minutes of riding, they were back at the rivers edge with the soft sandy banks. Following them into the river, Wapiti turned and headed upstream.

"You want me to go downstream?" Shawn asked, stopping his horse in the middle of the small river.

"No, they wouldn't turn back downriver now. Remember, they need to get those cattle south where no-one knows the old brands on them." Wapiti said, looking over at the river's edge for where it was they came back out of the river at.

They were being smart by staying in the middle of the small river, cause it would wash their tracks away quicker. After a couple hundred yards they came to a dead tree laying across the river. Looking to the smaller end on the east side of the river, he could see a few horse tracks in the shallow, calmer waters and where they had broken off a couple dead branches off crossing over the tree. He could easily see tracks on both sides of the tree, but the tracks quickly lead back into the deeper, faster flowing water washing their tracks out again.

With all the trees, brush, and large rocks along the river's banks made it almost impossible for anyone to ride through. So, for right now riding in the river was the easiest way to go upstream. After a good half mile plus they could see a large wide flat area on the east side of the river. Sure, it was timber covered, but it was a good two hundred yards plus wide rolling hills from the river's edge before the steep mountain ridge started upwards again.

Looking the area over while turning his horse in that direction, still watching the sandy, to small rocky edge of the river. But looking up at the small valley ahead at the same time. The heavy brush and large rocky bank just cleared at the top end of the wider valley when Wapiti saw horse tracks in the shallower water leading out of the river to the larger, flatter, grassier area.

Right off, they both saw the remains of someone's camp fire. Which the tracks they were following led right up to, then over to an area a few feet further away where they had tied their horses up for the night. They both climbed off their horses and started looking the area over. Shawn concentrated on the fire area, and Wapiti where they had tied up their horses.

Right off, Shawn saw two empty fifths of whiskey. "Looks like they had themselves a little party last night." He said walking around looking for any areas that might look like someone had slept on it.

"They all put new shoes on their horse's right here." Wapiti said, holding up one of the shoes. "Counting the shoes, there's five horses total." Then he started walking towards the green grassy, thinly tree covered rolling ridge that lay out in front of them.

"I've got four flat areas here in the grass where someone slept," Shawn said, pointing at the ground. Watching Wapiti walking through the grass going away from them. "Where you going?"

"There's both old and new shoes riding up and back down the valley right thru here." Wapiti said, looking back at the Marshal.

"Could be from someone riding the night watch on the cattle." Shawn said, pulling out his pocket watch, it was almost one o-clock. Just looking at the watch made his stomach grumble from being hungry. So he walked over to the pack horse and took the small grub bag off the horse and started making them each a PBJ sandwich.

He was taking his first bite when Wapiti came walking up so he handed him his sandwich. "What'd ya find out?"

"They had the cattle out across the valley over there." Wapiti said, taking the sandwich. "Thanks."

"That fire's dead cold, hours cold. So they must have pulled out just after sun-up." Shawn said, taking a drink off his flask, then taking another big bite off his sandwich.

"Freshest manure is about the same." Wapiti said, walking over to his horse, he grabbed his water bag and started dumping it out.

"Change mine too please." Shawn asked, taking out a large loaf of banana nut bread, cutting them each off a thick slice.

"Sure Marshal." Wapiti answered, walking over to his horse, getting the water bag, he headed back over to the edge of the small river. Trying to hold and eat his sandwich, while trying to empty out and refill the water jugs without getting his sandwich wet.

"I imagine they'll head out across this east facing ridge. It's easier to travel, less heavy limbs from the Fir trees." Shawn said, waving his hand downstream.

"You're probably right." Wapiti said, leaning over, refilling one bag and looking down the valley.

"They won't be able to follow the river much further…it turns and goes up in between the Middle and South Sister's volcanos." Shawn said, pointing. "A couple miles or so upstream the river comes to a goat trail that goes between Sisters and a small town called Elk Lake."

"They wouldn't want to take the chance of someone else taking that trail at the same time. They'd have to know anyone they came across would be wondering why they were taking the back road." Wapiti said, handing Shawn his water bag.

"Thanks," Shawn said, taking it and giving Wapiti his piece of banana nut bread. Then he took a big drink of the ice cold water. "Not really, not if they bought some land between there and the town of Crescent Lake."

"That makes perfect sense, being out here in the wilderness like this, with very few people coming through. They have well over one hundred head of breed cows and this year's calves, they stay hid for a couple years and most of the brands will be theirs." Wapiti said, tightening up his cinch strap.

"Sounds just like the same idea I was having." Shawn said, climbing up in the saddle. "From here on in they'll be easier to track with all those cattle tracks."

"That's true, even you'll be able to track them now." Wapiti chuckled out, turning his horse up river.

"I'll have you know, I was tracking Outlaw's long before you were ever born!" Shawn stated, following behind Wapiti.

It only took them a couple minutes to get to the place where the cattle had spent the night. Riding through the middle of the tracks, they started following them up the river over the timber covered rolling foothills. Just like the Marshal had said, after a couple more miles they came to the road, and just like the Marshal had said they would. They headed their herd down the barely visible road through the grass and timber.

"Shawn took out his pocket watch and looked at it, it was almost four o-clock. "Come on," he said, kicking his horse into a slow trot. "Maybe we can catch up to them by nightfall."

"Alright," Wapiti said, kicking his horse in the side, quickly catching up to the Marshal. "How far to the town of Elk Lake?"

"It's about thirty miles from Sisters this way." Shawn said

"So with those calves they'll be lucky if they make it halfway today." Wapiti said, taking a bite of jerky. "So how big a town is it?"

"Livery, Saloon of course, Trading Post, some lady started a restaurant in her house." Shawn said, thinking about the last time he was there. "The last time I was thru here, some Preacher was building a new church on the outskirts of town."

"How many people you figure live in and around it?' Wapiti asked

"I don't know…I guess fifty plus anyways." Shawn said, taking a drink off his flask. "Why are you so interested about it?"

"Just trying to think what we're going to do with the herd after we catch up to these Rustler's. We can't watch over them and try to herd cattle at the same time, so we're going to need some help getting them all back home." Wapiti said

"You might be onto something…we might not want to catch up with them till their closer to town, so we can get the help you're talking about." Shawn said, taking one more small drink off his flask before he put it in his pocket.

They had been riding at a slow trot for almost an hour, when Shawn held his hand up in the air and brought them to a stop. "Listen…I thought I heard cattle mooing."

They both started concentrating on hearing any noise that might be out ahead of them. After a couple long seconds, they both heard a couple more cattle mooing. "You think those cattle are the cattle we're looking for?" Wapiti asked

"Has to be, cattle only moo like that when they're being herded." Shawn said "Let's head up this side of the ridge and get above them." He said, pointing and turning his horse off the road and into the timber.

The ridge wasn't a steep ridge, more like the rolling foothills, only covered in timber. But they could still hear the cattle up ahead of them.

After a good slow hour and a half ride through the timber they could hear the cattle mooing from below them. But because of the thickness of all the timber, they could only see the tops of the trees down below them, and out across the mountain sides off in the far distance.

"We're going to have to wait till they set up camp for the night, so we can see their campfire smoke to know exactly where they are." Shawn said, taking out his pocket watch, it was well past six-thirty. "I figure we've traveled a good seventeen to eighteen miles today. They're not going to have any trouble getting those cattle to sleep tonight…This goat trail meets up with another goat trail that comes from Bend just a couple miles further up the road by Elk Lake itself, not the town. The town is another good eight plus miles further down the road…Anyhow, back to the Lake. About thirty years ago a man and his wife homesteaded well over ten sections of land around the lake."

"How much land is a section?" Wapiti asked

"Six hundred and forty acres." Shawn answered "Let's just say, it's a hell of a lot of land. Not to mention the water right's in the Lake as well."

"I see how you can own land, But How The Hell Do You Own Water?" Wapiti asked, in a loud whisper.

"Don't ask me how it all works, it just does…! Shawn stated, with an "I don't know" look on his face. "ANYHOW, back to the roads. Their ranch house is close to where these two roads come together…if we slow trot it from here, we should be at their ranch house by nightfall."

"Sounds good to me, maybe they'll let us sleep in the hay loft instead of sleeping on the hard ground." Wapiti said, kicking his horse into a slow trot. Sure there was a lot of timber, but it was mostly old growth timber with large grassy areas in between the trees.

After only about five minutes of riding they couldn't hear the cattle mooing below or behind them anymore, and Shawn made a point of pointing it out to Wapiti, as he kicked them up to a medium trot pace. Because of the lateness of the day, the shadows from all the timber was making it darker earlier and faster. After only maybe an hour they had to slow back down to a walk. It was getting hard to see too far into the timber.

Shawn looked out across the countryside to the east, the moon wasn't nowhere in sight. Looks like it's going to get dark on us real soon." He said, looking back over to Wapiti.

"How much further to the goat trail from Bend?" Wapiti asked

"Shouldn't be too much further up ahead." Shawn answered, taking a drink out of his flask. "Glad I have that fifth on the supply horse, cause this bottle's almost empty."

"ONE, last time I looked in the supply bag, there were two fifths. So I don't think you're going to be running out before we get back to another town." Wapiti said, with a big smile on his face. "I wish we had a couple beers personally."

"If we're lucky and find that ranch house before it gets too dark, they might just have a couple we could get off them." Shawn said, putting his nose in the air. "You smell smoke?"

"Yeah, I do." Wapiti answered, stopping his horse. Taking a big breath of air in through his nose and looking at the tops of the trees. Putting his finger in his mouth, he stuck it in the air. "The breeze is coming out of the south at only a couple miles an hour. So I'd say we're not too far from wherever that smoke is coming from."

"I agree with you on all accounts." Shawn said, kicking his horse back into a slow walk.

The ride seemed to be taking longer than it really was, because they couldn't see fifteen to twenty feet in front of themselves. After a long slow half hour they came out of the timber to the road.

Stopping, they both started looking around as to exactly which way was the ranch house from here. The smell of the smoke was heavy in the air.

"I say we follow the road towards Elk Lake." Shawn said, pointing down the road to their right.

"How sure are the lakes that way and not that way?" Wapiti asked, pointing in both directions.

"Cause just like you said, that smokes coming out of the south…unless I lost my sense of direction, that way is still south." Shawn said, turning his horse down the road.

It was a chilly, quiet, eerie night, tall timber lined the road and tens of thousands of sparkling lights in the night sky above them. They each could hear the pine squirrel's jumping from tree-to-tree out there in the total darkness. Their horse's hoof steps seemed to echo with every thud of them hitting the ground. They had been riding for a long quiet half hour when they rounded the bend and could see light's on in a cabin only a couple hundred yards in front of them.

"Sure would be nice if they had a cold beer." Wapiti said, looking over at Shawn, who was taking a drink off his flask.

"It might not be as cold as from a cold cabinet, but I'm sure they'll have a beer or two." Shawn said.

Shawn called out as they rode up to the hitchin' rail in front of the large two story cabin with a large covered front porch. "ANYBODY STILL UP…THIS IS U.S. Marshal Shawn Felton and Deputy Wapiti."

They both had just gotten off their horses and were tying them up when the front door came open. "Did you say U.S. Deputy Marshal Wapiti was out here?" they heard a man's voice say.

"YES, he's here too. I'm Marshal Shawn Felton and we were hoping on sleeping in your hay loft tonight." Shawn said, walking towards the man, holding his hand out.

"Please to meet you Marshal, I'm Casey Myers, please come in." He said, shaking Wapiti's hand too. "It's a real pleasure to meet you Deputy."

The three walked inside the large living room, then over to the dining and kitchen area. There were four men in their early twenty's setting around the fireplace reading books and Mrs. Myers was sitting in a chair mending a pair of socks. When she saw them, she instantly stood up. "Can I make you gentlemen a pot of coffee and something to eat?"

"If it's no trouble Ma'am, even a couple sandwiches would be nice." Shawn said, watching her walk towards the kitchen.

"I cooked a large roast for dinner, there's more than enough left for a couple sandwiches and please call me Ann." She said

All four men jumped up when they walked into the room and walked over to meet both Lawman. "Is it true you knocked out three Professional Wrestler's in less than two minutes in Prineville a couple days ago?" one of the men asked, shaking Wapiti's hand.

"Didn't even take him that long." Shawn said, in a bragatory voice. "He had to hit each man a few more times than normal, but in the end, he got to pour a couple pitchers of water over their heads to wake them up." Starting to chuckle. "These your son's Mr. Myers?"

"Call me Casey, please Marshal, and no. My two Daughters and their husbands are down at the ranch in the valley raising and putting up hay for the winter. These are four of my Cowhands that help me ride herd on over eight hundred head up here on the mountain in the summertime...This is Tom, Mile's, Hank, and Fred." Casey said, introducing the men.

"How much land do you have Casey?" Shawn asked

"I homesteaded three sections of good valley land outside Bend and fifteen sections up here around Elk Lake twenty five years ago. I own two thirds of all the water in that Lake." Casey said

"What do you do with the water, I mean, it's in the lake." Wapiti said

"I've built trenches around the mountain ridges on the south side, staying as high as I can, but still below the Lake so it flows downhill. I put in log spillways every couple hundred feet or so with a head gate feeds ten or more spillways out across the ridge. When I come to a split ridge, I split the trench again. Starting midsummer I open the head gate at the lower end of the Lake sending the water down both sides of the valley. Most I gain in elevation is a couple hundred yards uphill, but you run a steady stream of water out across each ridge for a week at a time, that waters a lot of countryside," Casey said, looking back and forth between the two men. "Hank, go get these men a couple cold beers out of the spring."

"Yes Sir Casey." Hank said, walking towards the back door. Just as Ann was handing each man a thick roast beef sandwich. They both 'thanked' her and started taking a bite When Tom asked how many scalps could he have now?

"He's up to forty-two now." Shawn said, with a serious look on his face. "Why, do some of you men want to try and take him on?"

"OH HELL NO." They all said, backing up a couple steps.

"I went over to John Day with Casey when he entered into that big poker game." Miles said, looking around at everyone. "We both got to see what he did over there. But I have to say everyone enjoyed that gauntlet run game you came up with Deputy, I wanted to go down to the other end and get another beating in, because that man had been at Casey's table and nearly broke him."

"I didn't last much longer after the gauntlet run whipping that man took. But I told Miles, if he went to the end and Deputy Wapiti found out you didn't play fair, he might make him run the gauntlet run himself, so he quickly changed his mind."

"That's exactly what happens to anyone that does hit a person twice." Wapiti stated, looking around at everyone

"I couldn't believe it when he came running back in waving his pistol and the shot you made, Marshal." Casey said. "I couldn't even see him through the crowd when you pulled the trigger. How you only hit him, I'll never know."

"I only hit what I'm shootin' at when it's less than thirty feet away from me." Shawn proudly said, standing full up. Just as Hank returned with two beer's and handing each of them one.

"How many men do you have up here?" Shawn asked

"These four, and three more out there on the mountain somewhere." Casey answered "Why, what's up?"

"We have some Rustler's coming up the ridge behind us." Shawn said, taking a drink off his beer.

"How many Rustler's and how many cattle do they have?" Casey asked

"Four Rustler's and over a hundred head of cows and calves." Shawn said, taking a bite off the sandwich.

"They'll definitely be stopping at the lake to water 'em." Casey said, looking back and forth between Shawn and Wapiti. "You men are more than welcome to sleep in the bunkhouse tonight and we'll set our trap up in the morning if you don't mind Marshal."

"It is late, and we need to get some rest." Shawn said "But could we bother you for another beer before we head out to bed."

"No problem Marshal, Hank, go grab these men two more beers." Casey said

"Right away," Hank said, walking towards the back door.

"Marshal, Deputy, I made an apple pie today. Would you gen-tlemen like a slice?" Ann asked

"That sounds real good." Both Shawn and Wapiti answered at the same time.

Ann returned with the pie as Hank came in the back door with two more beers. Thanking them both, Shawn, Wapiti, and the four Cow hands headed out the front door.

"Just grab your bedrolls and head for the bunkhouse Marshal, Wapiti, we'll put your horses up." Hank said, untying the reins.

CHAPTER 4

"Sure do appreciate it men, we've been up since before day-break." Shawn said, trying to untie his bedroll with one hand and hang on to the piece of pie and beer with the other.

"Here Marshal, Wapiti, let us get those for you." Both Miles and Fred said.

"Mrs. Myer's apple pies are too good to let them break-up and fall on the ground." Fred said, untying Wapiti's bedroll and handing it to him.

"Thank you very much Sir." Wapiti said, taking his bedroll. "How much money would one of you want to check over our horses tonight?"

"We wouldn't charge either of you anything." Hank said, leading the horses away. "Come on Tom, you do one and I'll do the other. Shouldn't take us very long."

"I hear ya Hank." Tom said, following him.

Walking into the bunkhouse, Miles lit a lamp so everyone could see. Looking around, Shawn could see a half dozen plus bunkbeds. "Does it matter which bed we choose?" he asked, walking towards an empty bottom bunk.

"You know it don't Marshal, throw your bedroll on any empty bunk you want." Miles said, walking over to his bed and laid down.

Within just a couple minutes it was all quiet inside the bunk-house, but Wapiti couldn't fall asleep. They'd be catching up to those Rustler's sometime tomorrow morning. Would they come in peaceful, or would they want to shoot it out. To his knowledge, they hadn't shot anyone in any of the people they'd stolen any cattle from. So if they were caught by a Lawman, they wouldn't hang, they'd go back to be Judged by a Judge and just end up doing a few years in prison.

Wapiti had been laying there thinking for a good half hour and was almost ready to fall asleep when the bunkhouse door slowly opened up, waking him back up. Instantly he reached for his pistol lying next to his head.

"Easy Deputy, it's just us." Both men said, whispering. Trying not to wake the others.

"Sorry," Wapiti whispered back. Lying back down trying to fall back asleep. Which to him, seemed to take forever. The next thing he could remember was the morning chow bell ringing, telling everyone to come and it.

Sitting up and looking around, he could see everyone else was up and gone. Standing up and stretching out, he quickly rolled up his bedroll and headed out the door. Seeing the large two story ranch house for the first time in the light. He couldn't believe it was only lived in half the year. It was bigger and nicer than most year round living homes down in the valley.

Walking over to the open dining table he sat all his gear on the ground and looked at all the food spread out across the table along with the other three Cowhands. Saying "Good Morning" to everyone, he sat down.

"What would you like on your plate, Deputy?" Ann asked, picking up a plate and put a large scoop of scrambled eggs on it.

"Little bit of everything Ma'am." Wapiti said, filling up a cup of coffee.

"Wapiti, this is Carl, Ted, and Mike." Casey said, introducing them.

They all quickly reached out to shake Wapiti's hand. "It's a Great Pleasure to meet you, Deputy." They all said.

"Not only do we get to meet the great Marshal Shawn Felton, but we also get to meet you Deputy Wapiti." Mike said, setting back down. "You're becoming MORE famous than the Marshal is."

"I like reading about all the fight's he's been in since becoming a Lawman…Truthfully, when we all heard the Marshal had hired an Indian Deputy Marshal, no-one gave you a second thought. Everyone thought you'd be run out of the first town you rode into." Mike said, jokingly.

"But he wasn't!" Casey said, loudly. "Fact, me and Miles got to see what happened in the first town he rode into. Like Miles said last night, Wapiti made everyone know he was the real thing and would be around for a while."

"I know I've enjoyed watching him fight all the fight's I've seen him fight in." Shawn said, pouring a small shot of whiskey in his coffee.

"Isn't it a little early to start drinking Marshal?" Ann asked

"He's thinking Ma'am." Wapiti chuckled, with a big smile on his face. "Least that's what he claims it does for him, helps him think."

"What's he thinking about?" Ann asked, with a small smile on her face.

"How to catch these Rustler's without getting anyone killed Ma'am." Shawn stated, taking a small sip.

"I find it makes men forget what it is they're supposed to be doing." Ann answered, with a big smile on her face.

They all set and ate their breakfast discussing all the fight's Wapiti had been in over the last five and a half months. After an hour of telling stories, they finished eating and Shawn said it was time to figure out how to get them Rustler's to give up peacefully.

"Tom, you ride down and watch the roads where the two come together. Hank, you cover the next gully over in case they try to track around and come out at the lower Lake. Miles, you and Fred cover the two gully on the west side. All of you make sure you have your binoculars on you, so you can see them from further off." Casey was saying

"We all carry them in our saddle bags as per your order's Casey." Hank said, pointing at his saddle bags.

"How we supposed to let everyone know which way they're coming from?" Tom asked

"Fire your rifle only once, that way they might think someone is out huntin' deer or elk and not give it a second thought." Shawn said. "Then whoever sees them first, after you fire that warning shot you ride back down towards the road. Then head back down the ridge towards us, we'll catch up to you as soon as we can.

"You Sure about firing a warning shot?" Casey asked "You sure it won't scare them off?"

"Not likely, like I said, using a rifle and not a pistol and only firing one shot. They'll think someone's out huntin' meat, not Rustler's." Shawn said, refilling his coffee. "Anyone else want another cup?"

"I'll have one." Wapiti said, holding his cup out towards Shawn, who refilled it.

"Let's all get saddled up and ready for them, you four, get going." Casey said, as everyone started walking towards the barn and all the horses.

Within ten minutes everyone was saddled up and the four took off down the road in two different directions. While everyone else headed back over to the table and sat back down with a fresh pot of coffee. Everyone was asking the Marshal how many men had he really killed since he'd been a Lawman. Some rumor's had his count to be over two hundred. Was that true, or were people stretching the truth a whole lot like usual.

"No, it's no bullshit story. According to Judge Monson, since I've been a Deputy U.S. Marshal or full Marshal over the last twenty plus years I've killed over two hundred men. But then you take in the ten plus years of being a Deputy Sheriff to Sheriff, my years as a Texas Ranger, plus add the war into it…I've killed well over three hundred men, probably closer to four." Shawn said in a serious voice, and with a sorrowful look as well.

"I was with Grant when he took Vicksburg." Casey said, looking over at Shawn. "By Your Looks, I'd Say You Were A Reb Sir."

"Yes Sir I AM…My parent's made me stay out of the war, but when I saw some of those Yankee's raping, then killing both Black and White women. Well Sir, I couldn't take no more. Captain Quantrill came through and I joined up with him for a short while. I went looking for those no good rapist's…I ended up in Appomattox when General Lee surrendered to General Grant, who later went on to be President of these here United States of America." Shawn said

"I was there too…" Casey said, looking at the other four young men sitting at the table with the same serious voice, but a sad look on his face and in his eyes. "That was the last big battle that pretty much ended the war. It took days to count the dead on both sides…I prayed to God at the end of that battle, that I would not have to ever kill another man for the rest of my life … So Far, he's answered that prayer."

"How about you Wapiti, have you killed anyone yet?" Mike asked

"NO, have any of you?" Wapiti asked, looking at the other three.

"NOPE," they all answered, and they hoped they never did. Fact, they all left their pistol's in their saddlebags when they went Saloon hopping. They only wore them out here, cause you never knew when you're going to come across a Timber RattleSnake. Some of them can get over eight to ten feet long.

"I wish more men left their guns outside like that." Shawn said "I've seen too many Youngmen Goated into pulling their pistol and their dead before they know it…It's better to be a live coward, than a dead fool."

"We like settling our disputes like Wapiti, we fight them hand-to-hand." Ted said, smiling at everyone. "Just are fight's aren't over as fast as the one's we've read about you fightin' in Deputy Wapiti."

"The stories I've heard and read about you Wapiti, is you are a HeadHunter, when he's thru with them, their noses are crushed and both eyes blackened so much that they can't see through all the swelling for days." Carl said, looking at everyone.

"We fight four and five men at a time in some of our fights too." Carl said, starting to chuckle. "But ours are two on three, four or vice versa. Not One Against three and four men at the same time."

Tom and Hank headed up the road going east at a full out run, as Mike and Fred headed west.

Within five minutes of riding Tom headed up the hillside next to the road going to Sisters. Keeping his horse at a good Gallup, he was over a mile up from the other road and three quarters the way up the ridge. When he stopped and took up his post, from there he could see the road cut through the timber for a good mile.

Hank headed on down the road for over a mile when he came to the next ridge. Turning his horse up into the timber, he quickly turned his horse angling his way up the ridge towards the top. He knew the only way he would know they were coming down this ridge would be from the mooing of the cattle from being herded. When he figured he was over a mile in and at the top of the ridge, he too, took up his post.

Mike and Fred headed west at a full out run, the ranch house set in between two ridge's. One was only a half mile most down the road and Mike split off going up the west side of the ridge. Climbing and angling his way to the top. After a good hour of hard riding he figured he was a good mile and a half up from the road. Being on top of the higher ridge he could see most of the lower ridge to the east of him. From there, with his binoculars he could see where the two ridges came together over a mile away. So he set up his post and waited for them to come over or someone else to fire their rifle.

"Fred continued down the road for another three quarters of a mile before he came to his ridge. Turning his horse, he too headed up the west side of the ridge. He too angled his way up the side of the ridge to where he could see over to the ridge on the west side of the one he came up. He knew Mike would see anyone coming over the ridge on the backside. So when he was high enough to see the ridges further west he set up his lookout post there.

All the men were getting restless while waiting for one of the four outlooks to spot the Rustler's and fire his warning shot. After an hour plus of storytelling Casey suggested they go play a game of horseshoes to kill the time.

Everyone thought it was a good idea too, so they all stood up and started walking over to the horseshoe pits. Shawn looked over at Casey. "You wouldn't know why someone would bring a herd down this way would ya?"

"It's a less conspicuous way south, well off the beaten path. Once they get on this side of the mountain, there's lakes and streams all the way to the Town of Crescent Lake." Casey answered

"Have you heard of anyone buying up land?" Shawn asked, tossing a horseshoe.

"Yeah, the Dolby Brother's, Brian and Craig, and the Garret Brother's, Brad and Pat. They came back from Alaska last spring with a shit load of gold and bought two big ranches and three smaller ones around Davis Lake. They actually paid more than the land was worth on the smaller ranches. But they wanted one large ranch" Casey was saying, as he threw his horseshoe. "Something like, twenty thousand acres all together…but they got all the water and timber rights too, so they'll more make out in the long run. But I think they ran out of money, cause I haven't seen any cattle around there yet. Not to mention, when I went to Crescent Lake last week I stopped in to introduce myself and tell them I had a couple hundred or so already bred heifers for sale. But no-one was home, so I went on into town, spent the night and thought I'd swing by again on my way home, but still, no-one was around, so I came home."

"Hundred plus head of bred cows, this year's calves, and four bulls to rebreed with, that's a nice herd to start with." Shawn said, taking a pull off his flask and offering Casey a drink.

Which he gladly took, then tossed another horseshoe, getting a ringer. "Haven't gotten one of those in a while." Casey said, handing Shawn his flask back.

Hank had been scoping the ridge all morning, and nothing was moving around except a few head of their cattle. He knew it had to be getting close to lunch time, cause his stomach was starting to growl out of hunger. Taking a raw red potato out of his pocket, he wiped it off and started eating it.

When all of a sudden he saw a large flock of birds fly up from around the top of the far ridge. Picking his binoculars up, he started looking through it. Looking over at the birds first, he could tell it was a flock of Crows. They could have been eating on a dead animal and something or someone scared them. Pulling his binoculars back towards the ground he kept searching but couldn't see anything. Slowly he started searching up the top of the next ridge over following it back down towards the road. But NOTHING! What had scared those Crow's into flight. Slowly he started looking the top of the ridge over just as he saw some cattle being herded coming over the top of the far ridge. Looks like they intended to ride around Myers ranch house, but still water the cattle down at one of the lower lakes.

Standing up, he quickly tightened his cinch. Climbed aboard and took out his rifle, firing one shot back towards the ranch house. Then turned his horse down the ridge and took off at a semi-fast trot going down the ridge through the timber.

Ann was just about to ring the lunch bell, when they all heard a rifle shot echoing off in the ridge to the west. Everyone came to a stop and started looking in the direction of the shot, then back at each other.

"Sounds like it's at least a couple ridges over." Shawn said, looking in the direction of the shot. "Let's ride gentlemen." He said, running over to where the horses were tied up at.

Ann rang the lunch bell. "You Men All Come By And Get Something To Take With You On The Way Out." She hollered out.

Everyone quickly tightened their cinch's up, climbed aboard as Ann was handing them each a hamburger sandwich and a couple pieces of fried chicken to put in their pockets to eat later.

Everyone quickly stuffed three to four pieces of chicken in their pockets, grabbed a hamburger sandwich and headed down the road at a full run with the Marshal and Casey leading the way.

"That shot sounds like they're coming in around the backside of the mountain." Casey yelled over to Shawn.

All three other outpost's stood up and looked in the direction of the rifle shot. Quickly they all tightened up their cinch's, climbed up in the saddle's and headed down hill back towards the road. Except Tom, he just headed over the ridge to his west to see if he could see them before he headed to the bottom and met up with Casey and everyone else.

It only took Tom about thirty hard riding minutes to reach the top of the next ridge over. Topping out, he could hear the cattle mooing somewhere down there in the draw under the cover of the timber. Turning his horse down the top of the ridge towards the gully as fast as his horse could go. He knew the Rustler's couldn't hear him way up here, so he wasn't worried about the noise from his horse's hooves hitting the ground hard and loud.

Shawn, Wapiti, and all the other's rode hard and fast past the first gully heading uphill and continued on to the second one, stopping when they got to it. Wapiti quickly started riding along the edge of the road looking for any tracks that Tom or Hank had left the road at and headed up the hillside. With the softness of the ground, he found his tracks easy. Turning his horse off the road and into the timber he started following them into the timber.

"What are you looking for? Wapiti" Shawn yelled out, looking up at him, then back at the other four men.

"Just making sure where these tracks were going. Looks like they headed up that side of the ridge, so I'd say they're from one of your Cowhands that came this way." Wapiti said, turning his horse back towards the group of men.

"How much further to the lake?" Shawn asked, looking over at Casey.

"If they're smart, and I think they are. They'd be smart to come down the next little draw there. That way they'd come out at the Lake and be well out of view from my ranch house and most of my men." Casey said

"Let's get down to that next gully." Shawn said, turning his horse he kicked him in the side and took off at a full run, with everyone right behind him.

It barley took them a couple minutes and they came to the mouth of the next little draw. Stopping, Shawn looked around at the lake behind them and the large meadow around the lake. "Alright now, we want to catch them out in the open. So you men get up there, over there, and a couple up there." Shawn said, pointing. "No-one shoots till I do, don't shoot to kill. Shoot at the ground at their horses feet, that'll make them rare up and maybe even buck a couple off unexpectedly. Then I'll call out to them, if they try and make a run for it, shoot their horses. I don't want to have to kill anyone unless there's no other way around it, CLEAR!" Shawn ordered out.

"Yes Sir Marshal." They all answered, heading in all the direction's Shawn had pointed out that he wanted them at. They all rode a good couple hundred feet up into the timber, tying their horses up to whatever they could find to tie them off to. A dead branch sticking up, a small tree, or even to a branch on a bigger tree. Then each one quickly ran over and laid behind a large bush, laying down dead trees, or anywhere else it would be hard for someone to see them and get a shot off in their direction.

They'd all been hiding for a good forty plus minutes when Hank and Fred came riding down the road at a slow trot. When they were almost directly below Shawn, when he stood up and called out to Them. "How far they away?" Shawn called out.

Startling both men as they anxiously pulled back on their reins, looking up into the area of the timber that the voice had come from. Then seeing the Marshal standing up from behind a large downed dead tree. "Sorry Marshal, you scared the shit out of us." Hank said, looking around at the others as they all started standing up and looking at them. "It'll take them a good two hours to come off that ridge...Mind if I go change out my water bag real quick Marshal?"

"No, fact, since we're all drinking warm water, let's everyone change out and get back into your hiding spot's." Shawn said, walking around the log and looking around at everyone else.

"Did you see 'em for sure?" Shawn asked, walking towards the road.

"Too much timber, but cattle only moo a lot when they're being herded thru country they don't like walking thru." Fred said, turning his horse towards the lake.

Even though it was late in the summer, the Lake was full and only a couple hundred feet off the side of the road. Everyone quickly started walking towards the lake, all the Cowhands were talking amongst themselves, how cool was it that they were getting to help the great Marshal Shawn Felton and Deputy Wapiti catch some no good Cattle Rustlers. They still couldn't believe Wapiti had fought three Professional Wrestlers and beat them all. Not one of them had even laid a hand on that Buck Indian, that sure would have been a good fight to have watched.

"What about the four the next night in Sisters." Carl said, taking a drink off his water bag as they all headed back to their hideouts.

Marshal Felton had given the Order that No-One was allowed to smoke till the herd of cattle got there and they had everyone in custody. Everyone was just sitting there watching and listening for anything coming down the draw. Every five minutes felt like ten, every ten, felt like twenty. They could hear and see the squirrels and chipmunks playing. Running up one tree, running out on the end of the branches and jumping over to the next tree.

A couple men had a couple chipmunk's run right up the top of the log next to them. Stopping, looking at them, then running off down the tree jumping over to another one and out of sight.

Shawn took out his pocket watch and looked at it, it was almost two-thirty. That makes it close to two and a half hours since Hank had fired his warning shot. They should be getting close to us by now, he was thinking to himself, looking at all the other men in the Posse that he could see.

After another long five minutes they could hear cattle mooing off in the distance. Shawn stood up and looked around for everyone, pointing up the draw. "They're coming!" he semi-yelled out. Then he quickly got back down behind his log out of sight.

It took almost another thirty minutes before the herd of cattle started coming out of the timber and heading towards the lake for something to drink. It took another five minutes for the entire herd and four Cowboys to clear the timber.

Everyone was waiting anxiously for the Marshal to make his move. It had been a long hot, hard, dry drive for the cattle and they were all thirsty and somehow they could smell the water, so they all speeded up and headed towards the lake on their own. The four Cowboy's slowly fell back from the herd riding towards each other.

They could all hear them talking, but really couldn't make out what they were talking about. When they were all within ten feet of each other, Shawn fired the first rifle shot at the feet of their horse.

Then everyone one else joined in, and many rifle shots started hitting the ground at the horse's hooves, scaring the horses into bucking, bucking two men off. While the other two fought to gain control of their horses.

"This Is U. S. Marshal Felton And My Posse, We Have You Totally Surrounded…So Please Don't Try And Do Something Stupid!" Shawn yelled out

"Where Are You?" one of the Rustler's yelled out, dropping the reins to his horse, holding his hands up in the air, looking around the timber line all around themselves.

"Right over here." Shawn said, standing up and walking out from behind his log. "All Of YOU, Slowly Reach Down And Throw Your Pistols In My Direction!"

"Yes Sir Marshal, just tell your Posse member not to get trigger happy." One of the Rustler's yelled back, as they all threw their pistols as far away from themselves as they could.

Slowly everyone stood up and headed down the hillside towards the Rustler's. They were all glad there hadn't been a shootout and no-one was killed.

"Alright, you two get off those horses and let me put these handcuffs on you." Shawn ordered out to the Rustler's. "Are these the men you were telling me about Casey?"

"I believe so, you men are the Garret and Dolby brothers aren't you?" Casey asked

"Yes Sir we are." All four men answered, holding their hands out so Marshal Felton could put the handcuffs on them.

"I know they stole the cattle, but the land is still legally theirs, isn't it Marshal?" Casey asked, looking back and forth between the Marshal and the four Rustler's.

"It Is, at least until someone can prove they stole the gold to buy it with." Shawn started saying.

"We found all that gold at our mine in Alaska." The four men all started yelling. "That land is ours fair and square." The taller, slender, elder brother shouted out.

"Sure, we stole the cattle, but the land was ours before we broke any laws." The taller, heavier set, elder brother, shouted out.

"What I'm getting at, is they have a lot of land that's going to sit empty for three to five years." Casey started explaining. "I have almost four hundred head of yearly bred heifers and a dozen bulls I could run on that land while you men are in prison."

"What's in it for us?" all four men demandingly shouted out.

"I'm getting to that." Casey said. "How about I run them on your land, since you own the water too, I'll give you men forty percent of all the calves till you get out of prison. By then, you could easily have three to four hundred head of cattle with your brands on them when you get out."

"That sounds like a pretty good deal." All four men started saying. Talking back and forth between themselves.

"How are we going to sign any kind of contract being arrest like this?" The taller, slender brother asked.

"I'd like to know how we're going to herd all these cattle and watch over these four at the same time." Wapiti spoke up, looking over at Shawn.

"Marshal, it's just before four now." Casey said, looking at his pocket watch. "I have about two hundred acres fenced off for my replacement heifers. We can put these cattle in with them, then when you get back to Bend. You can wire their rightful owners and they can sent a crew down to retrieve them."

"That's Fine Four These Cattle, But What About The Deal You Offered Us." All four men stated saying

"I'm not letting anyone run cattle on our property without an agreement signed ahead of time!" the taller, heavier set brother firmly stated.

"What's your name's?" Shawn asked, looking the four men over.

"I'm Brian Dolby and this is my younger brother Craig. He's Brad Garret and that's his younger brother Pat." He said, introducing everyone.

"It's getting late Marshal, how about you stay at my place again tonight and we can get this contract drawn up to everyone's satisfaction." Casey suggested.

"You two men go get our horses." Shawn said, pointing at Carl and Mike.

"We wouldn't be in this situation if you two wouldn't have spent, what was it Pat, five times the price per acre we paid for all the other land we bought, which would have left us with enough money to buy a few hundred bred heifers, not to mention, the bulls from P.O. Nicely to rebreed them with, and then we could have bought a few hundred more next year as well. So you two went behind our backs and bought that last section and a half at five times the regular price." Craig was disgustedly explaining, as Pat agreed with him, they did pay five times the price per acre all the other land cost them. And like he had mentioned before they bought the land. We all knew his asking price, so we were going to hold off a few years before getting a loan from the local bank and buy the land then. But like Craig explained, you greedy bastards just had to have that land!

"Yes Sir Marshal." Both men said, taking off at a slow run back up the hillside through the timber.

"The rest of you men, get your horses and round up that herd of cattle and head them back to the ranch house and the heifer field" Casey ordered out. "Don't worry if any of our cattle follow them in, we can separate them once they're all inside the pen with our heifers."

"Are you going to need any more help with these men Marshal?" Ted asked

"No, just go do what Casey asked you to do." Shawn said, as they all took off towards the timber and their horses.

"You Four Rustler's Listen Up…I'm Only Going To Say This Once!" Shawn said, glaring straight into each man's face. "I'm going to cuff one end of those handcuffs to your saddle horn so you can ride your own horse more easily. NOW, Deputy Wapiti is going to be riding the front door with that double barrel ten gauge loaded with steel balls, not bee-bee's …It'll take your head clean off if you should try and escape. I'll be bringing up the rear with my rifle in hand … You try and run, I'll kill your horse and you'll walk the rest of the way in with your legs in shackles. Do I Make Myself Clear On What Will Happen If You Try And Run On Me!"

"Yes Sir Marshal." All four Rustler's said, looking at that ten gauge in Wapiti's left hand, with one hammer pulled all the way back. "We won't give you any trouble Marshal." They continued saying.

Just as a couple men came riding up leading three horses, while the rest all headed over towards the lake to round up the cattle.

"Wapiti, hold that ten gauge on these men, as they climb up in their saddle's. One at a time I'm going to uncuff one hand so I can anchor it off around your saddle horn … You try to run on me and Wapiti will shoot ya with that shotgun." Shawn was explaining, while all four men were climbing up in their saddles.

"Don't worry about us Marshal." All four men kept saying.

"This ain't worth dying over." Brain said

"Casey, this is your deal you want to work out with these men. Why don't you ride on ahead and start drawing the contract up,

Now you said forty percent, Don't be changing it on them now and hold me up any longer than I need to be." Shawn said, locking Craig's handcuff around his saddle horn.

"I personally think we should get closer to fifty percent." Brad spoke out. "Like you said Mr. Myers, we own the water too."

"I'll go forty five percent and not one calf over!" Casey said, climbing up in the saddle. "That should give you a good couple hundred marketable steer's when you get out for cash to start over with."

"We'll take that offer." All four Rustler's said, watching Casey turn his horse and head down the road at a fast gallop.

It only took Shawn a couple minutes to recuff everyone and climb back up into his saddle. "Wapiti, you bring up the rear, the rest of you follow me. Now let's get moving at a slow trot."

"Yes Sir Marshal." Wapiti said, turning his horse back down the road. "Let's go." He said, kicking his horse but keeping his eyes on the four men, who quickly fell in behind him.

CHAPTER 5

It barley took them thirty minutes to get back to the ranch house where Casey was standing with a piece of paper on a clipboard in his hand. Walking over to the four Rustler's he handed it to Brian first. "Print your name's and sign your signature under it. I was thinking, I'll have another three hundred head of bred heifers I can add to the herd the following year, enlarging my herd and yours too."

Brain quickly read it over, it was simple. Mr. Myers would start out with running three hundred head of cattle, they would receive forty five percent of all the calves just as he had agreed to earlier.

"Hurry up!" Shawn yelled out, just as Ann came walking out of the house.

"Just reading it over Marshal." Brain said, signing the paperwork and handing it to the other's so they could read and sign it too.

"Marshal, a couple young men came by a couple hours ago and traded me seven grouse for fifty cents each." Ann said, handing him up two large pillow cases filled with food. "One has fried grouse and the other has some cornbread, zucchini bread, and honey butter."

"Thank you very much." Shawn said, taking them. Reaching in the bag, he took out a couple pieces and handed the bag over to Wapiti. Then, putting one piece in his mouth, he reached for his wallet with his empty hand. Taking it out, he handed Ann a twenty dollar bill. "Here Ma'am, thank you very much for feeding us."

Holding her hands up, Ann refused the money. Saying it was the least she could do for them.

Continuing to hold out the twenty dollar bill towards her. "Please take it Ma'am, I'll put it on my expense account and get reimbursed for it when we get back." Shawn said, smiling and winking at her. "So the State is paying you, not me."

"Alright, if you insist." Ann said, taking the money.

"It only took them ten minutes to sign the paperwork, refill all their water bags, give each man a couple pieces of fried grouse and they were heading back down the road at a medium trot trying to eat at the same time.

In no time at all they passed the goat trail road that led back to Sisters, but they kept riding down the main road back towards Bend.

After riding hard for a couple hours they topped over Mt Bachelor and could see the vast valley down below them. Shawn pulled out his pocket watch and looked at it, it was almost seven o-clock. If they were lucky they had a good hour before nightfall. He knew there was no way they would make Bend tonight. But they would easily make it early tomorrow well before noon at this pace.

They kept up the pace till the sun started setting behind the mountains behind them. "Slow up Wapiti." Shawn yelled out, slowing his horse to a walk and looking around for a good place to camp for the night. Which didn't take very long and they came across a large grassy area.

"That area right over there will do for tonight." Shawn yelled out, pointing the barrel of his rifle to the area he was speaking about.

Riding over, both Wapiti and Shawn dismounted, and Shawn walked back to the pack horse and took out the leg irons.

"Wapiti, you keep that ten gauge on these men till I get them shackled around that big pine tree over there." Shawn said, pointing his rifle again. Then walking over, he uncuffed their hands leaving the handcuffs attached to the saddle horn.

Then he started shackling one side to one Rustler's leg and the other end to another Rustler till he had them all chained together. Leading them over to the tree, having them circle the tree, he shackled the last shackle around Craig's angle.

"How we supposed to sleep changed up like this Marshal?" They all started asking.

"You'll sleep just fine!" Shawn said, walking back toward all the horses. Where Wapiti was in the process of unsaddling them.

Walking over to the saddles on the ground, he untied all their bedrolls and took them over to them and tossed them on the ground at their feet. "There ya go, now I advise you all to get to sleep as soon as possible, I want to pull out before sun-up."

"We're hungry." They all started saying

Shawn walked back over and grabbed the bag of fried grouse and took it back over to the four men. "Grab yourselves three, four pieces then eat up and get some sleep. I usually wake up around four-thirty." He said, taking a pull off his flask.

"You wouldn't have some more of that you'd be willing to share with us, would ya Marshal?" Brad asked, pulling out a couple pieces of grouse.

"I'll be right back." Shawn said, handing Brain the bag of grouse, then walked back over to the supply's. Pulled out a full fifth he filled his flask back up and headed back over to the four men. "Here, this might be the last drink you men get for a few years…Now, give me the grouse back so me and Wapiti have something to eat.

"Thanks Marshal." Craig said, handing him the bag of fried grouse and took the bottle of whiskey at the same time.

"You're welcome Youngman." Shawn said, reaching in the pillow case and took out a piece. "Eat up and get some sleep, we're pulling out before sun-up." He said, walking away and back over to Wapiti and handed him the bag.

"Thanks Marshal." Wapiti said, reaching in and taking out a couple pieces, then tossed the bag over to their supply pile a few feet away.

They both quickly ate, laid out their bedrolls and everyone fell fast asleep.

Shawn and Wapiti both woke up when a skunk came walking between them dragging the bag of fried grouse away. There was a half full moon in the sky, the smell from the skunk made them both roll over and set up fast. Wapiti was in front of him and when he set up shouting. 'HOLY SHIT' He startled and scared the skunk into spaying his self-defense mechanism, spraying over half of Shawn's head and shoulders.

"HOLY SHIT!" Shawn shouted out, jumping up out of bed, trying to get away from the smell. But no matter where he went, it followed him.

All the noise woke the four Rustler's up, at first they were scared awake from the screaming and shouting. Then looking over at the Marshal jumping up from his beds. After another few seconds the Rustlers could all smell the aroma of the skunk and figuring out what had happened and they all busted up laughing.

"DAMN YOU STINK!" Wapiti said, chuckling and looking over at the Marshal.

"Go To Hell...All Of You!" Shawn demanded, taking his shirt off. Walking over to the supply's, he opened up his laundry bag and grabbed another shirt and T-shirt. Grabbing a water jug, he quickly started pouring water into the T-shirt, while everyone was still laughing at him.

"You guys just go ahead and get up, we're pulling out in an hour." Shawn ordered out starting to wash his face and shoulders off. "Wapiti, would you please build a fire and put a pot of coffee on."

"Sure Marshal, no problem." Wapiti said, still chuckling a little.

With the moon light, it was easy for him to see and find wood for a fire. While the Rustlers were still carrying on about how funny it had been to see the Marshal get sprayed by that skunk. They were a good twenty feet away from him and it smelt like that skunk was still in camp.

Shawn had finished cleaning up when Wapiti put the coffee pot on the small fire. "Alright men, stand up." He yelled out walking over to the Rustlers. "Wapiti, you got that ten gauge ready."

"Sure Do Marshal." Wapiti yelled back, pulling the shotgun to hip level facing directly at the four men, he pulled both hammers back and they made a loud "CLICK".

"Tell him to drop those hammer's back one lock in case he trips and falls." all four men started saying at the same time.

"He's alright…Now here's what we're going to do. I'm going to unshackle you, then reshackle you each separately so you can saddle up your own horse…You can plainly see what the consequences will be if you try to jump me." Shawn said, unlocking one lock off each man. Then when they were all in single irons, he locked the other side around their other leg.

"Now, let's get saddled up." Shawn said, pulling out his pocket watch. "It's almost Five, if we hurry up we could be in Bend by late morning.

Wapiti was just tucking his cinch strap down when the coffee started to percolate out the pour spout. So he walked over and pulled it to the side to let the grounds settle.

Everyone quickly took his coffee cup out of his saddlebags and walked over to the fire. Shawn reached down and picked up the pot. Filled his cup first, then filled everyone else's cups. Nobody said much as they spent close to ten minutes, each drinking two cups before the pot was empty.

"Alright, now each one of you walk over to your horses and recuff your left hands for me." Shawn ordered out.

Which all four Rustler's did without hesitation cause Wapiti pulled that big ten gauge back out and was pointing it at them. "What if he trip's and that thing goes off?" Brain asked

"He won't have to move if you don't, so I suggest you men stand real still while I remove these leg irons." Shawn firmly stated "Now pick your feet up one at a time for me."

All four men did as they were told, and it only took a couple more minutes and everyone was saddled up and heading down the road. With the moon's bright light help they could see the road just fine, so Shawn kicked them into a medium trot.

They had been riding for a good twenty minutes or so when the sky to the far east ridge started lighting up over the edge of the planet. With the scattered clouds across the sky that slowly started turning lite orange color. Then within a couple more minutes the base was a reddish orange color at the bottom center, to orange in the middle, to a lite orangish yellow on the far edges. It may have only lasted for five minutes at the most. But it was one of the prettiest sun rises any of them had seen in a long while and they were all talking about it.

Shawn pushed them at a medium trot for a good hour, before he'd slow them back down to a walk for about thirty minutes. Then it was back to a medium trot again, he kept telling them that he wanted to make Prineville before it got too late.

After a good three plus hours of pushing everyone their horses were covered in sweat and were tiring out as they rode into the outskirts of Bend. Shawn turned them to go around town, till he saw the wire fence that went around Chris Hensley's ranch. Turning them up the street, he headed towards Chris Hensley's ranch house. Which only took them another five minutes to get to.

As they rode up to the water trough to water their horses, Chris came out and asked the Marshal if there was anything he could do to help them.

"You wouldn't mind swapping us out our tired horses for some fresh mounts would you?" Shawn asked, looking at his pocket watch, it was just past ten-thirty. "I'd really like to make Prineville today."

"No problem Marshal." Chris answered, turning towards a couple of his ranch hands. "You men go get six fresh horses out of the training corral."

"Yes Sir." The two men answered, taking off at a slow run.

"Alright, all you men, again, I'm going to uncuff the cuff around your saddle horn so you can resaddle a new horse...However! Wapiti is still going to be standing close by with that shotgun in case any of you decide to make a run for it." Shawn shouted out.

"Don't worry about us, we're not stupid Marshal." All four men answered, as Shawn unlocked the cuff from around their saddle horn. Just as the two ranch hands came leading six horses out to them.

"Could you do me one more favor Mr. Hensley. Would you please go down to the tele-graph office and wire everyone on this brand list. Tell them they can pick their cattle up at Casey Myers ranch at Elk Lake, not the town. His ranch house is close to the Lake itself." Shawn asked, handing him the paper with the list of brands on it.

"Sure Marshal, no problem." Chris answered "But how many times I have to ask you to call me Chris, Marshal."

Everyone quickly took their saddles off and put them on a new horse. They all started talking about how big and well dispossessed all the horses were. After they got out of prison and sold all their marketable steer's they'd be back to buy a couple new horses as soon as they could, they told Chris.

While everyone saddled their new horse, Shawn refilled all the water bags and gave one back to each man. They were just about ready to pull out when Mrs. Hensley brought them all out two thick ham steak sandwiches for each man.

"Here Marshal." Mrs. Hensley said, handing him a large paper bag with all twelve sandwiches in it. "Don't know when you men ate last, but this should hold you till you get to Powell Butte."

"Thank you Ma'am." Shawn said, looking at the bag. "How much do I owe you?"

"Nothing Marshal." Mrs. Hensley said, turning to walk away. "I won't hear any arguments about it either, You just watch your back door for back shooter."

"Always do Ma'am, and thank you for the food." Shawn said, riding over to each man and handing him a sandwich. "Alight, Wapiti, you take the front door again and I'll bring up the rear. Do you remember the way we came into town from the goat trail back to Powell Butte?"

"Sure do." Wapiti answered. "Let's go gentlemen." He said turning his horse up the street, making sure they were following him, which they were.

"That sandwich really hit the spot, '' everyone was saying. While they ate, but they all sure wished they had another one when they finished eating them. Just as they left the last street and headed into the timber.

"Everybody, kick it up, let's get moving." Shawn yelled out.

"Yes Sir Marshal." They all yelled out, kicking their horses into a medium trot riding through the Juniper and Ponderosa Pine trees. They were all surprised at how well and how fast all the horses would jump over, go around a tree or a large bush. They didn't even have to turn the horse, as if by pure instinct they were all running like they were chasing after something and it was getting away from them, so they were taking the shortest route thru and around everything. Many times the men got a branch in the face as their horse cut around the tree closer than he should have.

Within a half hour they were at the goat trail road that cut through the timber going towards Powell Butte. They all slowed down to a walk and started looking both ways up and down the road. After thirty seconds or so, Shawn ordered them to move back out at a medium trot.

After about an hour, Shawn yelled out to everyone to slow down and walk the horses for a while, which everyone did. Shawn could see the four Rustlers talking amongst themselves. He could hear they were talking about how many cattle they'd have when they got out of prison in a few years.

After a good half hour of walking the horses, Shawn ordered everyone back into a medium trot. With the cloud cover moving over head, it kept it cooler riding in the shadows from all the timber.

They'd only gone a couple more miles when they came across two men trying to cut up and remove a large size Douglas Fir tree that had blown over and completely blocked the entire road.

"HOLD UP!" Shawn yelled out, looking the two men and their mule team over. One man had a broad ax and was delimbing the tree, while the other man had a five and half foot long one man saw and was cutting thru the butt of the tree.

"Looks like you men could use some help." Shawn said, riding up alongside the tree.

"Not Really Marshal." The man with the ax yelled back. "Judge Monson gave us a fifty hours of community service for a bar room brawl over at the China Palace Lounge last week…he said this job he'd knock four hour for travel time and four hours labor, plus pay for our dinner and two pitchers of beer at the diner in Powell Butte before we came back home." One man started explaining.

"What he's sayin' Marshal, is if we finish up to soon and the Judge finds out, he just might add more time to our fine." The man on the saw yelled out. "But we thank you for the offer to help."

"Very well then, I'll tell Judge Monson it was at least two feet bigger in diameter so he needs to knock a couple more hours off your time." Shawn said, smiling. "Let's get going men." He ordered, pointing towards the top end of the tree.

Everyone did as he ordered and rode around the tree back to the road on the other side. Then once again, Shawn put them into a slow gallop the rest of the way into Powell Butte.

Riding into town, they rode over to the Livery and the water trough for their horses to get a drink. "Marshal, how about you take this twenty and go over to the Merc, get yourself a replacement bottle for last night. Then buy us one last bottle for tonight, who knows when we'll get to have another drink." Brad asked, holding out the money.

"Alright son, I'll do that for you." Shawn said, reaching over and taking the money.

Everyone climbed off their horses and started stretching their legs out. Which was even more difficult to do with one hand being cuffed to the saddle horn.

Shawn looked over and saw two boy's playing in the dirt in front of the closest house. "You Boys Come Here For A Minute!" He yelled out

Both boys looked up and over to the group of men. "You want us Mister?" one of them asked back.

"Come here, I've got a job for you." Shawn yelled back.

Both boy's stood up and ran over to him, seeing his badge right off. They came to a sudden stop. "Yes Sir Marshal, what can we do for you?" one of the boy's asked, respectfully but excitedly.

"I want you to go to the Merc and tell Tim you're in there for me. Then tell him I need four cold beers, two for each me and Wapiti, four pint bottles he has of Kentucky Bourbon and one fifth." Shawn said, handing the boy the twenty dollar bill. "You boys keep the change for your payment for doing the job for me."

"That Going To Be Over Seven Dollars." Brad yelled out. "We could use that extra money for when we get out."

"That's the price you have to pay for them to do the job." Shawn said, with a big smile on his face.

"Youngman, would you grab four more beers for us too?" Brian asked, holding out a five dollar bill. "You can keep the change from it as well."

"Yes Sir. " They both answered, as the second boy grabbed the money and they both took off running across the street to the Merc.

Shawn took a pull off his flask, then looked at his pocket watch, it was only two-thirty. They would be in town in time for an early dinner.

"Wapiti walked around and took all the water bags off every horse, dumped them out and refilled them with fresh cold water.

All the Rustler's thanked him for thinking about them too and changing out their water with fresh water. They all knew and told Wapiti NO other Lawman would have done that. They'd make the criminal drink hot water to make their trip back in more miserable.

It only took the two boy's maybe five minutes at most to return with everything in two big paper bags. "Marshal, there's over ten dollars in change left over." One boy said, holding out the money.

"I said all the change was yours for doing the job." Shawn proudly said, holding his chest up and out. "Sometimes I pay by the job, not the hour. So thank you boy's." he said, walking around handing everyone a beer, giving Wapiti two. "Here's something to drink for the next couple miles."

"Thanks Marshal." Wapiti said, taking them and opening one up and taking a big drink off the bottle.

"When we get to the outskirts of Prineville, you men all put your coats back on so you can put one of these pint bottles down your coat sleeve so no-one can see them." Shawn said, with a smile on his face, but a serious look in his eyes. "If the jailer sees them, he'll confiscate them as well. So you wait till he goes back out to his desk before ANY of you take your coats off, CLEAR!"

"Yes Sir, and Thank You Marshal, we really appreciate you doing it for us." All four men started saying at the same time.

"Thanks for warning us about when to take our coat's off too." Brian said, taking a long drink off his beer.

"Everyone, tighten your cinch's up and let's get out of here." Shawn ordered out.

Everyone did as they were told and they were heading out of town on the main road. Shawn had them walking their horses for the first couple miles so the horses didn't cramp up from drinking so much water.

Just like every trip before, there were family wagons, freight wagons, carriage's, and people walking on both sides of the road. After a good couple mile's the east bound StageCoach came running around them. Creating a large dust cloud, so they all brought their horses to a stop, covering their faces waiting for the dust to settle down.

After a long thirty seconds or so, Shawn ordered them to get going, and pick the pace up to a medium trot.

It took them just over an hour and they were riding down the hill into Prineville. "Hold up." Shawn called out. Riding over to the four men and quickly unlocked the cuffs around their saddle horns so they could put their coats on. Then, he quickly recuffed them, handed them each a pint, and they put them inside one sleeve as headed back down View Ridge until it turned into Northwest Third Street.

All the rustlers adjusted the pints in their coat sleeves as the rode down the street, the people were all coming out to see the Marshal and Wapiti bringing in some more Outlaw's, and once again, none of them were laying over the saddle. They were ALL setting up, which makes at least five, six groups of Outlaw's he's brought back in alive since Wapiti signed on as a Deputy.

Like usual, Judge Monson was standing outside of the Courthouse watching them ride in. When all six men rode up in front of him, he looked the Outlaw's over. "Did they give you any trouble bringing them in Marshal?" He asked, handing him a beer and calling Wapiti over to get his.

Thank you, Your Honor." Wapiti said, climbing off his horse and walked over, taking the beer, he opened it up and started taking a drink off it.

"How about us, Your Honor, we're thirsty too!" All four Rustler's shouted out, getting off their horses.

"You men will have to wait a few years before you get another drink of alcohol of any kind." Judge Monson, stated, staring into each man's face. Just as the Jailer opened up the side door leading into the jail downstairs.

Shawn walked over and started uncuffing everyone's hand and leaving the cuff around the saddle horn.

"Your saddles will be in the storage locker when you men get out of prison." Shawn said, watching them all walk towards the door.

"Now, Your Honor, we're both tired, dirty, and hungry...so if there's nothing else, we'll see you tomorrow at our normal meeting time." Shawn said, grabbing his horses reins and a couple of the Rustler's horses reins and headed towards the Livery Stables.

FELTON 11

THE GOLD STAGECOACH

CHAPTER 1

Wapiti rolled over and set up when he heard the door to the shack crack open and slowly open up, it was Griselda with a pot of coffee and a hot plate.

"Marshal awake?" Griselda whispered

"No," Wapiti whispered back, reaching over to a table between the two beds, he picked up a silver dollar and tossed it to her. "Thanks for the coffee Gris."

"Marshal's snoring like he got drunk last night." Griselda said, still whispering and smiling. Stacking up the two empty plates on the table.

Wapiti stood up and pulled his pants on over his long handles. "We woke up around nine when your Mom brought us in the pie, he said to save his pie, he was goin' Saloon hoppin'…He said he was tired of me having all the fun."

"We've only heard stories about him getting into fight in one of the Saloon's the next morning when he snores like that." Griselda quietly chuckled, having to temporarily cover her mouth while filling Wapiti's coffee cup and handing it to him. "With You, We've Got To See A Couple…Your Good Wapiti" she said in a louder whisper, picking up the dirty dishes and headed back out the door.

"Thanks." Wapiti said, taking the cup. "Think I'll go out on the porch and let him sleep."

Picking up the hot plate and coffee pot, Wapiti walked outside to the table and sat down at the table and looked across the street towards the bank he started thinking. How long would they be in town for this time, that nice soft bed sure made it nicer sleeping last night. He was thinking as Jose came running up beside him.

"Did you guys have to shoot anyone on your last huntin' trip?" Jose asked, in a semi-quiet voice.

"No, we had them out numbered." Wapiti answered

"I heard you guys brought in four Outlaw's," Jose says, sitting down at the table. "How'd you have them out numbered when there was only two of you?"

"We had a Rancher and his seven hired hands with us when we met up with them." Wapiti said, filling his coffee up. Just as Griselda brought him a plate full of food.

"Mom thought you'd be hungry, so she cooked this up for you." Griselda said, setting the plate on the table.

Wapiti looked down at it, three eggs over easy, many strips of bacon and two sausage patties, crispy hash brown potatoes, two pieces of toast, and a new hot plate for the coffee pot. "Thanks Griselda, this looks wonderful, tell her thanks." He said, digging in.

"When do you guys have to go back out? Do you think we can do some target practice today?" Jose asked, leaning over on the table.

"I don't know on either item." Wapiti answered, taking a bite of food.

"You going to be able to teach me how to fight today?" Jose asked, with excitement in his voice and demeanor.

"I' don't know about that either. We have a meeting with the Judge at one o-clock." Wapiti said, in between bites.

"What do you think he'll want you guys to do, or where to go?" Jose asked

"I couldn't answer that question either." Wapiti answered, as Shawn opened the door.

"You two sure are noisy." Shawn said, walking over and filling himself up a cup of coffee.

"Sorry Marshal," Wapiti said, in between bites and pointing over at Jose.

Shawn shook his head with a big smile on his face and started rubbing Jose on the top of his head. "He does get a little excited at time's...Jose, this coffee is getting low. Would you please go get us another pot?"

"Yes Sir Marshal, right away." Jose said, taking off at a full run to the back door to the restaurant.

"So'd you find any fight's last night?" Wapiti asked, just as Shawn reached over and took over half patty of sausage. "HEY!"

"Nope...You've taken the fight out of 'em." Shawn answered, taking a bite of sausage. "You still have three pieces of bacon."

"So how long you think the Judge will give them, and when do we go to Court over them." Wapiti asked, taking another bite of food.

"Don't know when their trial will be, but since all the cattle have been recovered and no-one was injured in any of the rustling. Judge Monson will probably sentence them to two to five years. If they're really good inside and don't get into trouble, they'll be eligible for parol at the two year point for, quote 'Good Behavior' ... But too many fight's, and they'll be doing the entire five" Shawn answered.

"Two Years Behind Bars, that would be almost like being in HELL." Wapiti said, shaking his head "Think about it, you live in an eight-by-twelve foot room, with another man, and if you're lucky, you get to go outside a couple hours a day...!"

"I hear ya." Shawn said "But I've seen men get out, rob the nearest bank they come to and are back inside within a couple months."

Shawn said "But now over in that new prison outside Pendleton they milk something like one thousand head of cows daily."

"They make them work inside?" Wapiti asked

"No, they don't make them, they pay them, I hear they start out at a quarter an hour up to seventy five cents an hour." Shawn said

"That's not very much money." Wapiti said, as Griselda and Jose brought out another pot of coffee and Shawn's breakfast.

"Thank you kids." Shawn said, looking at the plate full of food, as Wapiti quickly grabbed one of the two sausage patties. "HEY!"

"I want my piece back." Wapiti said, laying it on his plate and started cutting into it with his fork.

"That was only a half piece, give me half of that back." Shawn shouted, reaching out.

Wapiti quickly pull his plate back. "Your loss."

Shawn took a big bite of crispy hash potatoes covered in egg yoke, followed by a big piece of toast. Then he took out his pocket watch and looked at it, it was already a quarter to ten. Looking towards the back of the business down the alley way below them, he could see Judge Monson walking towards them.

"Griselda darling, would you please go in the shack and get me that extra coffee cup please?" Shawn asked.

"Sure, no problem Marshal." Griselda said, going inside the shack.

"Good morning Your Honor." Shawn said, as Judge Monson pulled out a chair and sat down, Watching Shawn pour a shot of whiskey into his coffee. "Sometimes I think you do that just to see if I'll get mad!"

"I Do, and It Does!" Shawn chuckled, with a big smile on his face. "But I need it this morning to help get rid of the hangover I have from last night."

"So tell me about these men you brought in yesterday?" Judge Monson said

"What's there to say, they stole well over a hundred head of cows with this year's calves. Plus four bulls from P.O. Nicely." Shawn answered, taking a bite of food. "All the cattle are accounted for and are waiting on their rightful owners to pick them up at Casey Myers Ranch at Elk Lake, by the Lake not the Town."

"Must be a skunk close by." Judge Monson said, looking back behind the shack towards the foothills.

"It's the Marshal." Wapiti spoke up with a big smile on his face. "The Marshal got sprayed by a skunk early yesterday morning when we were camped out…Carmen had him wash in tomato juice to help get rid of the smell. It helped some, but as you can plainly smell, he needs another bath."

"I remember smelling a skunk when you men came in yesterday, I just didn't put the two together." Judge Monson said with a big smile on his face. "So what happened?"

"Mrs. Myers fried us up seven Blue Grouse and put them in a pillow slip for our trip back, we all had a couple pieces right off the bat, then a couple more pieces for dinner and put the bag back with the other supplies. It was about four-thirty give or take five minutes, when this skunk came into camp and was dragging the bag of fried grouse off. He came right in between us, when we smelt him we both jumped up. Well Sir, that scared the skunk and he instantly blew his self defense system right in the Marshal's face and chest."

"That would have been something to see." Judge Monson chuckled, filling his coffee cup up and emptying the pot. "Young Lady, would you please go get us another pot and hot plate please?"

"Yes Sir, Your Honor." Griselda said, jumping down from the chair, her and Jose were kneeling on listening to them tell the stories about how the Marshal's last huntin' trip had gone.

"How Did You See The Skunk?" Jose asked

"The moon was up near full and bright, so we could see pretty well. I was looking that skunk straight in the face, and the Marshal was looking at the other end…It was priceless." Wapiti said, starting to chuckle harder, looking around the table at everyone.

"They give you any trouble coming in?" Judge Monson asked, with a big smile on his face.

"NOOO, not at all." Shawn said, taking a bite of food. "Peers, they hit a big strike up in Alaska, came back here and bought a big spread around Davis Lake. They bought out four, five places, but ran out of money before they bought any cattle … Seems the two elder brother's spent their cattle and living expense money for a few years on buying a hold out owner of only a section and a half for five times the other acreage price that they bought legally. They figured they could hide the herd for a couple years so most of the brands going to market in a few years would have all their brands on them."

"You think they might have gotten away with it Marshal?" Jose asked excitedly.

"With that much land to hide them in, YEAH, I've heard of quite a few rancher's starting out that way." Shawn answered, just as Griselda returned with a fresh pot of coffee and hot plate. 'Thanking' her, he refilled his cup.

The three had been talking for a good hour, the kids were listening intently on everything being said. When from down the street they could hear someone yelling out for the Marshal. After another thirty seconds or so a very heavily sweat covered horse came running in between the large opening to the street, the rider was still yelling out, "MARSHAL! MARSHAL!" as his horse came to a sliding stop and he jumped off stumbling and crawling trying to reach the Marshal.

Shawn jumped up and ran over towards the man as fast as he could go. Catching up to him, Shawn helped the man to his feet.

He could see dry blood coming out of the man's ear. Shawn knew the man's ear drums had been blown out from the percussion from an explosion. He was still just hollering out for the Marshal over and over again.

"JOSE, Go into the top drawer of my desk and get a pad of paper and a pencil." Shawn said, pulling his flask out and handing it to the man, telling him to calm down. It was going to be alright. But he knew the man couldn't hear him. The man quickly took the flask from Shawn and started drinking it down, he was extra thirsty from the long, hard, hot ride he had just made.

"Come over here and sit down Youngman." Shawn said, leading him over to the table.

Just as Jose came running out with the pad of paper and pencil. "Here Marshal." He said, putting them on the table along with another coffee cup. "Marshal, you want me to go get some more coffee?"

"NO Jose, you take this man's horse over to the Livery. Tell Gordy to pick the best three horses out of the ones we rode in on. Then run over to the Merc and tell Roger we need supplies for a week as fast as he can get them over to the Livery. Griselda darling, go get this man a pitcher of beer and a hamburger to eat please."

"Yes Sir, Marshal" Both kids answered, taking off running.

Shawn looked over at the man, who was taking another pull off the flask. Then he wrote a note on the pad of paper and pushed it towards the man. "What happened?" He asked, looking the man in the face.

"They robbed us." The man answered.

"Shawn grabbed the pad of paper and pencil and wrote down, WHEN, WHERE, HOW MANY. Then pushed in front of the man again to read.

Looking down at the paper, he quickly read it, then looked back up at the Marshal. "The road that takes you around Lookout Mountain to Deep Creek and Big Spring's mines on the North Fork." The man was saying.

"OKAY, OKAY..." Shawn said, pointing his finger back down to the pad of paper, pointing at How Many first. Then asking the deaf man at the same time.

"I only saw two, I was inside the new metal coach. First I heard two shot out the back and I saw both guards fall off their horses dead. Then barely a couple seconds later, I heard three shot's out front. Thru the porthole I could see another man had killed both front guards and the driver." The man was explaining, taking another drink off the flask. "This is empty, you wouldn't have any more would ya?"

"Wapiti, the bottom drawer of my desk." Shawn said, looking back at the man and pointing back at the pad of paper. "How Many and How Long Ago Did They Rob You?" He asked slowly, looking straight into the man's face.

"There was just two...I wouldn't unlock the door from the inside, so they blew the steel door open. The next thing I remember was waking up and they were gone. I slowly crawled out of the coach, caught one of the guard's horses and rode to town as fast as I could." The man was explaining as Wapiti handed him a near full fifth of whiskey, which he quickly took another drink off of. "I don't know how long I was out or even what time it is now. But I do remember, it had only been daylight for an hour most."

Shawn pulled out his pocket watch, it was almost eleven o-clock. "It's almost eleven, sun comes up around five thirty this time of year ... plus or minus and fifteen minutes, that means they have a good five plus hour head start on us. Not to mention the near two hour ride from here to where they robbed the coach at." He was thinking out loud, taking a pull off the bottle. "How far up the road towards the North Fork were you and which way did they go when they left?"

"WHAT?" the man yelled out

Shawn quickly wrote the two questions down on the pad of paper and pushed it back in front of the man.

"Only about a mile from the Ochoco River and the forks in the two main roads…It was easy to tell their tracks from all our horses, on my way to catch the closest horse I could easily see their tracks going back up the road towards the North Fork" the man answered. Thanking Griselda for the hamburger and taking a bite.

"What's that way Marshal?" Wapiti asked

"NOTHING, nothing at all. But they know they can't sell any of that gold ANYWHERE around here." Shawn answered, still thinking and speaking out loud. "They need to go east to a town before they can even start to cash any of that gold in for cash, John Day's the closest big town that way. But after they get off that road and start cutting over those mountains towards Dayville. That's some ruff, steep, rocky country going over and between Spanish Peak and Wolf Mountain. Then they have go over Battle Creek Mountain down to Dayville. If we stick to the main road, we should be able to catch up to them by the time they get to John Day if we're lucky."

"How much gold were you hauling?" Judge Monson wrote down, pushing the paper back in front of him.

"We only buy from the two big mines, so all the thousands of other hopeful dreamers sell their gold to the big mines. We make the trip once a month, but never the same day. So no-one sees us leave, we pull out around midnight." Reaching inside his shirt he pulled out the manifest, laid it on the table and opened it up. They all could see all the previous loads date's and amount of gold picked up at each mine.

Shawn grabbed the folder and started looking at it. He could see the Big Springs mine had cashed in three hundred eighteen pounds eleven ounces and twelve grams. Deep Creek mine had cashed in two hundred ninety pounds six ounces and fourteen grams. Shawn started adding both amounts up in his head as the man was reminding him it was in Troy weight, only twelve ounces to the pound.

Shawn finished adding everything up. "That makes a total of six hundred nine pounds five ounces and eight grams, give or take. That's a lot of gold, how did they haul it all away?"

"They took two of our six horses from our team, I also saw one empty packsaddle on the side of the road." The man answered "I noticed the rider bringing up the rear was leading a horse that looked like it was loaded down with extra packs to haul everything away with."

"That's smart, they don't know for sure how many horses they need, but you put three, four pack saddles on one horse, then steal as many of the other horses you need to haul it with." Shawn said

"Judge, why don't you take this man over to Doc Becky's and me and Wapiti will get ready to ride." Shawn said, patting the man on his shoulder and standing up. Taking the bottle from the man, he quickly filled up his flask and gave him the bottle back. Then headed into the shack to get his gear, which Wapiti was already doing.

Within five minutes they were walking out the door and heading towards the backs of all the buildings. Walking in between two they quickly stepped up on the boardwalk and headed across the street towards the Livery Stables. Everyone was watching them and wondering with those men killing everyone in the robbery, would the Marshal get to keep his streak of not killing anyone going to continue, or would he have to bring these men in over the saddle like the Old Marshal Felton was known for doing. It used to happen more often than not.

When Shawn and Wapiti walked inside the Livery stables they could see two horses saddled up and Gordy and one of the Kennedy boy's were loading supplies on the pack horse.

"Almost finished Marshal," Gordy yelled over. "I just finished shodding these three here when Jose came in and said you need three horses to ride out ASAP, or As Soon As Possible,"

"Appreciate it Gordy." Shawn said, putting his rifle into its sheath, then he tied his bedroll down.

"Jose said they killed five men in the hold up." Gordy said, tying the tarp off.

"That's what the lone survivor said, he was actually lucky. The explosion knocked him out so they probably thought he was dead too, or they would have shot him as well." Shawn said, reaching for the lead rope. "Tele-graph Chris Hensley in Bend and let him know we had to borrow these three horses, so I'll get them back to him as soon as possible. Judge Monson said he'd hirer a man to bring the others back this week allowing the lone rider to ride one of our horses back and lead the other two. He pays them a dollar a mile plus fifteen dollars a day for meals, and reambure-ses all hotel bills, but not the lady, they have to pay for their play-time away from their wives if they're married, in which case a fam-ily man gets a buck and a quarter cause his family has to be fed while he's out of town. But I hear tell the rider he uses tells his wife 'that's just a bullshit story, he only gets one dollar a mile. Figure fifty miles each way, full days hard, tiring ride. Trust me, we came from twenty or better miles south of Bend yesterday. I'm just glad we got one night's rest on a soft bed. Cause this next week isn't going to be, it's going to be that hard pad, lumpy as hell ground."

"I hope it's soon." Wapiti stated. "These damned horses get fidgety from the smell of Elk, I don't even want to be on him should we come across a bear or a mountain lion…It's going to be bad enough if we come across one or the other. But if we're close enough and that lion screams out, these horses are going to be unbroke again… and go totally berserk trying to get away from him as he leaps out of the tree branch or off a rock bluff on the side of the road."

"You're right about that." Shawn chuckling answered, climbing up in the saddle. "Their breed and trained to work cattle, the way they can run into and around the brush and trees is good … But if we come across a screaming mountain lion, let's just say, I don't know if I'm still that good of a Cowboy anymore."

"You men be careful." Gordy called out to them as they kicked their horses into a medium trot heading down the road out of town.

Shawn pulled out his pocket watch and looked at it, it was just past twelve noon. "Looks like we'll be sleeping on the ground tonight, cause I doubt we make Mitchell."

"I figured as much." Wapiti answered, pulling out a candy stick and started eating it.

"You're supposed to suck on those things, not eat 'em." Shawn chuckled, taking a pull off his flask.

"You drink whiskey when you think…I eat my candy sticks." Wapiti answered, taking another bite and crunchingly chewed it up.

"It's a damn good thing our prey isn't close by, cause they'd be able to hear your crunching a half mile off, with the echos, add a few more miles." Shawn chuckled, putting his flask back in his jacket pocket. "What Ya thinkin' about?".

"These men we're going after…They've already killed five innocent men…That's a Hanging Offence, these men 'WON'T' be wanting to give up very easy." Wapiti yelled back.

"If things go the way I hope they do, we should see them before they see us." Shawn said

"How we going to do that when we don't have a clue as to who they are or what they look like?" Wapiti asked

"Hopefully we can get a good description of them from a bank teller when they sell off some of that gold." Shawn said, taking a drink off his water bag.

The two had been traveling at a medium trot for a good hour when Shawn slowed them down to a walk and pointed up ahead on the road. "That's the road the robbery took place on."

"Why don't we go that way too?" Isn't it shorter that way?" Wapiti asked, as they rode past the road.

"Shorter Yes, Easier, I'd say HELL NO. If they try and go over the mountains between Table Mountain and Spanish Peak, that's some rough and rocky country, lots of black shale rock, cliffs, and large boulders. How anything grows up there is anyone's guess … it'll take them at least one full day's ride longer going that way" Shawn assuredly said, taking a small drink off his flask. "I bet they lose every shoe before they reach the top of the first mountain pass, with two more still to go before they can drop down into Dayville."

"Where's the closest place for them to get reshod at?" Wapiti asked

"That way, Dayville!" Shawn adversely answered

"How long will it take us this way to catch up to them in Dayville, if we can catch up to them by then?" Wapiti asked.

"It'll take us all of two days of hard riding." Shawn answered "But it'll take them two and a half minimum if they're lucky."

The two rode at a slow pace and talked for just over a half hour and Shawn kicked them back into a slow trot. They had the normal traffic as far as the wagons went, but there wasn't as many walking. There was also more log hauling team's hauling an average of two thirty three foot long log's with ten big draft horses pulling them.

"What do they do when they come to a steep mountain down-hill grade?" Wapiti asked.

"Each wheel on the wagon has six braking pads. Two top and button or center of wheel, then one at two o'clock, four o'clock, eight o'clock, and ten o'clock." Shawn answered

"This is going to be a long boring ride with there being nothing between here and Mitchell, then the same between Mitchell and Dayville." Wapiti said

"We'll get us an early dinner up here at Bandit Springs. There's a real good spring there and an older couple run a small café there in the summer time." Shawn said

"I remember…He also keeps his beer in that cold water trough next to their cooking wagon." Wapiti said with a big smile on his face. "That, and not having to eat your cooking tonight will be just fine."

"I agree with you." Shawn answered "This way we can ride further before we have to shut down for the night.

They'd been traveling at a slow trot for just over an hour when they saw the open dining area ahead. Slowing their horse down to a walk the last hundred feet in, they started looking the crowd of people over. There were at least three small families, three freight wagons, two carriages, and five Cowboys that were riding guard over cattle that grazed in the high country in summer time.

Riding over to the water troughs for the horses they climbed off listening to all the conversations going on around the table's and cook's wagon and grill. "I wonder what the dinner special is?" Shawn asked, loosening his cinch while their horses drank their fill.

"Whatever it is, it smells good." Wapiti said, doing the same thing.

After a couple more minutes they led their horses over to the hitchin' rail and tied them up, then headed towards the wagon and the grill. Ahead of them in line was one of the three family's order-ing their food first. But Shawn, Being An U.S. Marshal, just walked around the counter and back to the cold trough full of beer and vari-ous flavoring soda pops and picked two beers up and tossed one over to Wapiti. "You don't mind me helping myself like this do you?" Shawn asked, looking at the lady doing the cooking.

"Not at all Marshal, you know that." She answered with a big smile on her face. "You on the trail of some Outlaw's?"

"Trying to catch up to some Ma'am. " Shawn said, taking a drink off his beer.

CHAPTER 2

"WHAT THE HELL IS THIS!"** they all heard someone yell out. Which brought everyone to a stop and start looking around for who was speaking. "Who Says We Have To Share Our Beer With A Stinkin Redskin!" one of the five Cowboy's yelled out.

"You Know Who That Buck Indian Is?" the man sitting at the next table asked, in a serious semi-loud whisper and look on his face.

"OOOOOH, Is He The Great War Chief Wapiti, That's We've Been Hearing About Beating Up On Three, Four Men At A Time." The Cowboy chuckingly and disbelievingly said, standing up and laughing, looking around at everyone.

"There's Five Of Us, That Says You're Not Drinking Another Drop Off That Beer Boy!" another cowboy demanded, as the other four men stood up and turned to face Wapiti.

Wapiti took a long slow drink off the beer and looked over at the men. "Loser buys me and the Marshal's meals and drinks, plus two extra beers for the road."

"We have to fight you too Marshal?" the first Cowboy ask, looking over at Shawn.

"CAN I JOIN IN TO WAPITI!" Shawn asked with excitement in his voice.

"NOOO...! I don't need your help" Wapiti said, looking at the closest open area. "Why don't you men move over towards the road over there." He said pointing, taking the last drink off his beer.

"One More Thing Gentlemen...Throw those pistols on that table before you move over to the fighting area." Shawn demanded

"No Problem Marshal." All five men said, tossing their pistol's on the table but kept their holsters on. "This is going to be fun, we're going to be the first ones to teach this Buck Indian just how they felt about him and all his kind." They all kept saying, slowly walking over to the area Wapiti had pointed out, rolling their sleeve's up as they walked.

"I'll pay ten to one to anyone who thinks Wapiti will lose this fight." Shawn shouted out.

Five men against one, even Wapiti, ten to one odds...If these men were half as good as they talked and looked, they might be able to make some money on this fight. Within the next few seconds some men said they had five or ten dollars they could bet. When it was all counted up, there was one hundred dollars. They all made Shawn show them the money to cover the bets with.

The couple minutes it took for everything to be done and everyone in the fight area, with Wapiti standing about ten feet away from the line of five men, slowly looking them over as they walked towards him.

Jumping forward and landing about halfway between them, Wapiti landed on his left foot and did a one eighty spin catching the man in the middle on the side of his head, sending him flying sideways to the ground, giving him a severe concussion, because of the hard hit, his brain and body didn't work anymore, as his lifeless body laid on the ground

Continue around on his right foot he brought his right fist up into the man's sternum of the first man to his right, making him feel like his heart just exploded in his chest as he dropped to the ground, and his face quickly turned dark purple from the burning and lack of ability to breathe.. He could see the second man on the right had stepped backwards. So he quickly spun around on his left foot, he quickly ducked down under the man's flying right fist, and brought his own right fist into the man's ribcage, breaking the center two and severely cracking the next one on both sides. Causing the man to bend over in pain. Doing a quick three sixty turn around, he kicked the man in the head sending him flying a good ten feet backwards before hitting the ground, he too had a severe concussion and was laying lifeless on the ground.

Seeing the second man to his left throwing a right punch at him, Wapiti blocked it with his left and threw his right into the man's stomach, picking him a four plus off the ground. Taking every ounce of air out of his body. Grabbing a hold of the back of his head and shirt he picked his head up before driving the man's face into his rising knee, breaking his nose, and knocking him out cold.

He quickly turned to face the last man, who was standing a good five feet away. Wapiti quickly started walking towards the man. Who quickly threw his arms in the air.

"I Give Up." The man yelled out, walking backwards over to his horse, then he quickly mounted up and took off back towards the herd of cattle they were supposed to be watching over.

Everyone started calling him a cowards, chicken shit, your yeller, were just a few. But he didn't care...there was NO DOCTOR out here.

The cook brought Wapiti a bucket of water with a big smile on her face. "Here ya go Deputy, now you can wake 'em up."

Wapiti slowly started walking around and pouring enough water on each man's head till they started stirring arounds trying to remember what had happened to them, why was it hard to see, think, or try set up. The echoing ringing in their heads gave them all the worst headaches they'd ever had, not to mention everything was blurry and filled with hundreds of little white stars continually falling from the sky to the ground.

Wapiti asked the cook for another beer and to put it on these men's bill.

Wapiti continued pouring water over the four men's heads one more time, asking them if they remembered what had happened to them yet, or could they even remember that far back yet..

"What's your dinner special?" Shawn asked, grabbing another beer.

"Homemade style Chicken Noodle Soup, only I use grouse instead of chicken." The Cook answered

"We'll take a couple large orders please." Shawn said "For those of you keeping count…Wapiti is now up to forty-six scalps and one chicken shit.

Within a matter of minutes everyone had gone back to eating but still looking over at the four men still sitting on the ground still trying to remember what had happened to them.

After a couple more minutes they all helped each other up and asked if anyone had any aspirin. As they slowly walked over and sat down on the closest bench seat.

After the Cook dished up the Marshal and Wapiti plates she grabbed four beers and a bottle of pills, she walked over to the four men. "Here." she said, handing them each a beer. "These are five dollars a pill, Doc Becky in Prineville says she gives these to people with broken bones to take their pain away…You men have that much money on yourselves?"

"Yes we do." One of the Cowboy's said, pulling a twenty out of his wallet. "Can I get a couple extra please?"

"Only two pills each." The Cook answered "The Doc says these are made from opium, if you take more than two in any twelve hour period and mix them with alcohol they could kill you."

"I don't care, here's another twenty, now please give us all two pills please." Another one of the Cowboy's said, as they both were holding out twenty dollar bills.

The Cook quickly took their money, then counted out eight pills and laid them on the table.

All four men quickly thanked her, then grabbed both pills and swallowed them down. "Where'd Hank go?" one of the Cowboy's asked, looking around for their friend.

"He chicken out, while you four were trying to wake up. He was on his horse and lit out of here like a deer running from a mountain lion." Shawn proudly said. "By the way, thank you for the free beers and dinner gentlemen." He said, holding his beer up, then taking a long pull off it.

"Cookie…If we sleep this off here tonight, will you sell us some more of these pain pills in the morning. I'm starting to feel real good right now…" one Cowboy said, trying to hold up a shot of whiskey. "I almost don't hurt at all anymore…Here's a shot to Chief Wapiti of the Nez Perce Indian Tribe." All four men toasted a shot and drank it down, and a couple started giggling.

"Do you even remember how we got this way?" one of the Cowboy's asked, slurring his words.

"I do," another slurred out. "You told Deputy Wapiti he couldn't drink a beer with us."

"Then why is he drinking one?" one of the other Cowboy's groggily said. "These pills make everything cool…But I need to lay down." he said trying to stand up, but fell head first into the ground, out cold.

The other three were all laying over the table and quickly fell fast asleep within a couple more minutes.

"Those pain pills seem to knock you out pretty fast." Shawn said, taking a bite of food.

"That's why I can only give them two, like Doc Becky said, too much of a good thing can kill you." The Cook said, wrapping two large pieces of apple pie in wax paper. "These should hold together just fine, here's a couple plastic forks so you men can eat them just before bed time tonight Marshal."

"Thank you very much." Both Wapiti and Shawn said at the same time.

"Can I get two more beers I can put in my saddle bags for later tonight Ma'am?" Wapiti asked

"Yes Sir Deputy, I'll be glad to get you a couple just before you leave after you've both had your fill." The Cook answered

Shawn took out his pocket watch just after he took his last bite, it was almost five-thirty. "I don't know about you Wapiti, but after a plate and a half I've had all I can eat…So how about we get out of here, we still have a good three hours of daylight left."

"Alright Marshal, I don't think I could eat anymore either." Then he handed the Cook a five dollar tip for the food and good service. Then picking up his two beers, they headed towards their horses. Untying them, they lead them back over to the water trough for one last drink before they pulled out.

Which all three horses did take a small drink while they tightened their cinch straps up and in just a couple more minutes they were riding by all four passed out Cowboy\s. "They're going to have one hell of a hangover when they wake up." Shawn said, chuckling.

Everyone that heard him, agreed with him and started laughing about it. They all had gotten to see how Deputy Wapiti laid down the law, and could hardly wait to see or read about his next fight. They'd all be telling everyone about the fight they had seen. Wapiti against five men, four knocked out cold and one ran away faster than a jack rabbit could run with a coyote on his tail.

In no time at all Shawn had them back to a slow trot heading down the road. Catching up to and passing many slower moving wagons. After a couple more miles they came across a family of five walking down the road and packing everything they owned on their backs. Even the youngest child, who couldn't be much older than four or five years old, had a small pack on his back.

Slowing up, Wapiti took fifty dollars out of his pocket and handed it down to the man leading the way. "It's not much, but it should buy you all a good meal when you get to Mitchell."

"Thank you Sir." The man answered, taking the money.

"You're welcome." Wapiti answered, kicking his horse in the side to catch back up to the Marshal.

"You keep giving your money away like that, and you'll be broke before we get to Dayville." Shawn said, with a small smile on his face.

"I still have more money than I need for this trip." Wapiti said "Besides, I've seen you give money away to people too."

"I know you're right." Shawn answered "There's times I do and times I don't. It depends on the people and the situation... Truthfully I was going to give them a few dollars but I saw you reaching for your wallet so I kept riding.

The two had been riding at a slow trot for a couple hours when they came out on top of one of the ridges. Shawn slowed up and looked at the sun behind them, it was just barely above the mountain tops. "Suppose we should start looking for a good place to camp for the night."

"You think there might be a stream of water down in the bottom of the valley floor ahead of us?" Wapiti asked

"Maybe, it would be best for the horses if we ride down and see." Shawn answered, kicking his horse back into a slow trot.

Within ten minutes they were well over half way down and they could hear water flowing over to one side. Riding over towards the sound of water and in no time they could see a small stream barley a foot wide. But it was more than wide enough for the horses and they quickly started drinking their fill.

Shawn and Wapiti quickly dismounted and removed their saddles while the horses continued to drink water. In no time at all the horses were unloaded and thru drinking, so they led them over towards a grassy area with a couple trees. Tying a rope between two small trees, they quickly tied them off, laid out their bedrolls and fell fast asleep.

It was still dark out when Wapiti woke up, but with the light from the near full moon he looked at his pocket watch and saw it was almost five o-clock. Getting up, he quickly found enough wood to build a small fire and put the coffee on.

As it started to boil the aroma woke Shawn up, rolling over he asked Wapiti what time it was.

"Just a little after five." Wapiti answered, pulling the coffee pot aside for the grounds to settle. "I've got both horses saddled, we only have the pack horse left to load up."

"Thanks," Shawn said, setting up, reaching for the coffee pot to fill his cup.

"How far do you figure we are from Mitchell?" Wapiti asked, filling his cup.

"We should be there in just a couple hours at the most." Shawn said, taking a couple small sip's off his coffee. "We should be able to get something to eat for breakfast there."

It only took them ten more minutes to load the pack horse up, then they each slowly drank one last cup of coffee before climbing up in the saddle and heading back down the road at a slow trot. They had a long way to go, so they didn't want to overwork the horses.

It was just starting to lighten up over the mountain ridges to the east when they headed out. By the time they got to the top of the next ridge, the sun was directly in their eyes which made them both covered their eyes and Shawn pulled his cowboy hat down to try and block out the glare.

About halfway down the next ridge they came across a couple wagons that had camped together for the night and they both could smell the coffee cooking. Wapiti was just about to suggest that they stop for at least one more cup, when Shawn suggested it first. Slowing the horses down to a walk, Shawn headed towards the camp. "Hello In Camp." He called out

Right off everyone in camp could see the sun flickering off their Badges. "Come On In And Have A Cup Of Coffee Gentlemen." A Lady yelled out

Riding up to the closest wagon, they both dismounted taking their coffee cups out of their saddlebags. "Sure Do appreciate It Ma'am" Shawn said

"You men need something to eat, we don't have much, but we're more than willing to share what we have." One of the men said, as they came walking up to the fire.

Three young boys were all shyly and quietly talking and asking each other if that was really U. S. Deputy Marshal Wapiti, and which one should be the one to ask him if he really was him.

"Thanks," Shawn said, holding his cup out and looking around the camp. There were three families with eight plus children. He could see and hear the three ten year old and older boys talking. "Thanks, but we'll be alright till Mitchell. But a cup of coffee sure does sound good Ma'am." He said, looking over towards the three boys. "That's Him, the one and only... United States Deputy Marshal Wapiti boys."

"Really!" they all said slowly walking towards him. While ALL the grownups started shaking Wapiti's hand first, then the Marshal. "It a pleasure to meet both of you." They were all saying at the same time.

"Is It True You Beat Up Three Professional Wrestler's Out Of Portland?" one of the boys asked, excitedly while shaking Wapiti's hand.

"Yes I Did." Wapiti calmly answered

"Did He Ever." Shawn yelled out. "He knocked all three of those men out in just over a minute's time."

"That's what we heard." One of the women said "You sure you men don't need anything to eat Marshal?"

"Thanks Ma'am, but I'm used to a late breakfast, if I ate right now you'd mess my routine up and my body wouldn't work when it's supposed to." Shawn answered, pouring a shot of whiskey in his cup.

"Isn't it too early to drink whiskey Marshal?" one of the kids asked

"We've already been up for a couple hours son, so it'll be alright." Shawn answered, rubbing the Youngman's head.

"You guys chasing after some Outlaws Marshal?" one of the older boys asked.

"Yes we are son." Shawn answered, taking a drink off his coffee.

"What'd they do?" one of the men asked

"Killed four Guards and the Driver of an armored Stagecoach with well over six hundred pounds of gold on board." Shawn answered

"I can't wait till I'm old enough to be a Lawman." One of the boys excitedly yelled out. "How Old Do You Have To Be To Be A Lawman Marshal?"

"Depends...but IF YOU put that Badge on...you had better be able to fight in hand-to-hand combat and be able to shoot true, cause you may not get a second shot." Shawn said, in a serious voice and look on his face.

"Like Deputy Wapiti?" one of the other boys yelled out. "I'd like to be able to fight like you, Deputy Wapiti."

"ME TOO!" both the other two boys said.

"Would you teach us how to fight the way you do, Deputy Wapiti?" one of the boys yelled out.

"Don't have time right now guys." Wapiti said, smiling, taking a drink off his coffee.

"Sounds like that school Deputy Johnson suggested might not be such a bad idea." Shawn said, as one of the lady's was walking around refilling everyone's coffee.

After another ten minute's and one more cup of coffee Shawn and Wapiti thanked them for everything. Then tightened up their cinch straps and headed back down the road at a slow trot. The sun was higher in the sky, so it was starting to heat them up as they both removed their jackets.

Neither one said much of anything as they traveled down the road. They hadn't even gone a couple miles further and they were riding by another campsite with one wagon at it. Right off they could see it was a freight wagon and the Driver was just finishing hooking up the team of six horses so he too could get on the road.

Within another thirty minutes they were riding up to the town of Mitchell and Shawn slowed them down to a walk.

Wapiti started looking the little town over, it was like most small towns. A few dozen house's, Livery Stables, Café, small Mercantile store, and of course a couple Saloon's. They could see a jailer's wagon outside the Café, only all the prisoners were eating their breakfast from inside the cage.

Shawn started chuckling as they pulled up to the water trough to water their horses. "Looks like they learned their lesson about letting them out to stretch their legs and eat."

"Look like." Wapiti said, getting off his horse with his warm water bag. "Give me your bag and I'll fill them up with fresh water why you go in and order our breakfast."

"Sounds good." Shawn said, handing him his water bag. "But if we want to make Dayville tonight we're going to have to just get a couple ham and egg sandwiches to go."

"That's alright, but add a sausage patty and a slice of American cheese please." Wapiti said, starting to pump the pumps handle.

"That does sound better." Shawn said, walking away.

Wapiti quickly rinsed out and refilled the water bags, then checked and cleaned all the horse hooves out while waiting for the Marshal to come back out.

Shawn walked past the Jailer's wagon looking at all the men inside eating with one guard sitting on the driver's seat eating his breakfast. Walking inside he saw the other two guards and the driver sitting at a table eating their breakfast. So he walked over to the table, and waved the waitress over at the same time.

Shawn quickly ordered four sausage, bacon, egg, and American cheese toasted sandwiches to go, then he looked at the table of men. "I heard you lost the Carpenter Brother's on me." Shawn said, looking down at them with a big smile on his face.

"That was one of the other crew's, they don't work here anymore." One of the guards chuckled out, in between bite.

"We used to let the men do the same thing, never once in five years had I ever had anyone even think about running on me. They were all just thankful for the chance to walk around for a while." The Driver said.

"Now, the New State Law says they're only allowed out one at a time to use a bush to hide behind when shitting. If they have to piss, they can just move to the back of the Coach and piss through the door." One of the Guards said, shaking his head. "Like Tom said, we did it all the time and never had anyone run on us. But then, I also did a pocket search on those prisoners and DID catch a couple that had a key on themself. Those men were lucky them Carpenter brothers weren't killers, cause happening at night like that, they could have killed them guards before they ran off."

"I wonder whatever happened to them? The Carpenter Brothers I mean." The other guard asked

"They kinda got away from me. and Deputy Wapiti." Shawn chuckled out

"How do you kinda get away Marshal?" one of the guards asked, with a strange, questionable look on his face

"WELL, we chased them from Prineville to the coast." Shawn started explaining, as he spiked his cup of coffee. "We caught up to them in Redsport on the evening train. It was past dark-thirty so I decided to wait them out so no innocent bystanders would get shot in the crossfire. They were in the process of loading a herd of cattle onto a ship bound for China. When they rode out on to the pier, I thought I had them surrounded with no way out. But they rode their horse up the side on the loading ramp up into the ship...They got away, but they will be spending at least three months out on that ocean, then end up in a land where they don't understand what anyone's saying."

"Three Months Out There On That Ocean, nothing but water as far as the eye can see. That would be just as bad as being in jail." One of the guards said, chuckling. "Then once you get there, you have to get another ship to come back home." He continued saying, as he chuckled a little harder shaking his head. "That'd be called six months in the 'Hot Box' wouldn't it Marshal?"

"I feel the same way." Shawn chuckling as the waitress brought him his food inside a paper bag. "That'll be six dollars Marshal." The waitress said, handing him the bag.

Shawn took a ten dollar bill out of his wallet and handed it to her. "keep the change Darlin'…Well, you men have a safe trip. Everything works out and I'll have some more customers for your next trip." Then he walked back out the door and over to Wapiti handing him a sandwich.

"Thanks." Wapiti said, tucking his cinch strap down. Taking the sandwich, he quickly unwrapped it and took a big bite, then climbed up in the saddle.

Shawn did just the opposite, he climbed up in the saddle, then unwrapped his sandwich and took his first bite. Then turning their horses they headed down the road at a walk.

"These sure do taste good." Wapiti said, looking over at Shawn, taking another bite.

"Yes they do." Shawn said, taking another bite. "I just wished we had something better than water to wash them down with."

It only took them five minutes to finish eating their first sandwich, Shawn looked over at Wapiti. "You want your second sandwich now?"

"NO, it's a long way to Dayville and that sandwich will make for a good lunch. Besides, that first sandwich was more than enough, I'm not overly full, but comfortably full."

"I feel the same way, so let's get going." Shawn said, jerking on the lead rope and kicking his horse into a slow trot.

Wapiti was looking over the terrain as they rode. There wasn't much out there, but by red sandy foothills covered in Juniper trees. They hadn't been this way in a long time, but this time he noticed that some of the hillside had a rosy red color with a greenish to blue hue look to them. "What causes them to turn different colors like that?"

"They say there's all kinds of dinosaurs buried around here. That's why the hil sides turn so many different colors. About twenty years back, I'd just got stationed out here from Texas as a U. S. Deputy Marshal. It was rumored that the Larkin Brother's dug up two large ten foot plus wide prehistoric turtles out here somewhere." Shawn started explaining

"Randy and the twin's?" Wapiti asked, excitedly.

"No, their Uncle's, Roy and his younger brother's, Floyd, Johnny, and Bob. They were living in Dayville at the time." Shawn said "Anyhow, the Government came and told them that was protected land. No-One was allowed to dig out there. So they confiscated the two turtle's and told them that if they told ANYONE about really digging them up, they would all be sent to prison for a very long time."

"Is that a true story?" Wapiti asked

"I asked Roy about it during the poker tournament. He just gave me a funny grin and told me he was under a Court Order and wasn't allowed to say anything about it. But the look in his eyes told me it was true." Shawn said, looking over at Wapiti.

"UHHH…I wonder what they looked like?" Wapiti asked

"Roy told me he couldn't legally talk about them, but that they were on display at some big museum back east. The Smithsonian Museum it's either in Washington D.C. area or New York City area." Shawn said. But he said he saw a picture of them being added to the museum and the article stated. The actual location of where these were discovered is secretive and protected government property. Nobody is allowed to dig there, not even the government." he continued explaining.

After a couple hours of riding through the desert they came to the top of a long ridge leading downhill with a small stream in the middle. Riding over they watered their horses and walked around for a couple minutes stretching their legs and backs out.

"From here down to the John Day River will be an easy ride." Shawn said, walking over to the creek and splashing water into his face, then wiping it off with a wet handkerchief. Then he took out his pocket watch and looked at it, it was just before one o-clock. So he walked over and grabbed the bag of sausage, bacon, egg, and cheese sandwich and handed one to Wapiti.

"I figure we're only about twenty miles from Dayville, so we'll be in well before nightfall." Shawn said, taking a pull off his flask. "We're going to have to stay off the main road once we get to the valley leading into Dayville, then Wapiti will have to have to sneak into town and see if you see three pack horses, that would be recently reshod, or the blacksmith would be shodding them."

"You sure think out loud a lot Marshal." Wapiti said, climbing back up in the saddle.

"Don't worry about just how I think, just be thankful I try to figure things out ahead of time so we don't get shot." Shawn said, turning his horse down the hillside.

"You think they'll beat us in, into Dayville I mean." Wapiti asked

"Don't know, like I said, that's some rough country they're riding through, but with only a five plus hour head start they shouldn't be too far behind us." Shawn said, kicking his horse back into a slow trot heading back towards the road.

It wasn't long and they caught up to and past a carriage with a man and lady inside. After another couple miles they past a couple freight wagons and one family wagon loaded up with four kids riding in the bed of the wagon and they were playing with wooden toy guns. They pretended to be shooting at them, so Shawn leaned over backwards like he had been shot out of the saddle. Making all the kids start laughing, as they reshot him at least a half dozen times in the three, four minutes it took them to slowly pass the wagon.

Wapiti couldn't help but join in on the fun. Before long their mother was looking back to see what all the laughing was about, and right off she saw the sun reflecting off their badges. She smiled at them and waved as they rode by.

From the top of the ridge it only took them an hour and a half to reach the gorge that led down to the John Day River. Shawn turned them off the road and headed around the outside of the gorge.

Wapiti remembered the Carpenter Brothers had camped at the other end entering the gorge on the Dayville side, the side they were heading towards.

Which only took a long thirty minutes to ride around when they were coming down off the foothill to the road and river. Wapiti looked back up the gorge. That river cut through a sheer rock cliff that was every bit of a hundred feet high above the river on both sides. Because of the blackness of the rocks and turns in the river, he couldn't see very deep into the gorge.

Shawn led them directly down over the road and to the river and started riding back upstream towards Dayville. "Riding in the river like this, we'll be hidden behind all the trees and brush so no-one on the road can see us."

"The Carpenter Brothers came this way too, remember." Wapiti said "I wonder why they ended up on the road instead of staying out here out of sight?"

"Never know what's in a man's mind." Shawn said, taking a pull off his flask.

The ride through all the Willows and Cotton Woods, with the river flowing around made for a peaceful and relaxing ride in its own special way. Every now and then they'd jump a small flock of birds or a Doe and her Fawn. They'd usually only run a short distance before they realized we weren't a threat to them and they'd stop, take one last quick look at them, then go back to eating.

After a nice relaxing slow ride they came to a fence that went from the road to their right across a grassy meadow to the river and across the meadow on the other side, going up the sage brush ridge out of sight.

"This answers your question as to why those Carpenter Brothers ended up on the road." Shawn said, taking a pair of fencing pliers out of his saddle bags.

"What kind of pliers are those?" Wapiti asked, watching Shawn get off his horse and walk over towards the fence.

Shawn walked over to the fence and grabbed a hold of the top wire. "These are called Fencing Pliers, see how they open up and make this notch." He said, putting the barb wire inside the notch, squeezing the handles together, it quickly cut the wire in half. Then he continued on down cutting the other four strands of wire.

"Won't this piss the rancher off, cutting through his fence and leaving a large hole that his cattle will be able to get out through." Wapiti asked

"NOOO, you just do a couple eye loop splices and put the fence back together." Shawn said, leading his two horses.

"How you do that?" Wapiti asked, leading his horse through the cut fence.

"Like this," Shawn said, grabbing one end of the wire, he bent it over about eight to ten inches up from the end. Then he started wrapping the tail around the main wire a couple times.

"I hope he didn't stretch this wire extra tight or I won't have enough wire to do this trick with." Shawn said, reaching for the other end. "Here, hold on to this end and pull the wire to me, while I pull this side through that hole in your wire."

"Alright," Wapiti said, walking over and grabbing the wire and did as he was told and started pulling it towards the Marshal.

They were lucky, the wire was loose enough to pull the other wire thru the eye and wrap it back around itself. Then Shawn untied the first loop, pulling it tighter with the pliers and rewrapping it. "Roger got these pliers for me a couple years back when the smaller rancher's started putting this wire up around their land like this. Can't count the number of times I've had to use them."

"Looks like I need to get me a pair of those pliers when we get back home." Wapiti said, making a small loop in one of the other strands of wire.

"I wonder how far down the valley we have to ride before we come to the end of this man's land and we have to cut through another fence." Shawn said, pulling another strand of wire threw the loop and quickly tied them off. It only took them about twenty minutes to finish, but as usual Shawn was being impatient and wanted to get moving.

CHAPTER 3

As soon as they finished repairing the last strand, Shawn was back in the saddle and heading back upstream towards Dayville.

After about another half hour, they could see the cemetery up on the hillside, then the ranch house just over a small ridge. Shawn was asking Wapiti if he remembered how mad the Lady of that house had gotten when we put our horses in her barn out of sight.

WHEN They came around a turn in the river AND they came to the rancher who was in the process of mowing his meadow hay down. but not expecting to see anyone, the sight of another person startled all three men when they first saw each other from hundred feet or so apart, and out of pure instinct, Shawn pulled his pistol and was ready to fire.

"WWWOOOWWW MISTER," the Farmer yelled out, pulling back on the rein's to his team of horses. "YOU DON'T NEED THAT GUN!"

"Sorry Sir," Shawn yelled out, putting his pistol back in his holster. "You kinda took me by surprise Sir. Sorry about this, we had to cut your fence back there, but we spliced it back together."

"That's alright Marshal, who are you trying to sneak up on around here?" The Rancher asked "To my knowledge there are no Outlaw's working for anyone around here."

"When's the last time you've been in town?" Shawn asked

"Couple weeks, Why?" the Rancher asked

"The men we're looking for should be getting into Dayville shortly." Shawn said, taking a pull off his flask, riding over to the Rancher and offering him a pull off the bottle.

Which the man was more than glad to accept. "Names, Bob Thompson, Marshal, how can I assist you?" Bob asked, taking a big pull off the bottle.

"Well now, if the men we're after came over the mountain like I think they came, then they should be getting into Dayville just about any time now." Shawn started explaining, taking his flask back and took another small pull off it. "Almost empty, Wapiti, will you please find my fifth on the pack horse while I try and think this through."

"How much of the fifth are you going to need Marshal?" Wapiti said, turning his horse over towards the pack horse, grabbing the leather bag that held the fifth.

"I'm just refilling this one, ya little smart ass." Shawn said, turning back to Bob.

"What do they look like and what is it they've done Marshal?" Bob asked

"Couldn't tell ya what they look like. But two days ago they killed four guards and the driver of an armored Stagecoach stealing over six hundred pounds of gold." Shawn answered, taking the fifth from Wapiti "Thanks"

"How the hell did they haul off that much gold?' Bob asked, reaching for and taking Shawn's flask back.

"HEY!" Shawn yelled out "What the hell you doing?"

"I'm thirsty." Bob said, taking an extra long drink off the flask emptying it. Shaking it upside down he handed it back to Shawn with a big smile on his face. "So how'd they haul all that gold away?"

"According to the only living witness they had one pack horse loaded down with additional packs. Then they took two of the horses out of the team, loaded them up and headed due east back towards the mine's according to the survivor." Shawn answered

"What makes you think they'd come this way?" Bob asked

"The survivor said he followed their muddy tracks back up the road trying to catch one of the dead guard's horses." Shawn said

"If they killed everyone, how could there be a survivor?" Bob asked

"The man inside the Coach was only knocked out and not killed when they tied a couple pieces of dynamite to the steel door, blowing it open so they could get to all the satchels of gold inside." Shawn answered

"Good thing he was knocked out and didn't moan or they might have shot him too." Bob said "We get a few men like that around here once and a while…Men that would make sure there were No Witnesses to the crime, if you get my meaning' Marshal."

"Yes Sir I do." Shawn said, taking a pull off the fifth, then refilled his flask and handed the bottle back to Wapiti. "Me or Wapiti either one can't go into town for a look around, if YOU get my understanding Bob."

"Yes Sir Marshal I do, but you see Marshal, I really need to get my hay mowed." Bob started saying.

"It's been a few years, but I do know how to run one of these knew horse drawn mowers." Shawn said, getting off his horse and looking at his pocket watch, it was just past four o-clock.

"Let's go over to the house so I can let my wife know why I need to go to town so she doesn't get mad at me for wanting to go to town tonight." Bob said, with a shit eaten grin on his face. "She hasn't let me go to town for a couple weeks now."

"Wapiti, come here." Shawn said "Bob, show Wapiti how this contraption works so he can mow while I'm talking to your wife."

"Yes Sir Marshal." Bob said, looking at Wapiti. "You sit in this seat, squeeze this lever, which releases this pin allowing the two blades of cycle's to cut back and forth between the two cutting the tall grass. Push the hand forward till it locks in place, then head the team around the field. Try and keep your row's as straight up and down the field as you can...I understand if it's your first time mowing Deputy Wapiti, and it's a Great Pleasure To Get To Meet You." Shaking both their hands. "But this piece of machinery run's itself, you just have to steer the horses around the field. When you get to the end of each row, pull this lever back up until you make the turn and head back down the next row...I'm sure you can see how easy they are to operate."

"Sure, I can see how easy it looks to operate." Wapiti said, with a big smile on his face, climbing on to the driver's seat. "I don't know how straight my rows will be compared to the one's you've already done, but I'll do my best." Then he pushed the lever forward and slapped the rein's gently on the backs of the horses. "YEEEEE HAAAAA WWWW, now I'm learning something new. Marshal, give Bob a few extra dollars to pick up a couple beers while he's in town please."

"I'll see what we can do." Shawn said, leading all their horses across the field towards the gate.

"I thought Wapiti rode a black Medicine Hat not a Quarter horse, all though these are nice looking horses." Bob said.

"He does, but he's off doing his Studly duty's, if you get my meaning again." Shawn chuckled

"Yes I do Marshal, what is he breeding him too?" Bob asked, opening the wire and pole gate. "Sometimes the neighbor's cattle get in and eat my winter hay before I can get it mowed. That's why I fence all my meadow's all off."

"How much land you have?' Shawn asked

"Only two sections, but over a thousand of those acres are along the river here. I mow four hundred acres three times a year on this end of the valley. Then I have three pastures divided up equally going towards town. I graze a hundred and fifty cows and calves in each pasture for about three weeks. That gives me a month and a half before the cattle eat it down again." Bob said

"Sounds like a good plan to me." Shawn said, looking up at the front porch where he could see his wife standing watching them come up the road. "How long you been married?" Shawn asked, watching three young boys from three to ten come walking towards them.

"Who's with ya Pa?" the oldest boy asked

"Marshal Felton." Bob said

"REALLY, WHERE'S DEPUTY WAPITI AT, HE IS WITH YOU, AIN'T HE MARSHAL?" the boy asked, very excitedly.

"He's out mowing hay." Shawn said, pointing towards him.

"REALLY." The two oldest boys yelled out. They were only a year apart at the most.

"Can We Go Meet Him Pa?" Both boys yelled out again. "MOM, CANE WE, we got all our chores done, please." They both kept pleading with her.

"Go ahead." The Lady said. "Pleased to meet you Marshal, I'm Karen."

"It's a pleasure to meet you Ma'am." Shawn said, shaking her hand.

"What can we do to help you, and why is Deputy Wapiti mowing hay?" Karen asked

"I need you or your husband to go into town for me and see if some men we're looking for have come in yet Ma'am." Shawn politely said.

"What'd they do?" Karen asked

"They killed five men and stole over six hundred pounds of gold." Shawn said

"Why would they be coming here for?" Karen asked, with a doubtful look on her face.

"It's the closest town if they came over the mountain like I believe they did Ma'am." Shawn said, taking a drink off his flask.

"How much of that whiskey have you already drank?" Karen said, snapping at Bob.

"I only had one small pull off his flask when he introduced themselves to me." Bob answered.

"So now you're going to go to town and hang out on the Saloon side of the Merc aren't you?" Karen snapped at him.

"The Marshal needs my help Karen, I promise I won't get into any fight's, I promise." Bob said, smiling and giving her a small kiss on the cheek. "I Promise, only beer and only twenty dollars to play nickel, dime, quarter poker with."

"Here." Shawn said, opening up his wallet and took out a fifty dollar bills, giving one to each of them. "I'll pay for the beer and CHEAP POKER ONLY, and the other is for you Ma'am, would you please go into the house and get us something for dinner and cook it for us. You can keep the change for your time."

"Keep your money for the food side Marshal, I have more than enough food to feed everyone." Karen politely said, looking at Shawn. "But if Bob goes to town and gets into another fight and ends up sleeping it off in the town jail, there will be hell to pay...Do You Understand Me Bob!" She demanded

"Yes I do sweetheart, and I promise I won't let anyone piss me off or goad me into a fight." Bob said, walking towards the two story square house.

"Please come inside Marshal, I have some cold tea to drink." Karen said, seeing their two son's go running out to meet Deputy Wapiti, which put a big smile on her face. She didn't want her kids to be racist over the color of anyone's skin.

Shawn followed them inside and Karen filled him up a large glass of cold tea. Which Shawn quickly poured a couple good shots of whiskey into it out of his flask.

"You'd better drink only beer tonight, Bob!" Karen demanded again.

"Yes Dear, I promise." Bob said, kissing her on the cheek. "Now Marshal, what should I be looking for?"

"I doubt very much that they'll bring the gold into town, but coming over the mountains between Table Mountain and Spanish Peak is some rough country, so I'm bettin they'll need all their horses reshod. So look for two men leading three horses with or without packs on them. More than likely they'll be willing to pay the Blacksmith extra if he'd get them done in a hurry." Shawn said, looking back and forth between the two.

Shawn looked down at his pocket watch, it was almost five-thirty. "Looks like you'll be buying your dinner in town Bob." Shawn said, still looking at his watch.

"That'll make it all the more believable why I came to town in the middle of the week like this. I'll just tell them Karen is mad at me again, they'll believe that." Bob chuckled, giving her another kiss on the cheek. "Mind if I borrow one of your horses Marshal, both of mine are attached to that mower out there.

"Sure, but make sure you drop the bedroll or you might draw unwanted attention." Shawn said, taking a big drink off his tea. "If it's not too late when you come back, bring a couple cold beers with ya please."

"Sure thing Marshal." Bob answered, giving Karen one last kiss on the cheek before he walked out the door. Over to one of the horses, removing the bedroll off the back of the saddle, he quickly tightened up the cinch strap, climbed up in the saddle and headed towards town.

Wapiti was actually having fun, he was doing something he had never done before and probably wouldn't do again for a long time. He was just starting to make the turn at the end of his first row when he saw two boys running towards him. He was almost half way down the next row when the two boys came running alongside him.

One of them yelled out asking him if he was really U.S. Deputy Marshal Wapiti? "Yes I am." Wapiti answered, looking over at the two boys. He figured they were around seven to eight years old.

"Wait Till We Tell Our Friends In School That We Got To Meet U. S. Deputy Marshal Wapiti!" the other boy yelled out.

"You can't do that right now boys. FACT, we can't have you telling anyone we're in town." Wapiti started explaining. Then seeing the horses were veering off course, he quickly got them to move back over a couple feet.

"WHY NOT?" the oldest boy asked.

"Because if anyone finds out we're even close by, the talk will get out around town faster than a preacher's sermon, and if the men we're chasing hear about it, they will turn around and get back out of town before we can catch them." Wapiti said "So You Can't Tell Anyone Just Yet, OKAY?"

"When can we?' the younger boy asked

"After we leave town." Wapiti answered, trying to keep his eyes on both the horses and the boys at the same time. "Promise Me, you won't tell anyone till after we leave."

"Yes Sir Deputy Wapiti, we'll do as you tell us." Both boys answered

"Dad usually has me drive the team after all my other chores are done." The oldest boy proudly said.

"How do you haul it all off the field?" Wapiti asked

"After it dries out for three hot days, then we load it onto a flatbed wagon. Then haul it over to that big stacker there." He says pointing. "We can stack it almost twenty feet high and a couple hundred feet long by stacking one area then pulling the stacker back about ten feet and keep filling in the space between the two." The oldest boy explained.

"So the cattle eat the stacks of hay?" Wapiti asked

"Kinda, we put panel gates around the stacks so the cattle can't get into the stack itself. Then everyday Dad load's up the flatbed with hay and then unloads it around the field for them to eat it." The oldest boy answered.

"How long have you been a Lawman?" the youngest boy asked

"Around six months now." Wapiti answered

"Only six months and he's already more famous than Marshal Felton is." The oldest boy said, looking at his brother.

"Maybe so, but Marshal Felton is known for bringing the Outlaw's in dead…Wapiti's known for kicking the shit out of them and bringing them in alive." The younger brother proudly says. "I want to be a Lawman like Wapiti, I don't want to have to kill anyone."

"I've just been lucky so far and I haven't had to kill anyone, but I personally know of three times that without my gun, I'd be dead." Wapiti stated, firmly. "So if you put a Law Badge on your chest, you had better be ready to have to kill a man, and you'd better not hesitate or you'll be the dead one."

Karen watched Bob walk out the door, over to one of the horses, mount up and take off down the road. "What if these men you're looking for find out he's spying for you and shoot him Marshal." She said, turning and looking over at him.

"I doubt they'll even doubt anyone knows who they are or what they've done. So they'll just get their horses reshod, get a good hot meal and head back to wherever they stashed the gold." Shawn calmly said.

"Why would they stash the gold before coming into town, Marshal?" Karen asked

"That gold is all loaded inside Bank Labeled satchels, if anyone sees them they'd know right off what was inside them. That and the fact that they're only a couple two feet long and wide and weigh an average of fifty pounds each." Shawn said, taking another drink of cold tea.

"I sure hope you're right Marshal." Karen said, walking over to the wood cook stove and opened the oven door and all that wonderful smell of what was cooking filled the room.

"What's that wonderful smell?" Shawn asked

"Beef Roast Marshal." Karen said, raising the lid and pouring in another glass full of water. "I added taters, carrots, turnips, onions, and a couple cloves of garlic."

"All I know is it smell's wonderful Ma'am." Shawn said, sitting down at the table. "Just how far is it to town from here?"

"It's only a couple miles Marshal, and would you please quit calling me Ma'am and call me Karen?" she asked

"Sorry Karen, it's my Southern upbringing. We call every Lady Ma'am until we're told otherwise." Shawn said, with a big smile on his face. "You sure that roast is going to be big enough to feed me and Wapiti too?"

"More than big enough Marshal, we usually have enough for two dinners." Karen said, refilling their tea.

"Thank you Ma, I mean Karen." Shawn said, pouring another shot into the glass of tea.

"How much of that whiskey do you drink in a day, Marshal?" Karen asked, sarcastically.

"No more than I need to I assure you Ma'am." Shawn chuckled, taking a small pull off the flask before putting it away.

It only took Bob twenty minutes at a medium trot to make it into town. Slowing down to a walk when he got to the bottom of the little hill coming in from the west. There was a Stage Stop Café on the right side of the street, The left side was a small circle of business's, starting with the Dayville Mercantile followed by the Saloon with four bedrooms upstairs on the west side, a two story house facing the street, with a Doctor's sign on it. The Livery Stable on the east side, about a hundred fifty feet directly across the lot from the saloon. Seeing no-one out he slowly rode over to the Livery Stable, still looking at the fronts of the businesses behind him. There were a couple wagons at the Merc and a half dozen horses tied up in front of the Saloon.

Riding up just inside the door to the Livery Stables he got off his and picked up his right hoof, looking over at the Blacksmith who was in the process of shodding a horse. "BILL, you wouldn't be working on five horses, three that look like they might have been wearing pack saddles would ya?" Bob asked, pulling out his knife acting like he was cleaning something out of the hoof.

"As a matter of fact, I am, they came in about two hour ago." Bill answered, starting to stand up.

"Just keep working, I don't want to draw any attention. How many men?" Bob asked

"Two men, their packs and six hundred pound grain sacks are right over there. These horses have been ridin' hard. They cleared their feed boxes up within thirty minutes, so I gave them more hay and an extra bucket of mixed oats." Bill answered, finishing with the hoof, he walked over and picked up the next hoof and went back to work.

"What do they look like?" Bob asked

"What's with all the questions about these guys, who are they and what is they are supposed to have done?" Bill asked

"Killed five men in an armored stagecoach hold up and got away with over six hundred pounds in gold." Bob said.

"Just how the hell would you hear a story like that…You're so full of shit it ain't even funny." Bill said, starting to chuckle.

"No I'm Not!" Bob said, staring straight into Bill's face. "Marshal Shawn Felton and Deputy Wapiti are out at my place right now!"

"SERIOUSLY…or you just funnin' with me like normal?" Bill asked, very questionably

"SERIOUSLY…!" Bob said, dropping his horse's hoof. "Well, I guess we know what's really in those grain bags, don't we? The Marshal didn't think they'd bring them into town…so they've been in for a couple hours you say, think they plan on spending the night?" he asked, leading his horse over to the water trough.

"That's all gold laying over there?" Bill said, excitedly, but quietly. "I wonder if I could steal some of it before the Marshal takes control of it."

"I'm sure the Marshal knows exactly how much gold is in those bags down to the gram." Bob said "So again, what do the men look like?"

"Like everyone else…But they're the only stranger's in town so it won't be hard to figure out who they are when you see them. Plus the fact, they'll both be recently bathed and looking to play with one of the three young ladies that, how do I say it cleanly … OH HELL, you know what they're wanting to play with, and yes it is a game of poker, you poked her many times." Bill said, tacking in a nail and breaking the end that came thru off.

"So they've been over at the Saloon for a couple hours then?" Bob asked

"Yeah, this is the last one of their horses then I'm done for the night. I was going to go home, but now I think I might go over and have a couple beers tonight." Bill said

"You'd Better Not Speak A Word Of This Conversation With Anyone, And Damn it, I mean Anyone Bill!" Bob stern faced, and a glare in his eyes that showed the 'Gates Of Hell' were about to open up.

"NO SHIT SHERLOCK!" Bill stated. "But I'd like to get a better look at them."

"You said you were done for the night, so put your closed sign up and let's go have a beer together." Bob suggested.

"That sounds good to me, Fact, I'll even pay." Bill said, walking over, closed the inside office door, then walking outside he pushed the left side half of the two large double doors were fully open.

"Marshal Felton is paying for drinks and poor man's poker till they came in." Bob said, waving the fifty dollar bill. "I need to pick up a fifty pound bag of grain from the Merc first." He said, leading his horse back across the open area to the hitchin' rail in front of it and tied his horse up, then walked inside.

Quickly looking the store over, he could see there were only a couple other costumer's in the store. He walked to the back of the store where the grain was stacked, grabbing a one hundred pound bag, he thru it up over his shoulder and headed back up to the cash register and paid for it.

"Good evening Bob." The Cashier said, with a big smile on his face. "I haven't seen you in town since that fight a couple weeks ago."

"No Frank, that kinda pissed Karen off, so I've been in the dog house you might say." Bob answered, with a big smile on his face. "But I did pretty good considering it was three to one."

"I'd say so." Frank said, giving him his change back. "You going over to the Saloon tonight?"

"Only for one beer, I promised Karen I'd be back in time for dinner." Bob answered, putting the bag of grain backup on his shoulder and headed back out the door. Walked over to his horse and set the bag of grain on the ground, then walked back into the Saloon and up to the bar.

Walking across the room he saw two tables that had three to five men drinking and playing poker with chip's to make it look like they were playing high dollar poker. When it was really just nickel, dime, quarter poker. That way you could relax, drink a few beers and unwind. He also noticed that like him, most of the men weren't wearing a holster belt and pistol.

One table had the two cleaned up Cowboy looking gentlemen, eating dinner with two Lady's. Walking up to the bar next to Bill said to Tim the bartender and ordered a mug of beer.

"How you Doing tonight Bob?' Tim asked, filling his mug and handing it to him. "Thought the wife wouldn't let you come to town?"

"I talked her into letting me come into town tonight to get a bag of grain as long as I promised to be home for dinner around six. So I figure I can drink a couple mugs here, then buy a six pack of cold bottles off you to go home." Bob loudly and proudly answered, taking a big drink off the beer and looking over at the two men.

Bill was right, they were your typical looking person, nothing real special except for the fact that they were wearing pistol's with their holsters tied down firmly to their thighs. A rancher's holster would be tied loose, so the upper, heavier weight of the pistol would cause the pistol grip to fall down and away from its desired location for a faster draw. But a gunman's ties his holster firmly to his thigh so the pistol grip 'does not' move a fraction on a inch most incase he has to pull it pistol fast, like the Marshal had done on him a couple hours ago, which almost made him shit his pants. With one quick glace he could tell by their demeanor, they'd probably killed more than one man.

Turning back around, he called Tim over. "Those two men spending the night or just passing through?" Bob asked in a low voice.

"Staying, they rented two rooms. Went took baths, then grabbed on to those two young Lady's and asked them if they were hungry." Tim said "Why do you want to know what they're up to?"

"Just curious is all, how about another beer." Bob asked, drinking down the last of the mug and handed it back to Tim.

"Who do you think they are?" Tim asked, curiously.

"Couldn't even begin to tell you who they might be, and I really don't give a shit who they are. Like everyone else in town, I'm curious about stranger's coming through town is all." Bob chuckling answered

Bob was just finishing up his second beer when the two men and two Lady's headed upstairs. Getting six bottles of beer he put them in a small gunny sack that he was tucked into his back pocket. Paying for everything and gave Tim a one dollar tip and walked towards and out the door. Walking over to his horse he tightened up the cinch strap, opening the bag of beers, he put three in each side of his empty saddle bags. Then picking up the bag of grain, throwing it up on his shoulder, he cautiously climbed aboard the horse and headed out of town at a slow trot. He didn't want to break the beer bottles.

Shawn had been forced to sit in the kitchen and smell all that wonderful food cooking for well over an hour when Karen asked Shawn to pull the heavy roasting pot out of the oven and set it on top please.

"Yes Ma'am, I mean Karen." Shawn cheerfully said, jumping to his feet and walked over to the stove as Karen walked out the back door and rang the dinner bell letting the boys and Wapiti know it was dinner time.

Wapiti stopped the team and looked over towards the house. "What's that ringing sound?"

"It's dinner time," The oldest boy answered, "Here, back the team up a couple feet so I can disconnect the mower."

"Okay," Wapiti answered, doing as he was told.

"That's good." The oldest boy said, starting to unhook the horses. "Backing the mower up gives you time to get the two cycles cutting back and forth before they hit the tall grass again."

"That's a good thing to know." Wapiti said, unhooking the other horse

"We can ride the horses back to the house faster than leading them." The oldest boy said, leading the horse over to the side of the mower so he could climb up on the horse, then he pulled his little brother up. Seeing Wapiti already on the other horse they headed across the field towards the house.

They could see a rider coming up the road a long way off and two freight wagons coming from the west. Kicking the horses into a fast trot they quickly rode across the pasture, the road, and up to the barn and put the horses inside. Where both stall's already had filled grain and hay boxes. So it only took them a couple minutes to take the harness off them and head towards the house.

They were a good hundred feet from the house when they came out of the barn, but Wapiti could smell whatever it was that Karen had cooked and it smelt good, it made his hungry stomach start to grumble and rumble.

Walking into the back door, Karen told them to wash up while she started dishing up plates of food and setting them at different spots around the table. Wapiti quickly started pumping the handle at the kitchen sink and they all washed up. He noticed the Marshal sitting at the table all bright eyed and excited, wiping his mouth off and reaching for a plate full of that wonderful smelling food.

Wapiti quickly washed up and slowly started walking towards the table. "Right here, Deputy." Karen said, pointing at the chair. "I put some extra food on that plate for you."

"Thanks," Wapiti said, sitting down at the table. This was the first time they had ever had dinner at someone's home waiting for the Outlaw's to show up, it was actually nice and peaceful he was thinking to himself as he sat down in the chair.

The two boys were quietly talking about the story's they could tell about meeting Deputy Wapiti and Marshal Shawn Felton. They not only mowed hay with deputy Wapiti, but then, they had dinner with him and Marshal Shawn Felton.

"That's enough boys." Karen said, with a shy, happy smile on her face. "We've never had anyone as Important as you two in our house before. Truthfully, no-one in town has, and it's an Honor too."

"Thank You Ma'am." Both Shawn and Wapiti answered

"I thank you for letting us into Your Home Ma'am." Wapiti proudly said. "Your boys were telling me they wanted to be Lawmen too when they grow up."

CHAPTER 4

" I just want them to be happy with whatever they choose to do in their lives." Karen said, just as they heard a horse riding up outside.

Both Shawn and Wapiti stood up and walked towards the door. Opening it up, they could see Bob throw something large to the ground, then grabbed his saddlebags and tied the horse off.

"What'd Ya Find out?" Shawn asked, walking towards him.

"They're there." Bob said "Looks like they brought the gold in with them."

"REALLY, I'd never thought they'd bring that gold into town. That means we might have civilians in the way when we catch up to them." Shawn said, taking out his flask and taking a small pull off it and put it back away. "Does it look like they're spending the night?"

"Yes they are, fact, they were both heading upstairs with a Young Lady each when I left." Bob said, walking up to the door and holding out his saddlebags. "Here's your beer Marshal, I got six."

"Two apiece works for me." Wapiti said, grabbing the saddlebags, opening one side he handed each man a beer.

"Where's the gold at?" Shawn asked, opening his beer and walking back towards the table.

"In the Livery, just piled up against the wall with the packs on top like it wasn't worth a penny." Bob said, taking a plate of food from Karen, and 'thanking' her for it.

"That's smart, you act like it's worthless and NO-ONE would think twice about what is really there." Shawn said, taking a drink off his beer. "They'll probably want to party and relax tonight and pull out early for John Day to cash some of that gold in."

"I know they're relaxing tonight." Bob said, taking a bite of food.

"How are they relaxing tonight Pa?' the eldest boy asked. Looking around at all the adults.

"They have some special company with them tonight." Shawn said out loud. Then covered his mouth and turned away from the kids. "I gotta quit thinking out loud when children are around." He chuckled out.

"What kind of special company Mama? " Both boys asked

Karen's face turned a little red, as she shyly looked around at all the men. "What kind of company?' both boys asked again.

"A girlfriend." Karen answered

"GIRL'S...!" both boys yelled out. "What do they do with these girlfriend's Mama?" the eldest boy asked

"They play cards sweetheart." Karen said

"What kind of card games Ma?" the middle boy asked

"Poker, I think honey." Karen answered

'Yeah, it's called Strip Poker!" Bob quietly chuckled. Which made all the adults turn their faces away from the children.

"Marshal, How you going to try and catch those Outlaw's?" Karen quickly asked to change the subject.

"YEAH, How You Going To Catch The Outlaw's Marshal?" both boys yelled out.

"Not really sure just yet, but I want to be in town before anyone wakes up." Shawn said

"This is ranch land Marshal, most everyone is up and working before the sun's too high in the sky, you know that." Bob said

"That means we need to be out of here by five o-clock." Shawn said, pulling out his pocket watch, it was a quarter to seven. "You folks mind if we sleep in your hay loft tonight?"

"Non-Since," Karen said "We have an extra room with two single beds in it. You men can sleep up there tonight."

"Sure do appreciate it Karen." Shawn said

"I'm glad to be of any help to you we can be Marshal." Karen said, cleaning up the dishes.

"How can we help you Marshal?" the oldest boy asked

"Find those saddlebags with the beer in it." Shawn said, looking around the room.

"Here It Is Marshal, over here on the kitchen counter." The oldest son yelled out. Picking them up and handing them to the Marshal.

"Thank you Youngman." Shawn said, handing Wapiti and Bob another beer. "If we need to leave by five, we should try and get some rest."

"The beds are already made up Marshal." Karen said, pointing towards the door that the staircase was behind. "Right through that door, upstairs, second door to the right. Here's a small lamp you can take up with you so you can see where you're going in the dark tomorrow morning."

"Thanks for everything Ma'am, that was by far the best roast beef I've had the pleasure of eating in a long time." Shawn said

"Me too Ma'am." Wapiti said "I don't usually agree with the Marshal, but that roast was one of the best I've ever tasted."

"Thank you both, boys, take the slop out to the pigs please?" Karen asked

"AAAA MMMAAA, we were hoping the Marshal and Wapiti would tell us some more stories about Outlaws they've caught." The Eldest boy cried out

"I don't have time to talk about Outlaw's I've caught. Right now I have to think about how I'm going to catch these next two without any innocent people getting shot." Shawn said, taking a drink off his beer.

"I don't know about you men, but a cold beer relaxes me and makes it a lot easier to fall asleep." Wapiti said, holding the last beer up. "I'm going to take this upstairs, lay down on a nice soft bed and fall peacefully asleep."

"You men go on ahead and go upstairs and get some rest. I'll make sure these two keep it down to a dull roar." Karen said, looking back over her shoulder at them while she was washing the dishes.

"We'll be quiet Marshal, we promise." Both boys cheerfully said

"Thank you Karen, boys, we appreciate everything very much." Shawn said, as he and Wapiti went upstairs to their beds.

Wapiti hadn't even drunk half his beer and they both were sound asleep.

The next thing either one could remember was Karen opening the door and waking them up. "Coffee will be ready by the time you men get downstairs. The boys are in the bedroom across the hall, please try and not wake them. I don't want to have to deal with them this early. So, please don't wake them, they're both lite sleeper's."

"Yes Ma'am, we'll both be real quiet." Shawn said, lighting a match, he lit the small oil lamp so they could see what they were doing. It only took them a couple minutes to get dressed and headed down the hallway trying not to cause the floorboards to squeak too much and wake the boys.

Walking out the door and into the kitchen, Karen was handing them both a hot cup of coffee. "Sugar's on the table and cream is in the cold cabinet."

"We drink it black Ma'am, I mean Karen." Shawn said, taking a sip of coffee. "Can't pack creamer and sugar is just one less thing to worry about."

"How would you gentlemen like your eggs, I already have bacon, sausage, and hash brown potatoes cooked, so it'll only take a couple minutes to fry you up a couple eggs" Karen asked, pouring some bacon grease back onto the griddle.

"We both like 'em over easy Ma'am." Wapiti said

"Will You Please Quit Calling Me Ma'am, I'm not that old." Karen said, with a big smile on her face.

"Yes Ma'am, I mean Karen." Wapit said, sitting down at the table picking up a piece of bacon. "Trust me, I'm just trying to be respectful Karen."

"I know Deputy." Karen said, just as Bob came walking back in the door.

"Didn't figure you needed your packhorse right now so I just saddled up your horses." Bob said, reaching for a cup of coffee from Karen. "Thanks sweetheart."

"Don't need him right now, but I'd like him close by if we need to follow these men down the road aways till they're out of town so no-one gets hurt in any fire fight." Shawn said

"Like you said last night, they have to head for John Day to cash any of that gold in. The Café at the Stage Stop opens at seven, the Saloon don't open up till noon." Bob said "You men go ahead and go on in just as soon as you finish your breakfast, I'll load him up and follow behind you in about an hour, just out of town on the other side of the river is a very large red barn. You can't miss it…I'll put him inside it, Mr. Albert Derr won't mind. He's a Sheep

Rancher, But that aside, he's a real good guy and a dead shot when it comes to killing coyote's that get too close to his sheep."

"Most Sheep Ranchers are good shots." Shawn chuckling answered "But you don't think they'd notice a man riding thru around seven o-clock leading a packhorse one way, then an hour later you come back down the street NOT leading that horse. I know that would get my attention!" Shawn said

"I'll just ride back out around town the back way and get back here in time to start mowing before it gets too hot." Bob said

"Alright." Shawn said, as Karen set a plate with crispy hash brown potatoes and three fried eggs.

"As you can see, the sausage and bacon are on the table." Karen said, smiling. Watching them both already eating a slice of bacon.

"Thank you Karen." They both said starting to eat. Shawn took out his pocket watch, it was ten minute to five. "We need to be in town before daylight."

"Marshal, ride into town, just past the Stage Stop is Owens Street. About six, seven houses up the street, the Martin's have a big barn you can put your horses in, so they'll still be out of sight." Bob offered.

"NO, I don't want to be that far from my horse if they run on me." Shawn said, taking a quick drink of coffee, then another big bite of egg and potatoes. "But I do like your idea about bringing my supply horse thru in an hour, then riding back around town, and I don't have to wait around loading that horse up right now.... Can't tell ya how much we appreciate all your kind help and hospitality you've given me and Wapiti."

Shawn was on his third cup of coffee when he started topping it off with a small shot out of his flask. "Isn't it awfully early to start drinking Marshal?' Karen asked with a skeptical look on her face.

"He's thinking Ma'am, I mean Karen." Wapiti said, with a big smile on his face. "He claims that anyways when he starts drinking this early."

"Only when I think there might be guns involved and some innocent person getting shot when they shouldn't have been." Shawn stated, glaring into everyone's eyes. "I try to think everything out so there's no unnecessary gunplay. Judge Monson gets real upset when I bring them back in over the saddle as opposed too sittin' up."

"How many have you killed since you been a Lawman Wapiti?" Bob asked

"None yet." Wapiti said, taking a sip off his coffee. "Had to out draw one in La Grande a couple months back."

"Who'd you out draw?" Karen asked, refilling everyone's coffee.

"He Out Drew Tom Skerritt." Shawn proudly said, puffing his chest up.

"Tom Skerritt, I heard he'd killed over twenty men." Bob said, sliding his coffee cup towards the Marshal while he was pouring a small shot in his coffee.

Shawn looked over at Karen, who had her back to them washing up some of the frying pans. Quickly he dumped in a double shot in his cup before putting the flask away, winking at Bob at the same time.

Wapiti just chuckled a little and took the last bite of his sausage. "You about ready Marshal?"

"Yes I am." Shawn said, standing up and taking one last drink off his coffee.

"Here's your change from last night Marshal." Bob said, handing him the money.

"Keep it, I'll write it down in my expense book as room and board." Shawn said

"There's over forty bucks here Marshal." Bob said, still holding out the money.

"Told ya, room and board, plus tip for the cook and two hot meals." Shawn said, walking towards the door.

"That's too much Marshal." Karen said, grabbing the money from Bob and tried to give some of it back to him.

"No Ma'am, If we'd had to rent two rooms and pay for four meals at any Saloon or Café we'd have spent every bit of what you have in your hand. You've earned it, so go buy yourself something nice with it." Shawn said, shaking both their hands and following behind Wapiti.

It was nice of Bob to leave a small lantern on inside the barn so they could see what they needed to see. Quickly they both checked their pistol's to make sure they were loaded, then they tightened up their cinch straps and headed out of the barn at a medium trot.

In no time at all they were on the main road and heading towards town. There wasn't much left of the moon, but it was early enough in the morning that its light made it easy for them to see the road.

It barely took them twenty minutes to ride to the top of the little hill that led down into town. There were a few street lantern's lighting the City Center up. One in front of the Merc, one in front of the Livery, one over the town Doctor's house, office and recovery room, and one in front of the Stage Stop Cafe. They all were a good ten feet off the ground and they could see all the store fronts.

Riding over to the Livery, Shawn got off his horse and opened the door and walked inside trying to look around.

Wapiti held on to the Marshal reins and slowly looked the area over. Especially, up at the windows above the Saloon where the two Outlaws were sleeping. It may have only took the Marshal five minutes inside to verify their load of gold was still inside.

"Their stash and three packs are still up against the wall where Bob said it was stacked at." Shawn said, looking around. "There sure isn't very many hiding spots around here."

"No there's not." Wapiti whispered, still looking around. "One of us can hide behind those big trees just to the side of the Stage Stop up that street, he'd be able to see the front of the Saloon, Merc, and the Stage Stop real easy."

"I agree with you." Shawn said, just as a lamp came on inside the Stage Stop. Looking around Shawn realized it was starting to get light out. "You take the spot you picked out and I'll put my horse behind the Livery here and wait for them on the inside."

"It's only six o-clock, I thought Bob said the Stage Stop didn't open till seven." Wapiti said, looking at his pocket watch.

"They have to get up and get everything ready before the first Stage gets in. So I'm guessing there'll be one coming through shortly." Shawn said, looking over at the Stage Stop Cafe. "If we get our horses out of sight real quick, we could sneak over and get us a cup before they open up."

"Alright Marshal, I'll go hide my horse and meet you over there in a couple minutes." Wapiti said, turning his horse towards Owens Street, watching the Marshal work his way around the back of the Livery Stables.

Turning up the street he could see the morning light reflecting off a window only twenty yards at the most away from him. Riding up under the bows of the big CottonWood trees that lined the streets. Dismounting, he tied his horse up to the hog wire fence around the yard of the house just behind him. Then walking back towards the street but still staying well hidden in the shadows and out of sight waiting for the Marshal to come out of hiding first.

He was caught off guard when he heard Shawn walking up the street from the east. "Wapiti, where you at?" Shawn whispered out.

"Over her Marshal." Wapiti said, stepping out into the light. "I can smell coffee cookin' at the Stage Stop Cafe, but a light just came on inside one of the rooms above the Saloon."

"That's alright, we'll only be a couple minutes." Shawn said, walking towards the door, opening it up and inside with Wapiti right behind him.

"We're not open yet." They heard a Lady say.

"Ma'am, I'm U.S. Marshal Shawn Felton and this is Deputy Wapiti, we'd like a couple hot cups of coffee to go, we'll bring your cups back later." Shawn said, looking at the Lady, then back out the window looking at someone leaning out of the window above the Saloon, and they were looking over the little town center. The Merc to his right, Doctor's house and Office, then the corrals and Livery.

"Yes Sir Marshal, is there anything else I can get you to eat real quick." The Lady asked, filling two large metal cups up and handing them to them.

"No Ma'am, we've already eaten. But I wanted one more cup while I'm waiting for my prey to come out of hiding." Shawn said, pouring a small shot of whiskey into his cup.

"Who You Looking For Marshal. Maybe I can let you know if or when they come in here for breakfast." The Lady asked

"Not really sure what they look like, but I'll know 'em when I see 'em." Shawn said, taking a sip of coffee.

"I haven't seen any stranger's in town, Marshal." The Lady said, going back to putting bacon and sausage on the grill to cook. "I try to cook a few pieces ahead of the morning rush."

"They're here Ma'am, but please don't tell anyone we're in town. I don't want to spook them and end up getting an innocent person shot." Shawn said, walking back towards the door. Stopping and looking out, he could still see the man leaning out the window but talking back to someone else in the room.

Wapiti and Shawn both just stood there looking out the window waiting for the man to go back inside. They had been standing there for a good five minutes watching the man stand in the window with his back to them and obviously arguing with someone else in the room.

After a couple more minutes the cook came walking up and offered to top their cups off. They both thanked her and Wapiti handed her a couple dollars.

"No Thanks Deputy, the Law eats and drinks free in my place." She said, walking away.

Looking back out the window they could see the man was gone. So they quickly walked out the door and back into the shadows of all the trees.

"You get back inside there out of sight, I'll work my way back up the street and cross back over well out of their sight." Shawn said, pointing and walking.

"Sure enough Marshal." Wapiti said, walking back deeper into the dark shadows under the many large Cottonwood trees. All the time watching the Marshal cross the street and cut through someone's yard going back towards the backside of the Livery Stables and out of sight..

'This was the boring part.' Wapiti was thinking to himself, sitting on a block of wood and slowly drinking his coffee. He had been hiding and drinking for a good ten minutes and was just finishing off his coffee when two men came walking down the stairs from the room's above the Saloon.

Wapiti couldn't make out anything that was being said. But he could tell one of the men was mad for the other one paying his Lady with a couple gold nuggets out of one of the bags. Why the hell did he even need to open any of those bags up for, they had taken over two hundred dollars off the six men they killed while stealing the gold.

The other man started telling the first man to chill out, nobody will know they had anything to do with that robbery. It took place over eighty miles away and like they'd figured, everyone will think the robbers headed towards a bigger City, like Portland or Eugene to cash it in at.

"You never know who that Lady will tell how she got two gold nugget's weighing well over two ounces, and what she did do to earn them." The first man yelled back. "She was only a twenty dollar most, that's half of what that thumb sized nugget is worth, what a fool you are." He continued saying, shaking his head back-n-forth in disbelief.

"They'll know what she did to earn it," the second man said, walking up to the door of the Stage Stop Cafe. "They'll just think some miner came thru and paid her out of his pouch because he didn't have any cash to pay her with."

"I hope you're right, now let's shut up about it till we're out of town." The first man said, opening the door and walking inside the Stage Stop Café to get something to eat.

After a couple more minutes a couple other people came riding or walking up to the Café for their breakfast too. Within the next ten, fifteen minutes Wapiti had had three different people walk by him and had no clue he was even around.

Even though they had had a big breakfast themselves, setting there and smelling all the food cooking was making Wapiti hungry again. He was thinking to himself as the morning Stage from the east or John Day came pulling up alongside the Café and came to a stop. Then the Shotgunner jumped down and opened the Coach door and the passenger's started unloading and going inside.

Shawn quickly crossed over the street and through someone's yard walking towards the back of the Livery Stables. When he got close to his horse he spooked him and he wrestled against the reins holding him tied up and started whining a couple loud times.

"Settle down boy." Shawn said, padding him on the side. Calming the big horse back down. Then he crawled his way alongside the Livery Stable till he was just a couple feet from the end. With all the lilac bushes he was well out of sight from anyone coming or going to or from the Saloon to the Stage Stop Café.

Shawn's coffee cup was empty long before he was ready for it to be. Looking back and forth between the two buildings he wondered if he could get back in time for another hot cup before anyone came out. He wanted another cup, but he knew those men would be coming out soon. He could tell by the sounds of the conversation's going on inside one Hotel room's open window that one man was mad as hell at the other.

Within a couple more long minutes Shawn saw the two men come down the stairs from above the Saloon. Still arguing, but now he could still hear it was about one of them paying one of those young Lady's with gold instead of cash. Why had he done it, they had taken over two hundred dollars off the six men back at the Stage robbery two days ago.

Before Shawn knew it they were walking inside the Stage Stop Café. Within ten more minutes more people started riding up or walking right past Wapiti to get their morning breakfast. After maybe another thirty minutes at most, the Stage from John Day came pulling up out front of the Stage Stop blocking his view. He didn't like it, but there wasn't anything he could do.

Looking around himself again, he decided to go back out to the backside of the Livery and find a way inside and a place he could hide out of sight and let them load all that gold up first. It barely took him a minute to be back in the yard. Looking over towards the house, he could see a Lady standing in the window looking directly at him. Stopping, he waved at the Lady trying to hold his badge out from his shirt. Within a minute a man came out the back door with a double barrel shotgun.

"I'm U. S. Marshal Shawn Felton Sir, it would be in your best interest if you go back inside for a while please."

"Yes Sir Marshal, but you sure I can't help you?" the man asked

"No Sir you can't, I'd rather know you're safe inside your house so hopefully you don't get hit by any miss fired rounds of fast flying bullets." Shawn said, continuing walking towards the back door. Then looking around he slowly opened the door and walked inside. The holding pens were along the other side of the Livery. It was light enough that Shawn could see all the horses inside. There were a good dozen head of horses inside and four, five times that more in the corral.

After a couple more minutes someone came up and opened one of the two big door's then walked into the office. Shawn could see the man building a fire, then he took a coffee pot outside to the water trough and began filling it up with water. After another couple minutes he came walking back in and put it on top of the stove top. Walking back out of the office, he walked over to a grain bin and filled up two large buckets of grain and started giving each horse a little. Then he started pitching some hay into their hay bin's to feed them with. He was just about to put the pitch fork back against the wall when he saw Shawn hiding back in the corner.

Waving the pitch fork up-n-down he demanded that Shawn come on out or he'd be throwing this pitchfork directly at you Mister.

"Settle down Mister, I'm Marshal Shawn Felton."

CHAPTER 5

"Bob Thompson told me you were in town, but I wasn't sure he was telling me the truth or pulling my leg. "I'm Bill Munkers, it's a pleasure to meet you Marshal." Bill said, putting the pitch fork back and extending his hand. "Where's Deputy Wapiti at. I'd like to meet him too."

Shawn stepped out from the corner and shook Bill's hand. "He's outside there somewhere."

"Those bags over there really full of gold Marshal?" Bill asked, looking at the pile of supplies with the three pack saddles laying on top of them. He already knew the top one was filled full of real gold, because he came back after midnight and everything had shut down and EVERYBODY had gone home to sleep. Then he, like Marshal Felton came in the backdoor out of sight from anyone, opened up the top satchel and filled half a five pound metal coffee can full. Then closed it back up, restacked the pack saddles and left the way he came knowing NOBODY had seen him before he was safely back inside his house out of sight.

"They are if they're the men we're looking for Bill." Shawn said, with a serious look on his face. "I'd feel a whole lot better if you went over to the Stage Stop Café and got yourself something to eat before they come back around looking for the horses and supplies so you don't accidently get shot."

"I have to agree with you Marshal." Bill said. Looking over at the Stagecoach blocking the view of the café. "You make sure my pot don't boil over, I told those men yesterday I usually open up around seven-thirty, eight at the latest. So they'll be expecting a cup of coffee to drink while their loading back up."

"I'll watch it, you just tell 'em it's on the stove. But you got hungry waiting for them to show up." Shawn stated.

"Yes Sir Marshal." Bill said, walking towards the door. "You just be safe, I can tell by the looks in their eyes, they have no problem killing anyone that might get in their way."

"I will, and thanks for the coffee." Shawn said, watching Bill walk away.

No sooner had he cleared the Stagecoach and the coffee pot started to boil out the pour spout. So Shawn walked in the office and pulled it to the side of the stove, continuing to look out the small window towards the Café.

Starting to fill up his cup, he seen two men walking back in his direction. Putting both the pot and cup back down, he quickly worked his way back out of sight in the far back, darkest corner.

Within a couple minutes they came walking inside the Livery Stables and into the office to get themselves a cup of coffee to drink while they loaded up. Shawn could tell the one man was still upset over the other man giving that Lady not one, but two gold nuggets last night instead of paying with cash.

In no time at all they were loading their packs up with all the heavy bags of gold. Fact that was all one of the men could talk about, was what he was going to do with his half when they got back over to Baker City. With this kind of money he'd be able to buy a couple hundred acres and even a few head of cattle to start his own Ranch.

"Just shut up and get loaded, I want to make John Day today." The other man ordered out

"I don't know what you're so worried about, everyone would think they'd gone back towards Redmond or Madras and take the train to Portland." The other man chuckled out.

"I won't settle down till we are back in Baker City." The Obvious leader shouted out madly. "Now shut up and help me finish loading all this up."

It only took them five more minutes to load all three horses and saddle theirs up. Shawn kept his eye on them the best he could, all the horses inside made it hard for him to see more than head and shoulders briefly as they walked around. Slowly he stood up and started walking along the wall towards the more open alleyway to the front door. He was almost where he wanted to be when both Outlaws stepped out from behind the horses and headed towards the office.

"I wonder where the Blacksmith is this morning. I guess we'll just leave thirty dollars on the desk for grain and hay this morning." The Leader said

"HOLD IT RIGHT THERE GENTLEMEN!" Shawn said, pointing his rifle at them and taking one more step out into the open. But his left foot stepped into a bucket and he stumbled and fell towards the ground.

Both Outlaws quickly pulled their pistol's and each fired three to four shots in the Marshal's direction before they stopped.

Shawn just laid there, he knew he had been hit at least four times. So if he didn't play dead, he would be dead and he knew it. Wapiti was still outside, they'd have to go through him. Please make his shot's be true Lord and keep him from harm, Amen. He said, cautiously doing the sign of trinity. The Father, Son, and Holy Ghost cross across his head and chest. He could hear the men talking.

"Teaches that Lawman for trying to sneak up on us." One man said, As they both opened their pistols up and took out the empty cartridges and reloaded them with live rounds, then put them back in their holster. "Do you think we should go check and make sure he's dead?" One of the men asked.

"NO, if he ain't dead, he's not far from it, look as the blood puddling up under that board he's lying on." The probable leader spoke out.

Shawn watched them continue on into the office, then back out to their horses. They both looked in his direction one last time before they led their horses outside.

Wapiti could hear the people in the house behind him wake up and start moving around inside. After another five minutes he could smell their coffee cooking. But he knew his thoughts had to be on the Stage Stop Cafe and the two men they were waiting for to come back out. Looking over in the Marshal's direction, he wondered where he was hiding at. He knew he'd be somewhere where they wouldn't be able to see him, till he was ready for them to see him.

The Stage Coach had only been in for five minutes at most when the two men came walking out and around the Stagecoach heading towards the Livery Stables. Wapiti's hand slowly went down to his pistol, checking to make sure the hammer guard was off so as not to prevent his draw if and when he needed to.

The two men were joking and laughing as they walked inside the Livery. Wapiti's heart was beating a hundred times a minute, if not more. His hands were starting to sweat so he wiped them off on his pants, but keeping his eyes on the Livery Stables. What were they doing in there, what was taking them so long to come back out, were just some of the things he was thinking about. After a couple more minutes three more men came out of the Café, climbed back aboard their horse and rode right past him.

One of them noticed his horse being tied to the fence, so they slowed down and started looking in his direction when all of a sudden everyone heard over a half dozen pistol shot's coming from inside the Livery stables. The men turned their heads in that direction as Wapiti came out from the shadow's and started walking across the street towards the Livery Stables.

Within a matter of seconds people were coming out of the Café and the Merc to see what was going on. They all saw Wapiti cautiously walking towards the Livery, with his left hand, he was waving it backwards to let the people know they needed to stay back, so they did

Wapiti walked up to within thirty feet of the open Livery Stables door before he stood still to make his stand. He could hear the men talking about killing another Lawman. He hoped it wasn't true, but he couldn't think about the Marshal right now, he had to keep his mind on the men inside the Livery Stables cause they'd definitely be drawing their pistols against him without hesitation, so he had better be the one making the first move!

After a long two minutes the men came out leading their horses and laughing, "That's Far Enough Gentlemen." Wapiti stated, glaring at them, with his right hand barely an inch from his pistol.

Both men came to a stop and looked over at Wapiti standing in front of them. Then they both looked at each other, then back to Wapiti. "This Ain't No Fist Fight Chief! You Can't Out Draw The Two Of Us!" the leader shouted out, dropping his reins. "So why don't you just step aside and let us ride through."

"That Ain't Happening!" Wapiti demanded, looking each man over slowly. They had both dropped their reins and had their hands within a couple inches from their pistols and continued to slowly move closer. "I may not be able to take both of you, but I will at least kill you out Sir, You ready to die?"

"You Ain't That Good Chief!" the Leader said, as both men reached for their pistols.

Wapiti had been listening to the man talk, but his eyes were on their hands, so even though he was still talking, but probably close to the end, hoping to catch Wapiti off guard allowing them to draw first, so when their hands were under two inches, Wapiti quickly drew his pistol catching them off guard. It was as if the Great Spirit had slowed everything down into slow motion mode. Right away his pistol barrel was aimed dead center of the shorter man's chest, out of the corner of his eye he could see both men's barrels had just cleared leather, so he turned his barrel a fraction of an inch and pulled the trigger shooting the man just between his shoulder and collar bone. Causing his gun to misfire and the bullet barely missing his foot as his body spun around and his pistol went flying up through the air. Then he moved his barrel dead center of the taller, skinny second man chest, his barrel had cleared leather and was in the process of being brought up into firing position, so again Wapiti moved his barrel a fraction of an inch and pulled the trigger hitting him in the exact same place as the shorter man, with the same consequences, only his misfire wiped upwards zinging over Wapiti's head into the roof of the Stage Stop Cafe, as his pistol went flying upwards and his body spinning in the direction the bullet traveled as both bullets within a fraction of a second went into the front steps going up into the Doctor's office.

Still standing tall with his pistol in his hand still aimed at the two men. "Now! You Both Should Be Dead Right Now...I Don't Miss My Target At This Distance. The Marshal warned me about giving a man a second chance, claiming they'll still try to kill me. I also know that a whole lot of you Gun Fighter's like to carry a snub nose 38 in your back sides. If you even look like you're going to try and pull one on me, I'll drill you dead center. Do We Understand Each Other?" Wapiti stated, firmly.

"Yes Sir Deputy." Both men said, looking at each other, then looking down at the hole through their shoulders, which hurt like hell. "Don't Be Getting Excited Chief, I'm just going to throw out my 38." The Leader said, slowly reaching around with his left hand. Grabbing the pistol grip, he looked back over at Wapiti for a couple seconds.

"If that pistol comes even remotely towards me, you're dead Mister!" Wapiti said, still staring at the man.

Quickly, he tossed the pistol to the ground behind himself.

"Now You Mister!" Wapiti said, looking at the second man.

"I don't carry one Deputy." The man answered.

"Both of you lay face down in the dirt." Wapiti ordered, which both men did. "Somebody go check on the Marshal." He ordered out, walking over to the men laying on the ground.

Bill, the Blacksmith and three others took off running towards the Livery stables. They were only inside for less than a minute when someone yelled out that the Marshal had been shot and for someone to go get the Doctor.

"If he dies, I'll hang you both Here, Today!" Wapiti said, putting their handcuffs on them with their hands behind their backs. Then helping them to their feet as two men were packing the Marshal by his shoulders with his arms wrapped around their shoulders.

Wapiti could see the Marshal had a blood stain coming from his right shoulder, one, a foot and a half lower down in his lower rib cage, and one in each leg. "I'll be alright Wapiti." Shawn said, looking at both men in handcuffs and a bullet hole in each man's right shoulder. "I see you went against my advice and gave them a second chance."

Everyone started cheering and wanting to personally shake Wapiti's hand. His string of bringing them in alive was now up to an even forty eight scalps. But these two were far bigger than all but one of the other scalps. This time it wasn't with his fists, this time it was with his pistol, he had OUTDRAWN Two Gunslingers as they were called. Men who had out drawn and killed many men in their past, and they had been there to see him do it.

Wapiti put his pistol away and took out the double barrel ten gauge shotgun and pulled back one hammer, looking both men face-to-face. "This is loaded with half dozen or so steel balls, NOT BEE-BEE'S…You try to run on me at any point from here back to Prineville, I CAN BLOW YOUR DAMN HEAD'S OFF AT FIFTY YARDS, Do I make myself clear Gentlemen!" Wapiti demanded to know

"Yes Sir Deputy, We won't give you any trouble, so you can go ahead and drop that hammer." Both men started saying.

"One Hammer Will Always Be In The Ready Position!" Wapiti said "Now follow the Marshal over to the Doctor's Office. "Wapiti ordered, pointing the way with his free hand.

"What If You Trip And That Thing Goes Off." Both men said, cautiously walking through the crowd of people.

"Just hope I don't." Wapiti said, following the men to the middle back office. Wapiti could see the Doctor coming down the stairs as the men helped the Marshal into the office.

It took them less than a minute to walk it, but Wapiti was worried about the Marshal's wound in his rib cage. If that nick's a lung, they can be deadly. By the time Wapiti got inside, Shawn had his shirt off and the Doctor was looking at his wounds.

"You Two Men Set Your Ass's On The Floor Right There!" Wapiti demanded, pointing the ten gauge at the floor then back at them.

"Yes Sir Deputy, But if you're going to wave that ten gauge around, would you please drop that damn hammer." Both men said, setting down on the floor.

"How's the Marshal, Doc?" Wapiti asked, looking back and forth between him and the Marshal.

"I'll have to remove both bullet's…He won't be going anywhere for a couple weeks." Doc answered

"What's the jail like in this town?" Wapiti asked

"A stick jail house, you could pull it apart with a couple good saddle horses" Wapiti heard a voice behind him say.

Turning around he saw Bob Thompson walking towards him. "Thought you had hay to cut?" Wapiti asked

"It can wait, How's the Marshal?" Bob said sincerely, looking down at the Marshal setting on the table.

"I've been shot worse." Shawn said, taking a drink of whiskey, then pouring a good size shot in each wound, cringing each time the whiskey hit the wound. "I'm going to need a couple bigger bottles before this is over with…So someone break into the Saloon and get me a couple fifths.

"I've got the key right here." They heard a man in the crowd of people watching shout out. "I'll be right back." Then they saw him working his way back through the crowd of people.

"With you not being able to ride, I guess it'll be up to me to get these two men and all that gold back to Prineville." Wapiti said, looking back and forth between the two Outlaws and the Marshal.

"I'll ride with ya Deputy!" Bob said "You give me that shotgun and I'll ride the front door, we can tie the pack horses off to these two men's horses which will slow them down even more should they decide to try and run on us, it'll take longer to actually get all three horses up to running speed before you shoot their horses out from underneath 'em."

"That's the way I'd do it." Shawn said, taking another small drink off his flask. "I can pay you Deputy's wages to help him take the gold and prisoner's back to Prineville Mr. Thompson."

"My understanding of the LAW, any legally Deputized Lawman is NOT entitled to any reward from the robbery. But a Bounty Hunter is eligible for the reward ... I'll take the standing fifteen percent reward money as payment for services rendered. After all, I came into town last night looking for them, finding them, I could have tried to arrest them myself as a Bounty Hunter. But I didn't for safety reasons, but I had Wapiti back in case they only wounded him, I wouldn't have let them finish him off before riding out of town. So I came back out and informed you they were in town. Then you both spent the night at my house in preparation for this set-up you pulled off here this morning, and I have both your horses and pack horse waiting for us to pull out whenever we're ready." Bob said

"What about your hay, I thought you needed to get it mowed?" Wapiti asked

"It does, I'll just ride the Marshal's horse both ways and my boys will have my horses to pull the mower with." Bob said, looking back and forth between the Marshal, Wapiti, and the Doctor.

"I know it wouldn't be smart for you to try and take 'em back alone, Deputy." The Doctor said, with a stern look on his face.

"You're both right." Shawn said "It wouldn't be smart for Deputy Wapiti to try and take them back alone Doc ... And Mr. Thompson, You're Correct. No Deputized Lawman is entitled to Any Of The Reward Money. So I'll agree to your terms ... You get the reward money only when Deputy Wapiti gets those prisoner's back to Prineville, Clear!"

"OF COURSE MARSHAL." Bob said, with a big smile on his face. "I told Karen before I left this morning that if one of you got shot, I'd help the other get any survivor's back to Prineville. She said she'd cook a chocolate cake for our trip."

"ALRIGHT!" both prisoner's shouted out.

"What the hell you getting excited about, you're both crazy as hell if you think I'm sharing with you." Bob said, staring down at them.

Just then a man came thru the crowd of people with two fifths in his hands and handed them to Shawn. "Here ya go Marshal."

"Thanks Sir, you just keep a running tab on how much I drink while I'm here and I'll pay you when I leave." Shawn said, looking at the man.

"I'd make him put at least fifty dollars of that up front." Wapiti chuckled out with a big smile on his face.

"You folk's all get out of here so I can get these bullet's out before he gets lead poisoning." The Doc said, waving his hands at everyone, backing them up.

"Go Ahead." Shawn said, looking at Wapiti with pain in his eyes. "I'll be alright, should be home in a couple weeks most."

"Alright then, you men get up and let's get going." Wapiti ordered

"We're going." Both men said standing up.

"But Will You Please Quit Waving That Damn Shotgun Around With That One Hammer Pulled All The Way Back." The Leader said, walking towards the door.

"Just move it." Wapiti demanded. "Wire me in Prineville in two day's and let me know how he's doing Doc." "I will." The Doc answered, closing the door behind everyone.

Wapiti looked at Bob leading the prisoner's through the crowd of people, not only was he carrying a rifle, but his pistol holster was firmly tied down to his thigh. By the way he carried himself, Wapiti knew Bob knew how to handle himself and wasn't one little bit afraid to be tested.

Walking up to the Livery Stables, Bill already had the three pack horses tied off to two horse by a lariat and all four horses saddled up and ready to ride.

Wapiti walked over to both men, handing Bob the shotgun. "Here's how we're going to do this…I'm going to uncuff one of your hands then cuff the other end to your saddle horn so you can stir your horse. Bob will be riding front door with that shotgun, I'll be bringing up the rear with my rifle. You untie those lead ropes and try to make a run for it, I'll shoot your horse out from underneath you and then you'll be walking the rest of the way back to Prineville with shackles on, and I'll make you walk out in all the brush and rock not on the smooth level road … Do We Understand Each Other Gentlemen!"

"Yes Sir, Deputy, we do." Both men answered, walking over to their horses.

Wapiti quickly uncuffed and recuffed each man to their saddle horns, then they all climbed up in the saddle. "Bob, lead the way at a slow trot.

"Yes Sir, Deputy." Bob answered, looking at the prisoner and pointing the shotgun down the road. "Let's move out gentlemen."

Everyone kicked their horses into a slow trot and both prisoner's were asking Bob to quit waving that shotgun around with the hammer pulled back, it just might go off.

"That's Right, It Just Might Do That, so don't startle me." Bob said, riding beside the leader.

Wapiti looked down at his pocket watch as they headed up the little hill going west out of town, it was barely nine o-clock in the morning. He couldn't believe everything was over with so early in the morning, he was thinking to himself. Looking back towards town one last time. Then he started concentrating on everyone and everything in front of him.

It barely took them twenty minutes to get back to Bob's Ranch where all three kids and Karen came out to meet them. "Tommy, take my horse, unsaddle him and you two boys hook them up and get that hay mowed down for me. If it's all down before I get back in four, five days most, I'll pay you each fifty dollars."

"REALLY PA!" they both shouted. "We'll have it done before then, promise!"

"Where's the Marshal?" Karen asked, with a worried look on her face.

"He's at the Doc's, but he'll be okay Ma'am." Wapiti answered, reaching into his saddle bags and took out a small burlap bag. Jumped off his horse and walked over to a lone Ponderosa Pine tree amongst the Cottonwoods.

What are you doing Wapiti?" Bob asked, watching him fill the bag with pine cones.

"I'll show ya later." Wapiti said, quickly filling the bag he walked over and gave it to Bob. "When I say pull, you throw two or three of these in the air at the same time"

"What for?" Bob asked, watching Wapiti climb back in the saddle.

"Target Practice, it'll give me something to do on this long, hot, boring ride back home." Wapiti said

"Off Your horse, I Call Bull Shit!" the Leader spat out laughing.

"Bob, get three of those in your hands and when I say pull you throw 'em up in the air." Wapiti said, holding his reins in his left hand and hovering his right hand over his pistol.

"Ready when you are Deputy." Bob called out.

Just as soon as Wapiti yelled out "PULL" Bob threw all three in the air and they all went in three different directions. Wapiti pulled his pistol out and blew two out of the sky still on their way up, then the third had just started to come back down, and his bullet went thru the pine cone breaking some of it off but sending the remainder flying sideways thru the air a long distance before coming back to earth..

"HOLLY SHIT!" both Outlaw's yelled out, while everyone else was just as impressed and said so. "No Wonder he out drew us." One of the Outlaw said, looking up in the sky at the dust that still lingered in the air from the falling debris from each pine cone, then back at Wapiti. "Where'd you learn to shoot like that?"

"The Marshal, we practice on and off a horse every chance we get. Sometimes we come to a long meadow, he'll pick out a large Pine or Fir tree at the far end, then I ride at it as fast as I can shoot both pistol and rifle. Then when I get to the tree, we count how many times I hit it, I can usually get it at least a half dozen plus bullets in a tree now." Wapiti said, reloading his pistol and glaring over at the two Outlaw's.

Both the Outlaws looked into Wapiti's face and eyes, his face was stern, but there was a small twinkle in his eye, daring them to try and run on him. They both knew they wouldn't have a chance to out run him. So they would just have to take their chances with the Judge.

"There's a chocolate cake in this bag and a half dozen roast beef sandwiches for you men to eat till you get to Mitchell." Karen said, handing both bag's to Bob.

"Thank you Sweetheart, like I told the boys. I should be back in five days most." Bob said, giving her a small kiss, then climbed back up in the saddle and they headed back down to the main road and headed back towards Prineville.

"Wapiti was keeping them at a slow trot most of the way so as not to wear the horses out too fast so they could travel a few extra miles each day. Wapiti and Bob had each eaten all three of the roast beef sandwiches that Karen had made for them during the day on that long hot ride, their last just after they set up camp next to the river outside Mitchel and the prisoners were shackled around a tree. But Wapiti only fed the prisoner's the Marshal's salty corn biscuits and Carmen's hot peppered beef jerky. They all liked the flavor of the Hickory smoke jerky. But all the crushed large black pepper that Carmen put on it made it almost too hot to eat, because it burnt their entire mouth. So of course the prisoner's complained about not having something better to eat.

"Marshal says you need extra salt on these long hot dry days so you won't have a heat stroke. He usually eats a half dozen plus of them a day." Wapiti told them.

"That black crushed pepper on that jerky, that ain't hot, you want hot, just try some of Carmen's OO LA LA Salsa, Now that will set your mouth on fire." Wapiti chuckled out.

It had been dark when they got into Mitchell and it was dark when Wapiti woke up and built a small fire and put a pot of coffee on, letting the other's sleep while it cooked. Which also gave him time to make two ham steak sandwiches for him and Bob before he woke them up.

Holding the double barrel ten gauge on them while Bob unlocked their leg irons from each other, to relocking their leg irons so they could walk. Then he made the prisoner's load all the pack horses while he and Bob enjoyed their sandwiches and a couple hot cups of coffee watching them work.

When they finished loading everything, Wapiti had them saddle all the horses while they both drank the last two cups of coffee in the pot. Which upset the prisoner's because they didn't get to have a cup of coffee either.

Wapiti just handed each of them a water jug, a big piece of jerky, and a couple corn biscuit's. Which again the prisoner's complained about all the salt in the biscuits and the meat being too damn hot to eat.

They could just barely see the sky lighting up to the east when Wapiti headed them back down the road at a slow trot. It was the dark before the dawn, the darkest part of the night. For the first twenty minutes Wapiti could only see the backs of the prisoner's. Then a Redtailed Hawk let out a loud screech and the sound sent a chill up everyone's back, as they all looked around for the big bird.

Being this early in the morning, it was cold out, so everyone was wearing their jackets. It was just warming up enough to consider whether to remove them when they pulled up to Bandit Springs and the Chow wagon.

Wapiti made the prisoner's stay handcuffed to their horses but gave them each a cup of coffee while he waited on the Cook to cook him and Bob a couple sausage, bacon, egg, and cheese sandwiches each.

When the Cook asked what she could cook for the prisoner's, Wapiti told him nothing. They were on bread and water for shooting the Marshal.

The twenty plus people that had camped there the night before couldn't believe Wapiti was bringing in two GUNSLINGER'S ALIVE…They usually fight to the death, because the Judge is just going to hang 'em anyway. They both had dried blood bullet holes in their right shoulders. Had Wapiti really out drawn these two men, they were quietly asking each other, with their eyes on Bob and that Double Barrel Ten Gauge with one hammer pulled back and ready to fire. They all step further away from him and the prisoner's in case he tripped and that barrel went off.

FELTON/WAPITI HUNTIN TRIPS #8 - #12

Wapiti had the prisoner's water all the horses that they were attacked to, while he and Bob water theirs.

Wapiti only allowed the prisoner's to have two cups of coffee, while he and Bob had a couple more waiting for their food to cook. Then he loaded everyone back up and they ate their breakfast riding at a slow walk down the road.

The prisoners could smell the sausage patties from the sandwiches and it made their stomachs rumble for something good to eat. But all they had to eat were the salty, dry, hard corn biscuit's, and hot jerky. But thanks to the early morning chill, their water was semi-cool.

Before they knew it the sun was high in the sky and cooking down on them. Wapiti still kept them at the slow trot pace when they rounded the bend and the Ochoco River was close by. So he told Bob to pull over and water the horses.

Which Bob did, slowing the horses down to a walk over to the river's edge. From the long, hot trotting, all the horses quickly started drinking water.

"Can we get down and stretch our legs out a little, Deputy?" the Leader politely asked.

"YEAH, and everyone check your cinch straps while you are at it." Wapiti said, putting his rifle in the sheath, then he got off his horse. He quickly checked his cinch strap, then grabbed his water bag and started dumping it out. "Change the water in your water bag Bob."

"Was just about to do that." Bob answered, dumping his water bag out, walking towards the river.

"How about our bag's?" one of the Outlaw's yelled out. "Our water is getting real warm too?"

"TUFF! It can get as hot as coffee, I don't care. It's still wet and will keep you from dehydrating on me." Wapiti said, holding his water bag under the water filling it up. When it was full, it picked it up and took a big long slow drink off it. Then he dumped a little on his face and wiped it off. "Boy Does That Taste Good And Feel Good." He said, looking over at the Outlaws walking back to his horse.

"Everyone saddle up and let's get moving!" Wapiti ordered, climbing up in the saddle and taking his rifle back out. Then looking across the river at a large Ponderosa Pine tree about a hundred feet away, he aimed his .44-.40 rifle at a branch about four inches in diameter. Firing four quick shots into the green branch, it quickly broke off and fell to the ground. Looking over at the two Outlaw's with a big smile on his face, turning his horse back towards the road. "Let's get moving."

It hadn't even taken them five minutes most to water the horses and they were heading back down the road at a slow trot.

They had been passing many wagon's going both ways all day long. But by the way they were riding, Bob, out front with that ten gauge in the ready position, two men leading four horses in the middle, and Deputy Wapiti bringing up the rear with his rifle in the ready position. Everyone knew he was bringing in some Outlaws, but what took four pack horses to haul everything and Where Was The Marshal?

The sun was starting to set behind the mountains to the west when they came riding up on the outskirts of Prineville. "Just stay on the Main Street here Bob, it will take us right up to the Courthouse."

"Sure thing Deputy." Bob called back as people started coming out onto the street to watch Deputy Wapiti bring two prisoner's into town. Both setting up in the saddle not laying over it, but everyone could also see the two dried blood stained holes in both men's right shoulders.

The news had come over the tele-graph line two days ago that Marshal Felton had been shot and that Deputy Wapiti had out-drew these two men. He was proving he was a man of Honor, just looking at the holes in the men's shoulders, not in the center of their chest like Marshal Felton would have done. He'd have brought them in laying over the saddle, yet Wapiti obviously could have killed these two men, but chose not to…WHY? Everyone was saying to each other, watching them ride by.

Riding up to the Courthouse, Wapiti quickly unlocked the handcuff from their saddle horns. "Bob, just knock on that door over there and the jailer will open it from the inside in just a couple minutes."

"Yes Sir Deputy, let's go gentlemen." Bob said, waving the shotgun at them then towards the door.

"Would you Please drop the hammer on that thing, what if you trip going down these stairs." One of the Outlaw's shouted back, walking towards the door.

Wapiti turned and looked into the crowd of people. "Who Knows Where The Bank Manager Of The Oregon Trust And Loan Bank Lives At?" he shouted out.

"I do Deputy." He heard a voice yell out. "I'll go get him right away." Then he could see two men take off running through the crowd of people, then down the street.

"What's on all those pack horses?" a couple different people yelled out.

"GOLD." Wapiti said, looking over and seeing Bob and the two Outlaws walk through the door to the jail. Looking back around at the crowd of people. "Who wants to earn a twenty dollar bill?"

More than half the people said "I DO" and wanted to know what it was he needed done.

"I need someone to take these saddle horses and our pack horse over to the Livery and put them away for us." Wapiti said, untying his pack horse. Turning back around he saw close to a dozen men fighting to get a hold of the reins and lead rope then headed towards the Livery stables.

"What about someone to help you unload all that gold on the other three horses, Deputy, aren't you going to need help unloading them too?" One of the men standing in front of him asked.

"That would be nice, all those that help unload, I'll buy you each a fifth and a large pitcher of beer at any of the Saloon's in town." Wapiti said, leading the horses towards the Bank, just as Bob came walking back out of the jailhouse door.

"Here Deputy," Bob yelled over. "One of the Jailer's went up to the Judge's Office, and got us each a cold beer."

"Thanks." Wapiti said, stopping and looking back at him. "I thought we'd have to wait till everything was put away before we'd get a cold beer."

"Me too." Bob said, handing him a cold beer and they both quickly opened them up and took a long drink off each bottle. Reaching in his pocket, he took out a ten dollar bill. Looking over at a young teenage boy, he asked him to come over.

The kid stepped through the crowd of people and over to him. "Yes Sir, what can I do for you?"

"Go to the nearest Saloon and get us four more bottles of cold beers and bring them back to the Bank, we're going to be awhile." Bob said, handing him the money. "You can keep the change for RUNNING and getting those beers back here as fast as you can run."

"But they won't sell it to me, I'm too young." The boy said, slowly taking the money.

"You just tell them it's for Deputy Wapiti, tell them if they don't sell them to you, he'll be over shortly to deal personally with whoever refused you!" Bob said, with a big smile on his face.

"Yes Sir Mister, Right Away." The boy cheerfully said, as he and two of his buddy's took off running thru the crowd and up the street towards Moser's Saloon. It was over a couple blocks away so they were all tired from running when they stumbled through the door and into the Saloon.

Everyone stopped and looked at the three young teenage boys. "What are you boys doing in here?" one of the men standing up at the bar asked.

"De..Dep..Deputy WA..WAPITI Just came back into town… with those men that robbed the Banks gold Stagecoach last week…" one boy was explaining while trying to catch his breath. "He gave me this ten dollar bill and said to have you sell me as many bottles as it will buy, or he'll be up here to settle up personally with the person who refused to sell them to me."

Charley looked at all three boys and started to chuckle. "He's turning into more like the Marshal everyday." With that comment everyone that heard it started laughing. Because it was true…many times in the past a NEW bartender would refuse to sell a Youngman a fifth or a couple beers this late at night thinking they were lying. Then later when Marshal did return, he'd walked around behind the bar and threw the bartender out over the top of the bar crashing down on the floor on the other side and then he would fill his own beer mug up.

"How many men are with him as Deputy's?" Charley asked

"I think two, so that's three all together Sir." The boy answered, walking over to the bar, handing him the ten dollar bill.

"A twelve pack is six dollars and fifty cent's." Charley said, putting a small wooden crate on the counter and started putting twelve bottles of beer inside.

Charley could tell by the looks in the boy's excited eyes that they were definitely taking a couple beers for themselves. He couldn't help but chuckle a little at the thought. He could remember stealing mugs of beer from underneath the grand stands at fairs and rodeos when he was a kid.

It only took him a couple minutes to load the small crate up and get the boys their change. Then two of the boys picked up one side of the crate and headed back out the door.

Everyone in the Saloon was laughing and talking about anyone telling Deputy Wapiti he couldn't have a beer when he wanted one. They all started talking about the many groups of men that had tried to stop him from having a beer in the past. Fact, not less than a week ago, he took on three Professional Wrestler's and flat kicked their ass's. One of them was the Reigning West Coast HeavyWeight Champion and he gave Wapiti his Championship Belt...If he wanted a beer, not one of them was going to stop those young boys from taking the beer to him.

The three boys quickly started running as fast as they could back up the street towards the Bank.

"That man said to only get four bottles." One boy said, looking over at others helping him pack the crate.

"I know, so when we get down one more block, we'll hide all but four and this crate underneath the boardwalk or between businesses and come back later and get them." The boy said, with a big smile on his face.

"What if someone sees us?" the third boy asked, running alongside.

"They won't, they're all more interested in Deputy Wapiti and all that gold he brought in." the leader said

"Did You Guys See The Two Bullet Holes In The Shoulders On Both Those Outlaw's?" the Boy running alongside said, in a loud whisper.

"They said the Marshal got shot." One of the boys packing said, looking back at the Saloon a block behind them. "This is far enough, let's hide the beer under the boardwalk here."

"Alright," the leader said, walking over to the edge of the boardwalk and set the wood crate on the ground. Then they quickly pushed the bottles under the boardwalk, leaving the empty crate on top of the boardwalk, they took off running with the four bottles of beer towards the Bank. They could tell by the way everyone was still standing around they were still waiting for the Banker to show up.

"How Bad Was The Marshal Shot?" someone in the crowd shouted out.

"Did You Really Outdraw Those Two Outlaws? Do you know who they are Deputy? Those two men are none other than Jim Logston and Randy Long." someone else yelled out.

Wapiti just looked over at Bob, then at the crowd of people shaking his head. "No I don't know those names, and I don't give a shit either." He answered, leading the horses across the street towards the Bank.

"Well, they're semi famous gunslinger's, the marshal's telegram confirmed Jim has nineteen notched carved into both his pistol grips and Randy has seventeen." Another man boastfully explained.

"WELL, DID YA...! DID HE REALLY OUTDRAW THEM?" the entire crowd started asking, looking at Bob.

"Yes he did." Bob yelled out

"How'd he do it, from behind something?" someone asked

"NOPE, he did it just like you read about in those dime store story books. He did it at twenty paces, hitting both of them right where he aimed, then he challenged them to try and pull their back-up pistol." Bob proudly said

"Did They Try To Pull One?" someone yelled out

"NOPE, Deputy Wapiti warned them against that, said he'd drill them dead center if they tried." Bob proudly answered, following beside Wapiti.

"How Far Away From The Duel Were You Mister?" someone else asked out

"Like most of the other witnesses, I was in the Stage Stop Cafe drinking a cup of coffee and talking to the others when we heard the first half dozen or so pistol shots. So we all ran out to see what was going on and we saw Deputy Wapiti standing directly in front of them stopping their exit. After a long thirty or so seconds the two Outlaw's reached for their pistols. One of their bullet's landed in the dirt about half way between him and Deputy Wapiti and the other bullet went into the roof of the Stage Stop Cafe…" Bob shouted out so everyone could hear him.

"WHY DIDN'T YOU KILL THEM DEPUTY?" someone yelled out.

"Didn't feel I needed to." Wapiti answered, walking across the street, taking another drink off his beer.

"That makes three Gun Slinger's he's outdrawn." Everyone started saying, talking amongst themselves and following Wapiti towards the Bank.

They had only been standing around at the Bank for a couple minutes when the three boys came running up with their four beers. "Here Ya Go Deputy." One of the boys said, handing him two beers, breathing hard from the run back from the Saloon.

"Thank you boys, did they give you any trouble giving them to you?" Wapiti asked, taking the last drink out of his first beer.

"No Sir, they said they didn't want to fight with you over a couple beers. They were all talking about all the other people that have said you couldn't have a beer." The Boy said with a big smile on his face.

"YEAH, they couldn't give them to us fast enough." The other boy said, handing Bob his two beers just as the Banker came walking up. So all three boys took off running back thru the crowd of people and up the street while more people came down the street to see WHO and HOW Deputy Wapiti had brought in.

"Why My Bank Deputy?" the Banker asked walking up putting the key in the lock and unlocking the door.

"Your vault is supposed to be robbery proof." Wapiti said "You men that are close, grab a bag of gold and bring it inside. Then, one of you other men take these three horses back over to the Livery Stables, feed, grain, and water them."

"Yes Sir, Deputy." All the men nearby started saying and trying to one of the men that got to pack a bag of that gold inside the bank. Most were disappointed when they were all gone and before anyone could act, another man quickly grabbed the lead ropes to the three horses. Wapiti handed the man a couple dollars and went inside the bank following behind everyone.

They quickly crossed the room to the stairs leading down to the large caged room below.

The Banker quickly unlocked the cage door and the six men all stacked their gold bags up against the wall and walked back out.

When all six men were out the Banker quickly locked the steel door and they all walked back out of the Bank. Where Wapiti handed one of the six men two twenty dollar bills. "A large pitcher of beer is a buck fifty, and a fifth is five dollars, Right?" He asked, looking at the men who were nodding their heads and saying 'yes Sir Deputy.' as he continued talking. "Six fifths is thirty dollars that leaves you ten. buck fifty times six nine bucks, leaving a one dollar tip for the bartender or cocktail waitress."

"Thanks Deputy." They all said, walking up the street to the Saloon.

"Come on Bob, you can sleep in the Marshal's bunk tonight, he won't mind." Wapiti said, following behind the others.

"Appreciate it." Bob said, opening his last beer. "Being after nine o-clock like it is, I imagine we'll have to go down to one of the Saloon to get anything to eat tonight."

"I doubt it." Wapiti said, opening his last beer. "I'm sure Carmen will have something waiting for us to eat back at the shack."

The two walked up the street and could see two men walking out of the Livery Stables closing the door behind themselves and waving over to them as they turned and walked through the opening between the building's where they could see a light on inside the shack.

"Told YA So." Wapiti said, opening the door, walking in and looking down at the table. Seeing four plates, two with two large burritos on them, two with big slices of apple pie on them, a large pitcher of beer, two beer mugs, and a pot of coffee sitting on a warming iron.

"You think that jerky was hot…wait till you try one of these burritos, you'll be glad we have this beer to drink to try and cool our mouths down with." Wapiti chuckled, picking one up and taking a bite.

Both men sat down and slowly ate their dinner. Bob agreed it was spicy hot, but it added a nice flavor to it at the same time.

It only took them ten minutes most to finish eating and they both laid down and fell fast asleep.

Felton 12

THE MARCS FAMILY

CHAPTER 1

I t was just a couple minutes before seven, when Griselda and Jose opened the door and set their breakfast and coffee on the table. "What's for breakfast?" Wapiti asked, rolling over

"Three eggs over easy, hash brown potatoes, two sausage patties, six pieces of bacon, and two slices of toast each." Griselda answered, filling two cups of coffee, she handed one to each man as they set up.

"Thank You Young Lady." Bob said, taking the coffee and looking over at the large plate full of food. "Tell your Mom thank you too please."

"Yes Sir." Griselda said

"So you really did outdraw those two Outlaw's?" Jose asked, excitedly.

"Looks like." Wapiti said

"Did you get to see it, Mister?" Jose asked, starring Bob.

Both Wapiti and Bob walked over to a plate of food and set down. "Yes I did." Bob answered, taking a bite of bacon. "No-one that was there, could believe he let them live and only shot them in the shoulder."

"Did any of them have a backup snub nose .38?" Jose asked, still excited

"Yes they did and Deputy Wapiti challenged them into trying to pull it. He told them that if they did have one and tried to pull it, he would drill them dead center with his second shot." Bob said, in between bites. "The one that did have one quickly threw it to the ground using his left hand."

"How many notches did they have on their pistol grips?" Jose asked, looking over at Wapiti.

"Don't know, I didn't pick them up. I just handcuffed the prisoner's and went in to see how the Marshal was. When I came back out someone had already picked them up, so I couldn't tell you if they had any notches on them at all." Wapiti answered.

Jose looked over at Wapiti's bed and could see the Championship Belt laying across the foot of his bed. "When and where are you going to hang your Championship Belt up?"

"Don't know that I will." Wapiti answered

"Can I see it?" Bob asked

Jose jumped down from his chair and started towards the belt. "Is it okay Wapiti if he sees it?"

"YEAH, it's alright." Wapiti answered

Jose quickly picked the belt up and took it over to Bob.

Right off Bob couldn't believe how heavy it was. Looking it over he could see it was made from thick leather with a large oval solid gold plate in the middle and precious jems of all kinds around its edge's. The writing around the outside rim read. "West Coast HeavyWeight Champion" In the middle there was a design showing a muscleman standing at the base of one of the big volcanoes that lined the west coast. "This thing is heavy and very beautiful Deputy, I think you should fix it up so you can mount it on the chest of your horse." He said, holding the belt up.

"Might scare off some potential excitement." Wapiti answered, with a big smile on his face.

"It might make more men want to fight you Wapiti." Jose said, looking at him.

"How's that Jose?" Wapiti asked, in between bites.

"It might cause more men would want to try and take it away from you." Jose cheerfully answered

Wapiti reached over and took the belt then tossed it back on the bed. "It can stay there for now."

Just then Griselda came walking back in with a fresh pot of coffee and hot plate. "Mom figured your other pot would be getting cold by now." Both men picked up their cups and took a sip, she was right. They were almost cold.

"Give those to me please." Griselda said, taking the two cups she walked outside and dumped them out, then came back in and refilled them back up.

Bob took out all the change in his pocket and counted up one dollar and ninety five cents. "Here Young Lady, this is your tip for being our waitress this morning."

"Thank you Sir.' Griselda said

Wapiti took out his wallet and took out seven dollars and handed it to Griselda. "I can see and smell you cleaned the shack while we were gone. So five is for that and the other two are your tip this morning,"

"Thank you Wapiti, now I can order a new dress I want." Griselda said, just as Judge Monson knocked on the open door he walked in.

"Welcome back Deputy, Mr. Thompson, I'd like to extend my appreciation for helping Deputy Wapiti bring those prisoner's and the gold back safely." Judge Monson said, shaking his hand.

The Marshal always kept four upside down cups on top of the table with the salt and pepper in case someone else came in.

Griselda quickly filled one up and handed it to the Judge. "Here, Your Honor."

"Thank you Griselda darling." Judge Monson said, taking the coffee and sitting down.

"Me and the Marshal had an agreement on just how I was to be paid for my assistance, Your Honor." Bob said, taking his last bite of sausage.

"Yes Sir, I understand that." Judge Monson said, taking a sip of coffee. "That's why I came over so early and not wait till my usual one o-clock meeting with Deputy Wapiti…I'm sure you'd like to get headed back home as soon as possible."

"Yes Sir, I would Your Honor." Bob said.

"Here's how the Marshal laid it out to me in his tele-gram." Judge Monson started explaining. "You not ONLY gave them room and board, but you went into town for them to ensure the men they were looking for were in town. So you found and reported their whereabouts before anyone else, so you are entitled to the standing fifteen percent reward money. You assisted Deputy Wapiti with their safe return as an independent bounty hunter."

"That sounds about right." Bob said, walking over to the Marshal's desk and started opening drawer's till he found a bottle of whiskey. "So when can I pick up my reward money and head back home?" Setting back down, he poured a shot in his coffee.

"It'll take at least two days before all the I's and T's are crossed and dotted before I know exactly how much reward there will be. You're more than welcome to stay in town at one of the hotel's while you wait to find out the final tally. But with you receiving so much money, I can't see the bank being, or anyone else being responsible for that bill, except you Sir." Judge Monson said

"I understand that." Bob said, taking a drink off the bottle.

"What I can do, is make the money payable at any Oregon Trust and Loan in your account if you have one, if not, we'll open one for you and deposit the money in it.." Judge Monson said

"I hear they have a two percent charge on all cash withdrawals over a hundred dollars." Bob said, leaning back in his chair. "That's why I bank with Ole Yeller Savings and Loan."

"Me too." Judge Monson said, taking a drink of coffee.

"Not only DON'T I bank with Oregon Trust, but the closest one is in John Day and that's over thirty miles one way from my house." Bob stated.

"Alright, when you get home you and have access to your account number you wire it to me…Number Only, no bank names or anything else at all. That way if anyone else does see it, they won't have a clue as to what those numbers stand for…Then I'll have Oregon Trust deposit the full amount of the reward down to the last penny into your account at Old Yeller Saving and Loan." Judge Monson said. Then looking over at Wapiti. "Now to you Deputy, why the hell were you shooting at their shoulders!"

"You asked me to bring them to you to be judged with the death sentence." Wapiti said, with a small smile on his face.

"That took guts!" Bob shouted out. "I couldn't believe it when I saw their two bodies simultaneously spin backwards as his bullet went into their shoulder area and their pistols went flying up into the air misfiring. One bullet hit the ground a few feet in front of the man who's pistol it came out of, that means his pistol barrel had just cleared leather when it went flying. The second, the barrel was out, but he was still bringing it up high enough to pull his trigger, so when Deputy Wapiti's bullet went thru his shoulder, his misfire went high upwards. If it had been me, I would have been aiming and shooting dead center of their chest, if it was me."

"Anyone Else Too" Judge Monson snapped out, with a serious look on his face, "Don't get me wrong Deputy, I'm proud of you. But over the last twenty two years of being Circuit Judge here in Prineville I've heard of two Deputy's and one Marshal killed, because they tried to give the man a second chance like you did…what I'm trying to say is…please be careful. I don't want to lose you son."

"Appreciate it, Your Honor." Wapiti said "So now that you and Mr. Thompson have made your deal, I'm sure he'd like to get heading home." Shacking Bob's hand. "Bob, it's been a great pleasure to have you assist me. If we ever get back to Dayville, I'll be sure to stop in and buy you a beer…Your Honor, since we've already had our one o-clock meeting. If you two will get out of here, I can lay back down and relax for a little while." He said, walking towards his bed.

"Yes Sir, Deputy." Both men said, standing up.

"Like Deputy Wapiti said Mr. Thompson, I greatly appreciate you assisting him in bringing the Outlaw's and gold back here safely." Judge Monson said, shaking his hand.

"Glad I could be of assistance, Your Honor." Bob said, shaking his hand. "Deputy, it's been a great pleasure riding with you. If you ever need help in the future you know where I live. Now gentlemen, it's almost nine-thirty and I'd like to make it home by tomorrow night, so I'm going to get going. Waving good-bye to everyone, him and the Judge walked out the door.

"I'll see you tomorrow at one o-clock, Deputy." Judge Monson said, following Bob out the door.

Bob and Judge Monson continued talking as the Judge led them between the building's and over to the Livery Stables. Where they shook hands one last time before saying good-bye.

Bob walked inside the Livery and saw Gordy tacking a nail into a shoe. "Sorry to bother you Sir, but I need the Marshal's horse so I can take it back to him in Dayville."

"Just finishing him up right now." Gordy said, breaking the tack off.

"That's not the horse I rode in on!" Bob stated

"I know, the one you rode in on belonged to Chris Hensley out of Burns. The Marshal traded their worn out horses with some fresh horses of his. Because the Marshal didn't want to have to spend another night out camping, he wanted to get home as soon as possible." Gordy said, dropping the horse's hoof, stood up with his hand extended. "Gordy Miller, I hear you're Bob Thompson, it's a pleasure to meet you." Shaking his hand. "How bad is the Marshal shot up?" He asked, with a serious, concerned look on his face.

"One in his right shoulder, one grazed each leg...but he got one close to the bottom of his right lung...that's the one I'm worried about." Bob said, shaking Gordy's hand. "So I know my horse, now where's my saddle so I can get out of here?"

"Saddle is right over there." Gordy said pointing "I don't know how much longer the old couple will continue to have their chuck wagon at Bandit Springs ... I figured you'd want to get an early start so I had Carmen make you up a couple burritos and PBJ'S for your trip. But I see she also put in a few corn biscuits and jerky in the bag too. I like that black pepper she puts on it, sure, it makes it hotter than Haiti's, but it fills you up slowly if you suck on it." Gordy was explaining, putting the bridle on while Bob put the saddle on. "So how'd they manage to shoot the Marshal that many times?"

"He said he had them dead to rights when they stepped out into the open, but his left foot stepped into a bucket that he didn't see, it tripped him, causing him to fall forward to the ground. Said he heard at least six or seven shot's going off before he hit the ground. Said he knew he needed to play dead, or he would be. So he did, played dead. Said he laid there for a good three minutes while they finished loading up. Then he watched them walk out the front door and stop. The doors were wide open so he saw them stop, drop their reins and after a long thirty seconds he heard four pistol shot's and saw both Outlaw's gun's go flying out of their hands and their body spinning halfway around from the bullet hitting them in their shoulders. He said the next three seconds were the longest of his life. Wapiti had given those men a second chance, but where had their bullet's landed. Then finally he heard Wapiti tell them to not even try to pull a backup pistol from behind their backs. Said if they did, he'd kill them for sure." Bob said, tying the cinch strap off. "Said he looked himself over and knew the wounds looked worse than they really were."

"Did you see the wounds yourself?" Gordy asked, handing Bob the grub bag.

"YEAH, like I said, the one in his lower right rib cage is the only one that I was worried about. But he was breathing and drinking just fine." Bob said, chuckling

"What time of the morning was it and how many fifths of whiskey did he order?" Gordy asked, following Bob out the door.

"Just after eight and he ordered two fifths and told Tim the Saloon owner to start a tab." Bob said, climbing up in the saddle.

"I would have made him put at least fifty dollars up front." Gordy said

"That's what Wapiti said." Bob said, chuckling. Then turning his horse down the street he headed out of town at a gallop.

Wapiti was just lying in bed relaxing and wondering how the Marshal was. He knew he'd be alright in a couple weeks, but what is going to happen between now and then. If anyone robbed a bank or rustled a herd of cattle, he'd be going after them alone. He wasn't sure how long he'd been laying there daydreaming, when Jose slowly cracked the door open and looked inside.

Wapiti rolled over, looked at Jose and asked him "What's up?"

"It's almost one o-clock and Mom wanted to know if you were coming in for lunch, or would like me to bring it out here to you?" Jose asked

"I'll come in." Wapiti said, slowly setting up then standing up. "Sure wish you'd brought a cup of coffee with you." He said, walking towards the door.

"Can you start teaching me how to fight today?' Jose asked, with excitement in his voice walking alongside him.

"After I eat lunch I don't see why not." Wapiti said, smiling and looking down into Jose's excited face. "Maybe Griselda would like to learn too?"

"But she's a girl, why does she need to learn how to fight?" Jose asked

"Women need to know how to defend themselves too." Wapiti said, opening the back door. "You never know when or where someone might attack you. There's men out there that will sexually assault them, so they need to learn how to defend themselves too."

"I never thought of that." Jose said, following Wapiti over to a table and sat down just as the waitress walked up and filled Wapiti's coffee cup as soon as he turned it over.

"Today's lunch special is homemade chicken noodle soup with two rolls." the Waitress said

"Sounds good to me." Wapiti said, looking up into those dark brown beautiful smiling eyes and smiling face.

"Right away Deputy." She said, winking at him before she walked away. Wapiti just smiled back at her and started thinking about Cathey, it had been almost six months since he saw her. Her and her parents have been over a couple times, but they had always been out chasing Outlaw's and didn't get back in till after they had returned back to John Day. She used to write to him at least once a week, but over the last couple months they have been fewer. Fact, now that he thought of it, he couldn't remember the last time he got a letter from her. He was sitting there thinking to himself, when the Waitress returned, rubbing up against him as she set his food down and refilled his coffee.

"Is there anything else I can get you?" the Waitress asked, smiling and winking at him again.

"No Ma'am, this will do just fine for now, thank you." Wapiti said, picking up a fork and smiling back at her.

"You like girls?" Jose asked, looking back and forth between the two.

"Some!" Wapiti said, with a big smile on his face, taking a bite of his food.

Griselda came walking over and sat down in a chair. "When will the Marshal be back Wapiti?"

"Not real sure," Wapiti answered, taking a drink of coffee. "Figure no more than two weeks hopefully."

"Gris, Wapiti is going to teach me how to fight after lunch… you want to learn too?" Jose asked

"YEEAAHH I Would." Gris answered, excitedly. "Let me go ask Mom if I can." She said, jumping out of the chair and ran towards the kitchen.

A couple minutes later the waitress returned and refilled his coffee and asked if he needed anything else. He didn't, so she continued on around the room asking everyone the same question.

It only took Wapiti ten minutes to finish eating, putting a two dollar tip on the table him and Jose walked back outside. Looking over Wapiti saw two old feather filled mattresses lying next to the garbage cans. "What are those doing over there?" He asked, walking towards them.

"Mom bought us all new thicker mattresses, so she's throwing these out." Jose answered

Wapiti leaned down and picked one up and started looking it over. It was about five feet long and three feet wide. "This will do just fine." He said, rolling it up and walking towards the shack.

"Work for what?" Jose asked

"For you to hit and kick." Wapiti answered, seeing Griselda running up behind them.

Walking into the shack, Wapiti found a rope and an old T-shirt. He started tearing the T-shit into three inch wide strips. "What are you doing?" Both Griselda and Jose asked

"I'll double and triple these up, then wrap them around your knuckles to protect them, you'll see." Wapiti said, tearing eight strip's out of the shirt and tossing the rest in a small garbage can. "Come on." He said, picking up the rope and walked back outside to the mattress. Both the kid's anxiously followed behind him.

Laying the strips on the table, he grabbed the mattress. "Here, help me roll this mattress up. Gris, you grab that end, Jose, you in the middle." Wapiti was saying and pointing at the same time. Then starting on the long ends, they started rolling it up as tight as they could get it. Taking the lariat he wrapped it around his end, tied it off and cut it off.

"Won't the Marshal be mad at you for cutting his lariat up?" Jose asked

"I'll buy him a new one." Wapiti said, with a big smile on his face and starting to tie it around the middle, wrapping and tying it off, he cut it off and tied the top. Picking it up, he packed it over to a tree next to the shack. Laying the mattress back on the ground, he took out his knife and poked a hole through each layer about a foot down from the top and ran the rope through them all and tied them off. Looking for a branch big enough to hold it. "Jose, would you go grab me a chair so I can reach that branch."

"Yes Sir Wapiti." Jose said, grabbing a chair from the front table and took it over to him.

Wapiti put the chair where he needed it, stepped on top and tied the rope around the branch when the bottom was about two feet off the ground. Stepping down from the chair he half heartedly threw a couple punches into the mattress. "It'll do for now, but it needs to be a little heavier, so run over and get that other mattress so the garbage man doesn't haul it off."

"Yes Sir." Both kids said, taking off running over, grabbing the mattress and quickly returning.

"Just roll it up and stick it under the outside table." Wapiti said, picking two torn pieces of T-shirt up. After they had put the mattress away under the table. He called them back over and wrapped the strips around their hands and knuckles. "Try and hold this tail in your hands for now. I'll get you a set of leather gloves later to better protect your knuckles with.

Wapiti quickly wrapped their hands and led them over to the mattress. Asking both kids to stand back a couple feet, he took his stance in front of the mattress. "Now look down at my feet, place them shoulder width apart and facing my Opponent. I'm right handed so I hold my left out just a little farther, so I can block their punch with my left and set up my right for either an uppercut up under his rib cage or a direct jab into his face … But for right now I just want you to practice throwing your punches. Just like with a gun, speed will come in time with practice … So start with two straight punches followed by two upper cuts, then two over the top like this." Wapiti explained while he showed them how to throw each punch a couple times. "Okay. Jose, step to the line."

"Yes Sir!" Jose said, walking up to the mattress he started hitting it like Wapiti had shown him.

"Like this?" Jose asked, continuing to slowly hit the mattress a couple times.

"Step into your punches, bring your upper cut up with more power. Remember, a good upper cut up under the rib cage on a bigger man will not only taking their breath away, but also damaging their kidneys, so after three, four good upper cuts, he'll start bending over from the pain, which will bring his face and head down lower to your level."

"So then you can smash their faces into your knee, right Wapiti." Jose said, excitedly. Practicing throwing the punch in the air, then pretending he had a man's head in his hands, he slammed his head down into his rising knee.

"That's about the size of it." Wapiti said, with a big smile on his face. "Another thing you can practice on doing while I'm gone, is stand a little further back from the mattress like this. Stand on one foot, try to make a one eighty spin and kick the mattress mid-level to head high, like this." He said, spinning on his right foot, he brought his left foot around hitting the mattress mid level sending it swinging almost up into the tree. "That's why I need to add the other mattress."

Both Jose and Griselda took turns practicing how to spin around on one foot and kick the mattress. But they both kept tripping over their own two left feet and couldn't make it all the way around. "This is hard to do." Both were saying as they kept trying.

"I bet if you practice at least one hour a day you'll be able to make that kick before the Marshal gets back." Wapiti said smiling. Looking at his pocket watch, he could see it was almost three o-clock. For the first time in a long time, he was actually having a day off to relax and do something fun for a little while.

The three had been practicing for well over an hour when the waitress from lunch brought out a small pitcher of beer, an empty mug and two mugs full of root beer. "You all look like you could use something cold to drink." She said, putting everything down on the table and started pouring Wapiti a beer. "I'm Nichole Anderson, some of my friends call me Nicky." She said, handing him his beer.

Wapiti looked the five foot plus tall Young Lady over, he figured she weighed around one hundred fifteen, and it was all in the right places. Those big brown smiling eyes could make a man's mouth get all tongue tied and his brain go BBBLLLAAAAA, just trying to think of something to say to her like right now.

"UUUHHH, thank you, Nicky is it?" Wapiti asked

"Yes it is, I see you're teaching the kid's to fight … Maybe you could give me some private lessons later." Nicky said, with a big smile on her face and winking at him. "I better get back inside." She said, walking away.

Wapiti couldn't help but watch her walk away. Both Jose and Griselda would come over and get a quick drink, but would quickly return to practicing on spinning and kicking the mattress. "Why don't you take turns punching the mattress for a couple minutes at a time. Here's ten dollars, later, one of you go down to the Merc and get a stopwatch to time yourselves with."

"Okay Wapiti, but for right now could you time us with your pocket watch?" Jose asked, starting to punch the mattress.

Wapiti took out his pocket watch and looked at the second hand. "Stand in close, start with two straight jabs, then two upper cuts followed by two over the top" He kept explaining. "Move your feet so you brace yourself from falling backwards when you throw each punch. Slowly work your way around the mattress while you're throwing your punches. TIME! Okay Gris, it's your turn.

"Okay." Griselda said, walking over to the mattress and started hitting it the way Wapiti had shown them.

"That makes you tired fast." Jose said, breathing heavily and taking a drink of root beer.

"The more you practice the easier it will get." Wapiti said "The more you practice, add thirty seconds to each round till you're up to five minutes each round, then add more rounds." Wapiti said, with a smile on his face. "TIME GRIS."

Griselda came walking over breathing hard, picking up her root beer, she took a big drink. "This is fun."

Wapiti stood up and walked over to the mattress till he was a couple feet from it. "Stand like this, just a little sideways." He started explaining "Practice kicking up as high as you can without losing your balance on your planted foot. Then after the kick, plant your foot bringing your fist around in continuing around on the one eighty spin either bringing your outside fist into the mattress, or bring your inside elbow high into the mattress, throat height...Kick your first opponent and drive him back out of your way. Which gives you all the time you need to hit and deal with the second person. But after you elbow him or hit him with your fist, follow after him first. Don't worry about the other's yet...Follow after your one victim, reach out and grab his shirt with your left and start pulling him back towards yourself while you're throwing your right with everything you have into the man's nose. This will cause both his eyes to water up, and should also break his nose, setting up a second full punch into his face that if the first punk didn't knock him out, it will knock him down and out of your way...Or, instead of your second punch hitting him in the face again. Bring your second punch up into his stomach, that will take all the air out of him, bending him partly over while giving you time for at least two more face shots."

"Or drive his face into your knee, right?" Jose said, excitedly.

"That's right Jose." Wapiti said "So now come back over here and start practicing the kick and follow it with either a punch or elbow...Jose, you first."

"OKAY." Jose said, excitedly. Walking over to the mattress he practiced a couple slow kicks spinning punches, then told Wapiti to start timing him. "Make it a two and a half minute round." He said, starting his practice session.

"How long do we have to practice till we're as good as you Wapiti?" Griselda asked

"My Dad said he started training me as soon as I could walk. But if you keep practicing four, five days a week, an hour each time. You should be able to protect yourself in about six months. But here you don't have anyone throwing punch's back at you while you're practicing. So just remember to stand in tall and throw your punches like you've been training to do...You'll probably both hurt the next morning, but nine times out of ten that person won't try you a second time." Wapiti said, taking the last drink out of his mug. Then he emptied the pitcher into it, filling it up one last time. The three had been practicing all afternoon when Carmen came out telling them it was dinner time.

"Let's go." Wapiti said, picking up all three empty mugs and pitcher and headed over to the staircase and upstairs and inside. Where the room had a wonderful aroma from whatever it was Carmen had cooked for dinner. "What smells so wonderful?" Wapiti said, walking over to the table.

"Pork Roast, slowly baked in butter and garlic, baked potato, and corn on the cob. Carmen answered, dishing him up a plate full. "There's more corn keeping warm in a pot of hot water atop the stove."

Setting down, Wapiti pulled the plate closer to him. "Wapiti, would you like a beer for dinner?" Griselda asked

"No, but I would like a glass of cold tea please." Wapiti answered, cutting into the roast and took a bite. It was moist and tender and tasted excellent and he told Carmen so.

"Thank you, would you like some jalapeños?" Carmen asked

"What for, this isn't Mexican food." Wapiti said, putting butter into his baked potato.

"We eat jalapeños with everything." Jose said, taking a bite of roast then a bite off a grilled jalapeno pepper.

Cautiously, Wapiti picked up a grilled pepper, took a bite of pork followed by a medium size bite off the pepper and started chewing. The roast tasted good but the pepper was burning his mouth and he said so reaching for his tea and taking a big drink.

Everyone started laughing at him. "Just like the Marshal, you'll get used to it if you stick around," Carmen said.

"Mom, did you see Wapiti was teaching us how to fight?" Griselda said, with excitement on her voice and on her face. "He says, girls need to know how to protect themselves from boys and men who might want me to be their girlfriend, but I don't want to be his girlfriend. This way I can beat him up before he can beat me up."

"Yes I did, and he's right, so you both keep practicing what he's showing you." Carmen said, walking away.

It took them a good forty five minutes to eat dinner. Wapiti had had two big pieces of roast and three ears of corn. He was totally stuffed and said he felt like he had made a pig out of himself and eaten too much.

"You see the Marshal's five inches of the roast is still left over. So it looks like it's going to be pork roast sandwiches for lunch tomorrow." Carmen said, picking up the dirty dishes.

"Sounds good to me, that garlic and butter gives it a wonderful taste…I bet that would even work on a beef roast too. Wapiti said, taking the last drink of tea in the glass.

"She does beef roast this way too." Griselda said, helping to pick up the dirty dishes and taking them into the kitchen.

"Thank you for that wonderful dinner." Wapiti said, looking down at his pocket watch, it was just past seven-thirty. "I think I'm going to go get me some clean clothes, take me a bath and go to town for a couple cold beers tonight."

"You have clean clothes right over there." Carmen said pointing. "You're starting to act more like the Marshal … After a long huntin' trip, he goes down to the Saloon to relax and usually gets into a fight. He says a good fist fight between him and two, three other men at the same time. That's the best part of his relaxation time." Stating to chuckle. "But he usually has dried blood on his shirt's and has a fat lip or a black eye the next morning … But I haven't seen one drop of blood on the chest area of any of your shirt's, only on your sleeves from their flying blood and the right knee area on your pants leg."

Standing up, he listened to Carmen and he started chuckling. "He's right…! There is nothing like a good fight to help a person relax. But Yes … I have been hit more than once." Wapiti said, picking up clean clothes and two towels. "This will be the first time in a long time I get to sleep on a nice soft bed as opposed to sleeping on that hard ground." He said, walking towards the door. "See you in the morning."

"Good night Deputy." Carmen and the kids both said.

CHAPTER 2

Wapiti walked downstairs and took a quick extra long hot bath and got dressed. Taking out his pistol, he checked to make sure it was fully loaded, it was. So he put it back in his holster and tied his holster firmly down. Putting his knife and sheath in between his belt and holster on his left side. Walking over to the back door of the restaurant he yelled up the stairs that he was leaving. Unlocking and opening the door, he waited for someone to come down and relock it behind him. He was just about to yell out again, when Jose opened the door and came running down the stairs.

"I'll be glad when I'm old enough to go down to the Saloon's and relax the way you and the Marshal do." Jose said

"You'll be old enough before you know it." Wapiti said, smiling. "But Remember, the more you drink the stupider you get. Those that drink mostly whiskey are usually mean drunks. They think it makes them invisible, and they want to start a fight over just about ANYTHING, ANYONE will argue with them about."

"Who usually wins?" Jose asked

"The sober one." Wapiti answered "A couple beers can help relax you after a long, hard day and help you fall asleep faster. But too much and you'll spend the night Praying To God, hoping to stop throwing up." Starting to chuckle.

"I'll remember that." Jose said, closing and locking the door.

Wapiti walked out through the space that had the view of the Old Yeller Bank. Looking up at the sky, he could see the sun had already gone down behind the mountains and it was getting dark fast. Stepping up on the boardwalk he could see two men, one on each side of the street. They were taking the unlit lantern's down, refilling them, relighting them, and hanging them back up with an extension pole on a large hook about twelve feet off the ground on every street corner and one in the center of the block. Looking up and down the street while he walked towards Moser's Saloon he noticed at least a dozen horses tied up outside. Other than a couple other men riding their horse and one lone wagon the streets were empty. With it being in the middle of the week, most people were home sleeping for work tomorrow. It only took him a couple more minutes to walk the block and a half over to Moser's Saloon. Stopping at the door, he looked up the street and could see at least a dozen horses tied up outside Buxton's Saloon too. Walking inside he could see a half dozen men standing up at the bar talking amongst themselves. A couple men were talking with a couple Young Lady's that worked there. One table had three men playing poker with chips, one had five men playing with cash money. Wapiti took a second look at the gambler wearing a fancy suit and hat. He knew right off that he gambled for a living. Continuing towards the back where Dave usually set, Charley handed him a beer as soon as he sat down.

"How's the Marshal really?" both Dave and Charley asked

"He should be alright in a couple weeks." Wapiti said, taking a big, long drink off the mug, drinking almost half.

"How'd they get the drop on him?" Dave asked

"He said he thought he had the drop on them … Said he was hiding in the back dark corner of the Livery Stables waiting for them to step out in the open first. When they did, he went to step out, but still staying in the shadows. Said just as soon as he stepped out to tell them to freeze, his left foot went into a bucket, sending him stumbling to the floor. Said he was about half way down when they started shooting in his direction. Said he counted them firing seven shots at him as he felt the four burning places as the bullets went inside or thru his body. Said he had to play dead or he would be DEAD..! Wapiti was explaining.

"So you really outdrew those two Gunslingers?" Charley asked, with the same look of excitement on his face that Jose gets.

"Yes I did." Wapiti answered, taking another smaller drink.

"Why'd you only shoot them in the shoulder and let them live?" Dave asked

"Cause I knew I could out draw them." Wapiti said, still looking over at the fancy dressed gambler. "How longs he been in town?"

"He came in last week-end." Dave said, looking over at him. "No-one's accused him of cheating yet. So, he's either lucky, or real good. Because between here and Buxton's he's taken close to a thousand dollars off everyone around here."

"I can't believe people are still sitting down at any table that he's setting down at." Charley said

"I've seen him somewhere." Wapiti said, still looking at the man. "JOE DALTON..!" He yelled out.

Everyone in the place stopped and looked in his direction. "DEPUTY WAPITI, how the hell you doin?" the Gambler yelled back, laying his cards on the table and standing up.

"Charley, fill me up another mug please." Wapiti said, watching Joe straighten up the cash pile in front of him.

"HEY, where you going with all our money!" one of the men demandingly screamed out.

"It ain't your money anymore." Joe said, putting the thick stack of bill's in his inside jacket pocket. "I've been wondering when you and the Marshal would get back to town." He said, walking towards Wapiti.

"HOW YOU KNOW HIM?" both Dave and Charley asked, watching the gambler walk towards them.

"Met him in John Day during the poker tournament, you could say he took third place." Wapiti said with his hand extended, shaking Joe's hand. "Dave, Charley, I'd like you to meet Mr. Joe Dalton."

"I've been hearing and reading about all your fights in the newspaper." Joe said, shaking everyone's hand. "Is it true you took out three Professional Wrestler's at the same time?"

"He sure as the hell did." Dave yelled out. "I got to watch it from one of my upstairs windows…I don't think it took him much more than a minute to knock them all out cold."

"I had the pleasure of seeing him fight in John Day, then the first night in Pendleton at the Cavalry Fort where he took out six Trooper's in not much more time than that." Joe said, smiling. "Charley, how about you set us all up a double shot."

"Sure thing Mr. Dalton." Charley said, setting four double shot glasses on the bar and filled them up.

Wapiti grabbed the shot glasses and handed one to everyone. "Cheers To Your Health." Then everyone drank their shot down.

"How about another one." Joe said, asking Charley to fill them back up.

"None for me." Wapiti said, turning his shot glass upside down. "I'm not a big firewater drinker, I'll still toast with ya, but with my beer."

"So how do you know he took out six Trooper's in Pendleton?" Dave asked

"The Marshal forced me into being a part of his Posse taking the gold back to Sumpter." Joe said

"We heard someone stole the gold out of the Fort by blowing a hole through the thick log wall." Dave said

"That's what I heard too." Joe said, drinking his shot down. "I didn't stick around to find out, me and Colonel Love have an agreement that I don't play cards against any of his Trooper's again."

"Again, how many times have you had troubles with him?" Wapiti asked

"About four years, ever since he was CO in Baker City." Joe said, with a big smile on his face. "Most of those Troopers have never gambled before and are real easy to bluff."

"You ever run back into them Larkin Brother's again?" Wapiti asked, curiously

"YEAH, in August they have a town celebration, Miner's Jubilee, large fair, small rodeo…" Covering his mouth, he started chuckling. Looking around making sure no one was listening, he started speaking in a low voice…this is a long story, so don't interrupted me." Taking a quick drink. "You remember the initial gold robbery in Sumpter, Butch, Sundance Kid, and Kid Curry, who's alias, alias was Young, Jones, and Smith."

"YEAH, Curry was Smith." Wapiti said, curiously.

"Well, I met Mr. Brigham Young and Harvey Jones that weekend at a big bull riding blow-out that they and the Larkin Brother's came up with…five hundred dollar purse, you could enter as many times as you wanted, they had hundreds of rider's, some re-entered hoping on getting a scored ride, some hoping for a better score to make the last fifteen buck-out." Joe was excitedly explaining, stopping long enough to drink down a couple big gulps of beer, then he continued. "Like me they were staying at the fanciest place in town, the Baker City Grand, I think is its name." beginning to chuckle a little more. "Oregon Trust and Loan just built a new bank at the corner of Washington and Main Streets, they dug a hole under the last thirty or so feet of the bank and cemented it in with a steel ten by twelve feet wide double doors in the back that came up into the cement sidewalk, covering for the staircase underneath, also the steel doors lock inside ... Under Baker City there is a maze of underground opium tunnels that the Chinese people are still digging ... Anyway they had this big bull only bucking competition to get the town drunk, just like in Sumpter..." stopping to take a drink, but chuckling more so he spilt some on himself. "They bring the gold down from the Sumpter under Cavalry protection weekly, then once every month or so the gold is transferred by train to the Denver mint. Come Monday morning after the bucking competition the Cavalry arrives at the bank right after sunrise to load all the gold to be shipped out that morning ... Only, there wasn't as much gold as there was supposed to be ... they figured someone stole more than four freight wagon loads of gold, not to mention over another two hundred thousand in cash."

"We read about that robbery in the paper." Dave asked curiously. "What makes you think they were involved."

"Me and the Marshal talked about it too..." Wapiti said, starting to chuckle "Randy does shit just to prove it can be done, plus he always has a back door plan making it hard to prove they were anywhere near the robbery." Wapiti was explaining.

"I thought they thought the Chinese tunnel diggers stole it?" Charley asked

"Where would you put four freight wagon loads of gold ... That's a hell of a lot of gold!" Dave said

"Marshal figures Randy played Robin Hood with it, you know, that man over in Europe, he stole from the rich and gave it to the poor ... the Marshal said he wouldn't put it past Randy to give it all away to various houses around town. Think about it, are you going to report a bag of gold you found on your front porch … I think not." Wapiti quietly said.

"But why would he rob it, just to give it all away like that?" Charley asked

"Who knows why Randy does what he does, but their aunt Patty in Pendleton said he wanted to use an all bull bucking rodeo to pull off the Sumpter robbery. But his brother Larry has a mean ass roan, even bit of eighteen one hands tall. They bet ten men couldn't ride him for eight seconds." Wapiti was explaining, stopping to take a drink of beer. "I saw that horse launch both Randy and Colonel Love twenty feet or more into the air, plus a big black First Sergeant Randy Lacy. Then when they were done and Larry took the flank strap off, that big horse wasn't tired of bucking. Larry jumped over into the saddle and that roan hit the sky, sending him sky high… Well now, he got everyone to bet that he wouldn't throw him again. He no longer got his feet in the stir-ups and that horse hit the sky again, the Marshal blew the eight second whistle twice and was about to blow it a third time when that horse took off at a full run around that arena."

"So you still didn't answer why you think he, Randy Larkin and his brothers were involved?" Dave asked

"Someone had to give them the idea … What'd the newspaper say, over two hundred thousand in cash was missing too … That's what they kept and split between them, I'm sure there were some Chinamen involved somehow, who else dug that short tunnel down the outside wall of the bank but them … Randy was the brains behind it, I'll guarantee that." Wapiti said, taking a drink. "Think about it, that bucking competition was just a cover for the actual robbery." Wapiti said, with a big smile on his face, drinking down the last of his beer.

Wapiti, Dave, and Joe had been talking for a couple hours when two men started yelling about which one of them was going to take a certain Young Lady upstairs. Within a couple more minutes one man threw a punch at the other, and all hell broke loose. Everyone close by backed up out of their way. While the two continued to duke it out. Within a couple minutes they both had black eyes and bloody noses when Dave asked Wapiti to break it up.

Slowly Wapiti started walking towards the men and yelled at them to break it up, but they wouldn't. By the time Wapiti reached them, one man had the other in a headlock and was punching the man in the face with every chance he got.

"I Told You Men Enough Already." Wapiti said, grabbing the man on top by his free arm holding it in place, making the man stop and look up. Allowing the other man to get free, spinning around and punched the man in the face before he saw Wapiti, then he too stopped fighting.

"Dave thinks you've both have had too much to drink tonight and if you don't leave right now, he thinks I should arrest you both for Drunken Disorderly, UNDERSTAND!" Wapiti said, looking back and forth between both men.

"But I want to go upstairs with her." The second man said, pointing at a Young Lady leaning up against the bar.

"Sweetheart, I ain't going upstairs with either one of you bloody drunken fool's." the Lady chuckled out. Then everyone in the room started laughing at them too.

The two men looked at each other and slowly started walking towards the door. Wapiti watched the two men walk out the door, then he walked back over and picked up his beer.

Dave thanked him. "Least they didn't break up any furniture like you do, Deputy." Charley said, setting a new full mug of beer in front of him.

"Thanks Charley." Wapiti said, taking a drink off his beer. "How much longer you going to be in town for Joe?"

"I don't like staying much more than a week, week and a half in one town. So I figure on taking the Stage to Madras in a couple days. WHY, you going to run me out of town before then?" Joe asked, smiling and taking a big drink off his beer.

"NOPE, not unless you get caught cheating." Wapiti said, with a serious look on his face.

"I Don't Have To Cheat." Joe said, proudly. "I can tell what most people are holding by the way they look and act. It's easy to figure out who you can bluff and who's trying to bluff you."

"Good card players are good at that, reading people's faces and knowing what their cards are by their actions." Dave said "Me, I can't bluff for shit and I hardly ever get a winning hand, so I only play nickel, dime, quarter poker, that way I don't lose as much money."

"Believe it or not, I've walked away from a lot of nickel, dime, quarter poker games with over a hundred bucks plus by the end of the night." Joe said, smiling and taking a drink off his beer.

The three talked till them, Charley, and three Young Lady's were the only ones left in the Saloon. Dave looked up at the clock behind the bar, it was almost midnight. He hadn't been open this late in the middle of the week for a long time. "Wapiti, Joe, I hate to break up the re-union, but I need to close up and get home or my wife will be madder than hell at me."

"Alright." Wapiti said, as everyone shook hands one more time and the Lady's followed them towards the door. Asking both Joe and Wapiti if they wanted any company for the night, none of them would even charge Deputy Wapiti.

Joe started laughing and looking the Young Lady's over, grabbing ahold of the hand of a tall slender blonde. "Wapiti, I bet you're the only Redskin that any white woman would freely lay down with... How about you come with me, darlin'."

"Yes Sir." The Young Lady answered, leaning in close to him.

"How about it, Deputy, you want to come home with us tonight." A shorter blonde asked, smiling and moving her hip's back and forth.

"No thanks Lady's." Wapiti said, shaking Joe's hand one more time before he headed back up the boardwalk. Just as he cleared the back of the buildings he could see a light on inside the shack. He knew what that meant and it put a big smile on his face, because he was actually a little hungry.

Walking inside he saw the two inch thick extra large slice of banana cream pie on a plate setting next to the lantern. Picking it up, he quickly ate it down, and boy did it hit the spot. After he finished it, he laid down and quickly fell fast asleep before he knew it.

The next thing he could remember was someone slowly cracking the door open to the shack. Rolling over, he could see it was Griselda with a pot of coffee. "You awake yet Wapiti?" she asked, walking over and setting the hot plate and coffee pot down on the table.

"I am now." Wapiti said, setting up. "Thanks for the coffee Gris."

"You're welcome." Gris said, filling up and handing him a cup. "So, did you get into any fights last night?"

"NO, just got to break one up." Wapiti answered, taking a couple sips of coffee.

"The Marshal usually ends up being part of the fights he breaks up." Gris said, with a big smile on her face. "Mom's making huckleberry pancakes for breakfast or would you like something else?"

"That sounds real good, but could you ask her to add a couple orders of bacon too?" Wapiti asked

"Yes Sir Wapiti, I'll be right back." Gris said, walking back out the door.

Wapiti pulled his pants on, picked up the coffee pot and hot plate, he headed outside and set everything on the table. Slowly looking towards Old Yeller Bank, he could see a small lantern lit inside the first window. That was to let him know that the Banker was inside working already. Looking at his pocket watch he could see it was just passed eight-thirty.

He was refilling his coffee for a second time when Gris returned with his breakfast. Reaching into his pocket, he pulled out two silver dollars and gave them to her.

"Thank you Wapiti." Gris said, taking the money. "Is there anything else I can get you?"

"Not right now, but could you bring me another pot of coffee in about twenty minutes please?" Wapiti asked, pouring syrup over the top of his Huckleberry pancakes.

"Sure will." Gris said, walking away as Jose came running up.

"You going to be able to teach us more about fighting today Wapiti?" Jose asked, excitedly.

"I don't know, I'll have to wait and see what the Judge has planned for me to do." Wapiti said, taking a bite of pancakes and boy if those huckleberries didn't make them taste better.

"You don't have to see him till one, you could teach us till then." Jose said

"I need to clean my guns and get my duffle bag repacked with clean clothes in case I need to pull out real fast." Wapiti answered, taking a couple bites of bacon, then a drink of coffee.

"OOOH...ALRIGHT." Jose said, disappointedly. "Guess I'd better get my chores done so I don't get into trouble." He said walking away.

"If I'm still in town this afternoon I'll teach you some more." Wapiti yelled at him.

"Thanks Wapiti." Jose said, excitedly, taking off running.

Wapiti was just finishing up his breakfast when Gris returned with his fresh pot of coffee and hot plate and set them down on the table.

"The Marshal likes to eat his breakfast out here usually too." Gris said, picking up the dirty dishes. "When will he be back?"

"As soon as he's able to travel he'll come back home, figure two weeks most." Wapiti answered, dumping out his old coffee and refilling it with fresh, hot coffee.

"What will you do until then, I mean you can't go chasing after Bank Robber's and Rustler's alone, Can You?" Gris asked

"If I have to…I will." Wapiti answered, taking a drink of coffee.

"I hope you don't have to go out alone." Gris said, picking up all the dirty dishes, coffee pot, and hot plate and headed back to the restaurant.

Wapiti stood up and walked back inside the shack and got his cleaning kit and rifle, then went back outside, sat down at the table and started cleaning his guns.

Looking up, he could see Sheriff Shaver walking towards him. "How you doing Wapiti?" Twick asked.

"Just fine Twick, how about you?" Wapiti asked, pointing one hand towards the door. "Go on inside and get yourself a cup, Gris just brought this pot out."

"Alright." Twick said, walking into the shack, grabbed a cup and returned to a chair at the outside table. Filling his cup up, he looked over at Wapiti. "I seen the two bullet holes you put into those GunSlinger's … I come over here and practice all the time, but I don't think I could outdraw anyone yet, forget two." Twick said, with a serious look on his face.

"Got to admit it, the best practice I've got was from shooting at all the flying Pine Cones and Corn Biscuit's." Wapiti said, running the cleaning rod up and down the barrel of his pistol. "Having two or three different objects to shoot at all going in different directions at the same time has made me a much better shot."

"With as much time as you two spend on the road you must get in a lot of practice." Twick said, taking a drink of coffee.

"Not for the last four plus month's we haven't been able to, because we've been chasing Outlaw's and that gunshot can be heard from a long distance off." Wapiti said, changing the cloth patch on the cleaning rod and started running it down the barrel a couple times, then down through the bullet cylinders.

The two had only been talking about thirty minutes, when they could hear a kid's voice calling out for the Sheriff over and over again. Stopping, they both started looking towards Old Yeller Bank and could see the boy coming out of the Sheriff's office still yelling for the Sheriff.

Twick stood up, whistled at the boy, and started waving his hand in the air. The boy saw him, and started running towards them, still repeatedly calling out. "Sheriff, Deputy Wapiti, HELP, HELP, They Robbed My Dad's Bank Last night." The Boy kept repeating, till he reached them.

Wapiti caught the running Young Man by the arm spinning him around. "Now calmly and tell me what happened?"

"Three men came into our house just after dark last night. They took all of us over to the bank, put a pistol up against my head and told Dad that if he didn't open the safe he'd start by killing me, then everyone else one at a time before lastly killing him if he didn't get unlock it." The Boy was explaining

"Did he open up the vault?" Twick asked

"Yes he did, That's Why I Told You They Robbed The Bank!" the Boy demanded out, glaring at him. "HAVEN'T YOU BEEN LISTENING!"

"Which back did they rob?" Wapiti asked

"The Oregon Trust and Loan." The boy yelled out. "Come on, I can answer your question on the way back to the bank."

"Alright," Wapiti said, wiping the oil off his pistol then laying the rag on the table and started reloading it as they walked. "Where's the rest of your family?" He asked, putting the pistol back in his holster.

"Still tied up at the bank." The Boy answered "I got myself untied and Dad told me to come and get you instead of untying them."

"That was smart of him, now let's get to the Bank." Wapiti said, taking off at a medium run. With the rest of the town running to catch up to them to see for themselves what happened.

Wapiti stopped at the door and turned around to face the growing crowd of people, holding his hands above his head. "Now everyone shut up and listen up, I'm only going to say this once. I need time to look everything over before ANYONE can come into the Bank…If you do come in after I close these doors behind us, I'll have Sheriff Shaver arrest you for impeding an investigation. Just so you know, that carries a fifty dollar fine or five days in jail."

Then he turned and walked inside, closing the door behind himself. "Over Here." The Boy was yelling, holding the door open that went back behind the counter. "Hurry Up!"

Wapiti and Twick semi ran across the room, through the door and back to the stairs and down to the caged room with the vault and four people lying tied up on the floor with their hands and feet tied together behind their backs.

"Thank God You Finally Got Here." The Banker yelled out.

Pulling out his razor sharp knife, he quickly cut them free. "So how many were there?" Wapiti asked, looking around at the spilled gold on the floor.

"Three, they broke my back door down about ten o-clock last night. What time is it now?" the Banker asked, hugging his wife and other two children. The middle son who was about five, the elder seven, and the little, just over two, three most.

Wapiti could see the dried tear stains running down their cheeks on his wife and two younger children. Taking out his pocket watch he looked at it "It's almost ten-thirty, ya know for a bank that's supposed to be robbery proof, you've been robbed twice in just as many weeks."

"What Would You Have Done If They Were Playing Russian Roulette With One Of Your Children, he pulled the trigger twice on empty cylinders thank God!" the Banker yelled directly at Wapiti.

"I'd have done the very same thing and I wouldn't be able to unlock that vault fast enough either." Wapiti said with an understanding look on his face, looking around the room. He could see four of the bank satchels of gold were still stacked against the wall. Four had been cut open and all the gold loaded into something else to carry it in. "So how much did they get and how did they pack it out of here?"

"We had some major land sales this week, so counting our operating fund of twenty thousand and one hundred and five thousand in cash that was supposed to be shipped out on the next bank stagecoach tomorrow. That they stuffed into a couple duffle bags. Then they cut open those gold bags and filled their saddlebags up as full as they could them." The Banker said

"Did you recognize any of them?" Wapiti asked, looking back up the steps where he could see more gold dust and nugget's laying on some of them.

"NO, they kept their faces covered under a pair of Lady's black nylon stockings pulled down over their heads." The Banker said "But when we came from our house across the Alley to the Bank, I couldn't help but notice the brands on their horses." The Banker started explaining.

"How did you see their brands, there wasn't no moon last night?" Twick asked, looking around at all the spilt gold laying on the floor. He sure wished he could pick up a couple of the bigger nuggets, chuckling at the thought.

"I have a lantern that I light every night on a lamp post in the back of my yard, so it light's up the Alleyway and the back of the Bank as well. That way I can see if anyone is trying to break into the Bank from my back window. I purposely bought the house directly behind the bank." The Banker was explaining. "All three brands had an older rocking 'A' brands I'd say were probably their original brand when they were born, just below the rocking 'A' are two zeros, I'd say they were a good ten plus years old."

"What makes you think they were zeros and not O's? Wapiti asked

"O's are round, zeros have longer sides, so they look like this 0." The Banker said, drawing both in the gold dust laying on the floor. Their brands looked like this 00." He said, mixing the gold dust around and drawing the brand in the gold dust again.

"How do you know the age of the brands?" Wapiti asked

"I used to be a stock buyer, new brands are black. The longer they live the brand turns into a tan color. Then after about ten years, the hair around the brand will start growing over and covering the outer edges of the brand. Making it harder to see, but still very visible, like the rocking A brand was." The Banker explained

"I'd say whoever robbed you was waiting for me to bring that gold back. That way they would get more than twice as much money in one robbery." Wapiti said

"I'd say your right Deputy … Let's go over to the Courthouse and see who those brands belong to." Twick said, handing the Banker a gold nugget that was about half the size of his fist. "I just wanted to see how it would feel to hold a gold nugget this big. Felt pretty good." He said, chuckling

"Your right Sheriff." Wapiti said, looking over at the Banker and his family. "You folk's going to be Okay?"

"Yes," the Banker said, with one arm around his wife and holding his young daughter in the other. "I noticed that on two of their pistol grips, they had at least a dozen or more notches on them."

"Thanks for the info … Don't let the info on their brands get out, I don't want no wide posse following me" Wapiti said, walking back up the steps and out the front door. Where hundreds of people had gathered in the street waiting to hear what had happened. They all started shouting out questions like who, when, and how much money did they get.

CHAPTER 3

"Wapiti just started pushing his way through the crowd. "The Banker can explain it to you better than me, so get the hell out of my way!" He demanded pushing two men backwards into the people behind them, sending a couple stumbling over to the ground. So those close to them quickly started backing away from him, kinda cursing him out by saying, 'He's starting to act more like the Marshal, with his pushing his way through a crowd instead of waiting on them to move.' as they quickly gave them more room than needed, as the Banker and his family came walking out the front door and everyone turned their attention to them. Wapiti was walking to the Courthouse as fast as he could. He could see Gordy was changing a wheel on a freight wagon when he came walking up to him.

"So did that robbery proof bank got robbed again, did it?" Gordy asked, looking over at Wapiti.

"YEEEAAAHHH It did!" Wapiti said, disgustedly. I'm going over to the Courthouse and look at the brand register.

"Jose already came by to tell me to get your horse ready, so I did. I'm just waiting on Rodger to bring a few more supplies over. I should have you loaded up and ready to go, long before you're ready to ride Deputy." Gordy said. Tightening down on the wrench and nut as hard as he could.

"Thanks Gordy." Wapiti said, continuing down the street towards the Courthouse, with Twick right beside him.

"What are you doing in here instead of out there chasing after those Bank Robber's?" Judge Monson asked,

"The only thing I have to go on is a brand, so I'm going to the registry and look it up." Wapiti said, continuing down the hallway till he came to the State Registry Office. Walking in, Wapiti looked at the man sitting behind the counter. "Get me the State Brand Registry, and I mean right now!"

"It's right over here Deputy, just a minute." The Man said, walking over to a cabinet, he pulled a drawer open and took the book out, then started to turn back around to Wapiti, but he was taking the book away from him and laid it out on the desk.

"Each page cover's one year, you can see the first page is 1850, this year's is the very last page." The Man was explaining, watching Wapiti turn it to the last page to the year 1892. "As you can see each page has forty lines, But we usually only get a dozen new brand's most a year. He started explaining.

Wapiti was going backwards in the book, running his finger down the line that showed what their brand would look like, wishing the man would shut up. He had gone back eight years when he found the double 00 brand. Starting back at the name, he could see the owner was Carl Marcs of McKinney Butte Road.

"Where's there a state map?" Wapiti asked looking around.

"Over there on the back wall." The office man said, pointing.

"Anyone have any clue as to where McKinney Butte Road is?" Wapiti asked, walking towards the map.

"Just west of Sisters." Twick said, running his finger across the map till he came to where the road split off the main road. "Just a couple miles northwest of Sisters here."

Wapiti took out his pocket watch, it was twenty after eleven. "If I get out of here within a half hour, I can make Sisters before nightfall."

"Wapiti, I've got a bad feeling about these men … I don't want you taken any chances out there alone. I know I said it was up to a Judge to Judge a man with the death sentence. But if they draw on you…You shoot to kill, UNDERSTOOD YOUNGMAN!" Judge Monson said, with his hand on his shoulder and a serious look on his face. "I'd hate to hear you shot to wound and they shot to kill. Don't give them a second chase son."

"Yes Sir, Your Honor." Wapiti said, turning and walking towards the door.

"You want me to ride with you?" Twick asked, following him back down the hallway.

"No Twick, I'll be just fine." Wapiti said, walking outside, then over to the Livery.

Gordy was just finishing loading up the pack horse when he walked in. "I'm just finishing up, Deputy."

"I won't be needing the pack horse for this trip, just give me my ammo bag and the grub bag with corn biscuits and jerky, that's all I'll need for this trip." Wapiti said, taking the reins to the Medicine Hat. It sure was nice to have him back, he could push him faster, longer than most horses. Leading the horse outside, he first put the grub bag string around his saddlehorn, then the ammo bag, followed by his water bag before climbing aboard. Then headed out of town at a fast trot going around wagons and narrowly missing a couple pedestrians crossing the street.

Wapiti kept the Medicine Hat at a fast trot up the hill going west out of Prineville. Just like every other time there were all kinds of people on the road. Freight wagons, wagons, carriages, and even people packing everything they owned on their backs going in both directions. All hoping for a better life in another town.

It took just over an hour and Wapiti was pulling into the Livery Stables in Powell Butte to water his horse. The Blacksmith came out to see where he was going and who was he chasing after without the Marshal?

Wapiti took his water bag off and started dumping it out. "Three men robbed the Oregon Trust and Loan bank last night."

"I thought that Bank was built to be robbery proof. Doesn't this make the second time that Bank has been robbed now, and they haven't even been open for a month yet." The Blacksmith said, handing Wapiti a pint bottle.

"No thanks, but I wish you had a cold beer, it's hot out here today." Wapiti said, starting to pump the handle on the pump.

The Blacksmith looked over and saw two boy's playing marble in front of the Merc. "One of you boy's run inside and get Deputy Wapiti two beers and make it quick."

"Yes Sir." Both boy's answered. Jumping up and running inside and quickly returned with two bottles. But they hadn't told the owner who they were for, so he thought they were stealing them, so he came running out right behind them. "You boys get back here or I'll tell your parents." He was yelling out watching them run up to Wapiti and gave them to him.

"Deputy Wapiti wanted a beer Sir." One of the boy's yelled back at the store owner.

"I'm sorry Deputy, I thought they were stealing from me." The Merc owner said "Who you going after by yourself?

"Three men robbed the Oregon Trust and Loan again." The Blacksmith said

"So who were the robber's?" the Merc owner asked

"According to the brands on their horses, it was someone from the Carl Marcs Ranch, which is up McKinney Butte road on the other side of Sisters." Wapiti said, taking a long drink off a beer. Reaching into his pocket, he pulled out a one dollar bill and handed it to the Merc owner. "This should cover the cost of the two beers. Then he reached into his pocket and pulled out all his change, which wasn't much. a three quarters and dimes, two nickels and a couple three pennies. "Here, you boys split this for running for me." He said, dumping it in the closest boys hand.

This made both boys get excited, cause now they would have money for candy and a sarsbirilla.

"Did you say Carl Marcs, him and his two boys have been under investigation a couple times for suspicion of robbing a couple Big Bank Job's. All over fifty thousand dollars or more per robbery, that way they don't have to rob anything else for a couple years." The Blacksmith said "They're also known for leaving no living witnesses."

"I've heard they've killed over thirty people in their robbery's." the Merc owner said.

"I've personally have saw him and his oldest son Sam kill over a dozen men between them over the last ten years in gun duels." The Blacksmith said "You go up against them, Don't Even think about giving them a second chance Deputy. They're fast and deadly"

"Thanks for the info." Wapiti said

"I don't charge the Marshal for a pint of whiskey, so I damn sure ain't going to charge you for a couple beers." The Merc owner said, holding his hands up and taking a couple steps backward.

"I much appreciate it." Wapiti said, handing the dollar bill down to the closest boy. If either of you are around when I come riding into town in the future, I'll give you a dollar tip for running and getting me a cold beer. Provided it's in the afternoon or later." He said, tightening his cinch strap. Then he drank down the last of the first bottle of beer and handed it to one of the boy's so he could get the two cent deposit back on it.

Climbing up in the saddle, he 'thanked' everyone for their help and information, then he kicked the big Medicine Hat in the side and took off towards Redmond at a fast trot. Riding past a sign that read Redmond 8 miles, Sisters 29 miles, taking out his pocket watch, it was just past one. At a medium trot, he should be able to cover the eight mile in an hour. Twenty nine divided by eight is three hours and five miles…so call it four hours. Add three more that he'd have to walk and allow his horse to rest, that's six hours. So I should get in around dinner time. Wapiti was thinking to himself as he rode up to the outskirts of Redmond. Slowing his horse down to a fast walk he continued down Main Street towards the Livery Stables looking at every brand he rode by for that 00 brand all the way to the Livery, not seefinding it.

He figured they had probably spent the night in a nice hotel room here last night. If they were smart, they would have already rented the room earlier so they wouldn't have to wake anyone up to get a key to a room when they got in late last night, or actually, early this morning. Depending on how far their ranch is from Sisters, they just might want to spend one last night relaxing playing poker and with the Lady's before returning to their ranch and hiding all that gold and cash in a stash somewhere on their ranch. But nowhere near their house and barn yard. They'd know that if they were suspected every square foot of their house and barn yard would be searched. Wapiti was thinking to himself as his horse finished drinking.

Then he turned and headed back up the street toward Sisters. He could see everyone was stopping and watching him ride by. The news had come across the tele-graph line about the robbery of that new supposed robbery proof bank. Everyone was wondering who he was looking for, and even more importantly, could he bring them in alive, the Marshal wasn't with him this time.

It only took him twenty minutes and he was heading out of town at a medium trot. His mind started thinking about the Outlaw's again. They already had a good hiding spot to hide everything so they could slowly spend it. Their Brand's had been seen by many witnesses on the streets, but no-one has ever found any money proving they had anything to do with the job. Or, any horse with both brands to prove they did it. The only horses they could find were the ones with the double OTT brand. They raised and sold horses, so their brands were all over the countryside by now.

But if they don't think anyone is on their trail yet, they'll definitely want one last night to relax with a couple Lady's. The Blacksmith in Powell Butte said if it was Carl Marcs and his two sons, they were known for leaving no living witnesses. They had killed over thirty innocent people in their robbery's in the past. So No-one could identify their faces and no-one ever found any money. Why did they leave this Banker and his family alive? Could it be that they did have some heart and couldn't kill children. Had that been the difference as to why they didn't kill anyone this time.

There wasn't as much traffic on this road like there was between Prineville and Redmond. Sisters wasn't as big a town and it set at the beginning of the vast wilderness stretching out to all the surrounding volcanoes off in the far distance where very few people lived or even ventured into. So there wasn't as much traffic going either way. What there was for the most part were empty freight wagons coming out and loaded freight wagons going in. He was just passing Cline Falls trail head when he could see the eastbound stagecoach and all its dust coming at him. Slowing his horse to a walk, he waited for the Stage to catch up to him. Turning his horse around backwards just before it passed him, he waited a good minute for the dust to settle down before heading back down the road at a medium trot towards Sisters. He started thinking about the three Outlaw's he was going after again. They were known killer's and proud of it, that's the only reason why a man carved a notch on his pistol grip. It was a way of bragging on how many people he'd killed. But how many of those had been face-to-face and how many had been in the back. What would he do when he came face-to-face with them himself? Could he outdraw three men before one of them shot him? One thing for sure, he would not be giving these men a second chance. How would he even know if they were in town, they'd probably stable their horses at the Livery. So he'd start looking for their horses there first. If they were spending the night in Sisters, Tom Chandler would know, he'd also know which Hotel, Saloon, or Brothel they'd be staying at.

As it got later in the day the shadow's from all the tall Pine and Fir trees shadows covered the road making it cooler outside. He was just about ready to put his jacket on when he came to the outskirts of Sisters. Slowing his horse to a walk, he started looking at all the brands on all the horses tied up in front of all the businesses he rode by. Concentrating on the Merc and Saloon's, but no double zero brands. Riding up to the Livery he took out his pocket watch, it was just past seven-thirty, he'd made good time. Dismounting, he led the horse inside and called out for Tom.

"Back here." He heard him yell out. So he continued towards the back still looking for the double zero brand till he found an empty stall to put his horse in for the night. Seeing Tom shodding a horse next to the empty stall, he led his horse in and tied him up.

"Good to see you Deputy, what are you doing here?" Tom asked

"Looking for some Bank Robber's." Wapiti said, taking his bridle off. So he could more easily eat the grain in the grain box and the hay in the hay bin.

"I heard that robbery proof bank got robbed again." Tom said, dropping the horse's hoof and stood up. "What brings you this way?"

"Their horses have two on brand them." Wapiti said, taking his saddle off. "One is double zero, the other is an 'A' with a rocker bar under it. The double OTT, or zeros brand belongs to Carl Marcs that lives around here."

"He does, him and his two boys … and they're in town tonight." Tom said, looking out the two front double doors.

"I looked at most of the brands on the streets and in here and I haven't seen those brands." Wapiti said, looking over at Tom.

"You won't either." Tom said, "When they ride the three with the rocking A brand on them, they always tie them up outback of Ole Lady Johnson's place behind her lilac hedges about three-quarters of a block down the street." He said, pointing towards them.

"Why they tie them up there and not inside the Livery?" Wapiti asked, walking towards the back door.

"I don't know, they do it at least once a year." Tom said, following Wapiti outside. "See, they're tied up over there out of sight from anyone in town."

"Don't make sense to hide their horses when everyone will see them in town tonight." Wapiti said, looking back and forth between Tom and the horses.

"They're not riding their usual horses." Tom started explaining, taking out his pint of whiskey, taking a pull he offered it to Wapiti.

"No thanks, I'll wait for a cold beer … What do you mean they're not riding their normal horses?" Wapiti asked

"When Carl came into town eight, ten years ago. He bought himself two stallions and one gilding, all half-brothers. Then he went out and rounded up over thirty nice looking Mustang mares to breed them to. Ever since his first born colts were two and a half years old and older, they ride them into town so people could see what their stock looked like. They usually keep those three hidden out on the ranch out of sight." Tom said "But every time they ride those three, they tie 'em up out back there."

"I think I know why they hide them out now. Wapiti said, looking back at them. even from here he could see they were very nice looking horses, the one on this end was well over seventeen hands, two most, and the backs of the other two appeared to be the same within aa inch. " What do they look like?" Wapiti asked, walking back inside.

"Average, little over six feet, Carl goes a good two hundred. Both the boy's, Sam and Chip, go a good one eighty, Sam ninety pounds. They usually don't wear their pistols, but they are today." Tom said

"Any idea as to where they are?" Wapiti asked, walking back towards the front double doors.

"They're over at the Broken Ranch Saloon, Brothel, and Café." Tom said nodding across the street towards the business next to the Hotel he and the Marshal usually stayed at when they're in town, he'd stay there again tonight.

Wapiti looked at his pocket watch, it was almost eight. "They have good food?"

"YEAH, they do, but that place gets wild some nights." Tom said, with a real serious look on his face. "Whiskey, Women, and Poker don't mix. There's a fight in that place just about every night."

"Sounds like my kind of place." Wapiti said, with a big smile on his face. "Take care of my horse please." He said, walking out the door. First he walked over to the Hotel for a room for the night. Walking in the front door, the owner came running in from the Café side asking him how could help him.

"I need a room for the night." Wapiti said, signing his name and badge number on the registry book.

"Yes Sir Deputy, how about room three at the top of the stairs." The Owner said, anxiously and nervously handing him his room key. "Is there anything else I can do for you?"

Wapiti looked around the empty room. "I want you, and I mean only you to bring me a pot of coffee at five A.M. Don't tell anyone you're doing it, understand!" Wapiti said in a loud whisper and a stern look on his face, taking his key and putting it in his pocket.

"Yes Sir Deputy, I'll set my windup alarm clock. Do you need cream and sugar?" the Owner nervously asked.

"No Sir, Just black…Thank you." Wapiti said. Walking out the door and over to the front door of the Broken Ranch Saloon.

Everyone stopped what they were doing and started staring at him. He just took a quick look around the room, seeing three tables with men and women sitting at them and three men and one Lady's at the bar. He walked over to a table just inside Café side where he could see four people eating. Setting down at a table so he could look back in the Saloon side.

Before he got set down, the waitress was handing him a menu and filling his water glass. "Dinner special is Salisbury steak Deputy."

"That sounds good to me." Wapiti said, taking a drink of water. "Can I get a beer to drink please?"

"Yes Sir Deputy, I'll be right back with both." The Waitress said, walking away.

Wapiti started looking the Saloon side over, he could see one table that had three Cowboy's casually playing poker with chips that probably weren't really worth anything cause they only had enough money to buy their drinks with. He could only see half of the next table and they too were playing with chips, but high dollar chips. Five dollar, ten dollar, and twenty-five dollar chips. One man at the table had a Young Lady sitting on his lap, telling him he'd been playing poker long enough, now it was time for him to play with her.

Wapiti was chuckling about that, when the waitress set his food and beer down in front of him. "Is there anything else I can get you, Deputy?" She asked

"Not right now, but I'll probably need another beer shortly." Wapiti said, with a big smile on his face, picking up his knife and fork.

"Yes Sir Deputy, I'll keep an eye on your mug level and make sure it never gets less than a quarter left and I'll bring you a fresh beer." The Waitress said, with a big smile on her face.

Wapiti thanked her and briefly watched her walk away before looking back into the bar area. He couldn't see much of the bar area or the other table of people on that side. But he sure could hear them talking. He couldn't make out exactly what anyone person was saying, but he could tell someone was partying on that side of the bar.

Wapiti slowly ate his dinner and enjoyed two beers, when the waitress returned with a third beer and asked him if he needed anything else.

"Just my bill please." Wapiti said, looking down at his near empty plate. "On second thought, here's twenty dollars, take a big slice of banana cream pie over to the Hotel and tell the owner to put it in my room. Keep five dollars for your tip and leave the rest with the pie, Please."

"Yes Sir Deputy, there's enough money here to get you two slices and still have money left over." The Waitress said, taking the money.

"Sounds good to me." Wapiti said, wiping his mouth off with his napkin and standing up.

"Be careful in there Deputy, There's a couple back shooter in there tonight." The Waitress said, with a serious look on her face and in her eyes.

"Thanks for the warning." Wapiti said, stretching out this way and that with his back, then rolled his shoulders and stretched his arms out, before placing his right hand on his pistol, using his thumb, he flipped the tie down loop of leather off the hammer, then walked around the half wall into the bar side. He could see two more tables. One was empty and one had three men that fit his description to a T, they were playing poker with cash money.

Everyone stopped what they were doing and started watching Wapiti walked into the saloon side. Walking halfway down the bar before he walked in and ordered a fresh beer please.

"Yes Sir Deputy." The Bartender said nervously. He'd read many stories in the newspaper about men that didn't want to allow him to have a beer. THREE had been Professional Wrestler's all at the same time. "What are you doing in our neck of the woods Deputy?" the Bartender asked, filling a new mug and handing it to Wapiti.

"OH, the Judge has me out looking for Cattle Rustlers." Wapiti said leaning up against the bar, facing the tables and speaking loud enough for those close by could hear. "I don't know how he expects me to try and bring in the Rustler's and the cattle at the same damn time, when I'm all alone."

"I'd just leave the cattle." The oldest son of the three men he was checking out said.

"What, just let them run wild, what will their owners say?" Wapiti asked

"Piss on them, just wire the Circuit Court in Prineville with their last known location, and let the owner come and get them back himself." The father said, discarding two cards. "You play poker Deputy?"

"NOPE, that's a game I've never played." Wapiti proudly said.

"Grab that empty chair and sit down." The Father said, pointing over at the chair.

"No thanks, I don't make very much money to wear this badge. So I'll keep what I have on me. "Wapiti said, smiling at them.

"One of you Young Lady's go get Chief Wapiti a tray of chips to play with." The father said, looking at the two Lady's sitting on the laps of each of his son's.

"Here Deputy." The Bartender said, handing him a tray that had two full rows of each color.

"Thanks." Wapiti said, picking them and his beer up, he walked over to the table and sat down. "So how are we going to do this?"

"Call your white's five, your red ten, and your blacks twenty dollars." The father said, shuffling a new hand of cards. Then telling him that every hand starts out with everyone putting five dollars in the middle, which everyone did, only theirs was cash money.

"This game is called five card draw." Carl said, dealing the cards. "First you bet what you have in first five cards. Then you can discard up to four cards and get four new cards. Then we all bet one more time and someone raises if they want. Then we all show our cards and see who really wins."

"OOOKAY," Wapiti said, slowly starting to pick up his cards. "So what happens with the cash I win during our game tonight, do I have to give it back." He asked, looking at three aces, and a king and queen.

"Hell Yes Chief, we'll let you keep whatever you win." The eldest son said. "By the way, I'm Sam, that's Chip, and Dad's name is Carl." He said, as they all started shaking hands.

"Obviously you all already know my name." Wapiti said, shaking their hands.

"Hope to shout, your fist's and feet are legendary." Carl said, looking at his cards and betting twenty dollars.

"That's one of these black chips right?" Wapiti said, tossing it in the middle.

"Yes it is." Sam said, putting a twenty dollar bill on the table, he discarded two cards.

Wapiti kept the three aces and the higher king and discarded one.

"Looks like Deputy Wapiti is trying to catch a straight." Chip said, discarding three cards.

"I don't know what I have." Wapiti said, picking up his card, seeing it too was a king.

Carl raised twenty on his new hand and Chip bumped it up twenty. "That's forty dollars to you, Deputy." Chip said

Wapiti threw in his two black chips. "Now what do we do?"

"Lay your cards down and see what everyone's holding." Carl said, laying his cards down. Showing two pair's, six's and Jack's.

"I just have this." Wapiti said, laying his cards down, revealing his Ace's over King's full house.

"Holly Shit, looks like Wapiti win's this hand." Sam said, pushing the pile towards him, then picking up the cards, he started shuffling the deck.

Wapiti restacked his chips and stacked his cash up. "Do I have to replay the cash or can I keep it and keep playing with my chips?" He asked, with a big smile on his face.

"You have to play all your cash money before you can use any more chips." Carl said, filling a shot glass and handing it to Wapiti.

"No Thanks, Carl." Wapiti said, holding his hand up. "I don't drink firewater, only a couple beers."

"OOOH, Come OOON." All three said, egging him on. "Winner of every hand has to have a shot of whiskey." They all continued saying.

"No Thanks, I'll just take a big drink off my beer." Wapiti said, taking a big drink off his beer.

"So you ever kill anyone Deputy?" Sam asked, smiling with a darkness in his eyes.

"No Sir I haven't, have you?" Wapiti asked

"YEP, Twelve!" Sam answered, pulling his pistol out and showing Wapiti the six notches on each side of the hand grips. Dad has seventeen on his … Chip can't hit the broad side of a barn with his pistol, he doesn't have any notches."

"But I can shoot the head off a grouse or sage hen at a hundred yards." Chip proudly spoke up. "You can't do that, if I put a notch in my rifle stock for every animal I've shot and killed, there wouldn't be any room left to put any more notches and you know it."

"You're both right Chip." Carl said "He's brought more game back for eaten than the both of us combined and you know it."

"What is the one thing you feel gives you your best advantage over the other men you've drawn against?" Wapiti asked, picking up a new hand of cards.

"Men that have never been in a duel yet will always hesitate for a fraction of a second their first time. By then, my pistol is already halfway out of my holster and their dead within the next two seconds." Carl said, betting ten dollars and discarding one card.

"That's what the Marshal told me too." Wapiti said, looking at a king high straight from three different suits in his hand, raising twenty dollars.

"We were in town a couple weeks ago when you took four Cowboy's on in a fist fight … But fighting with a gun is a whole lot different than with your fists." Carl said, putting his money in the pill in the middle of the table. "Not only had you better not hesitate, but your first shot better be true, you may not get a second shot."

"What about one man up against two or more, which one do you shoot at first?" Wapiti asked, laying his hand of cards down and dragging the pile of cash back towards himself. Taking a second look he figured he had close to five hundred dollars in front of himself. Too bad he couldn't get out while he was up like this. Oh Well, he was having fun and enjoying himself with these men. Sure, he knew he'd have to face them face-to-face tomorrow morning before they pulled out with all the gold and money on them. He couldn't let them think he was really looking for them and not Cattle Rustlers.

"Why's the Judge got you out chasing Rustler's when someone just robbed that new bank in Prineville yesterday?" Carl asked

"Don't have the slightest idea who they were." Wapiti said, with a serious look on his face, discarding four cards, and picking up four more, three of which were Queen's to go with the one he kept, giving him four of a kind.

"Didn't anyone get a look at them or their horses?" Sam asked, picking up his new cards.

"No, they had their faces covered with Lady's nylon stockings, and the banker has his mind concentrating on one of them holding a pistol to his eldest boy's head." Wapiti said, raising twenty dollars.

"Looks like Wapiti is catching on real quick on how to play this game." Sam said, putting the twenty in the pot and looking at all the cash in front of him.

"Beginner's luck." Carl said, laying a small mixed straight. "Beat that Deputy."

"I don't know if I can." Wapiti answered, laying his cards on the table, revealing his four queens.

"That beat's ya Pa." Sam loudly chuckled out.

The four had been playing for a couple hours and Wapiti was having fun. On top of that he had a large stack of cash in front of himself. Both the Young Lady's that were sitting on Sam and Chip's laps were saying they were tired of waiting on them to go upstairs with them. Telling them if they didn't go soon, they'd be sleeping alone cause they were ready for bed.

They all played one more hand which Wapiti won with a straight spade flush from six thru Jack. Looking down at the pile of money he knew he had close to a thousand dollars in front of himself.

Standing up he looked at the stack of money on the table, he knew he couldn't keep it. But how would he explain having all this extra cash, picking up the multiple stacks, he tossed it back to Carl. "Thanks for teaching me how to play, but if I show up with that much cash on myself, they'll think I took a bribe off the Cattle Rustler's I'm supposed to be looking for." Wapiti said, shaking everyone's hands and heading out the door back over to his Hotel room and some much needed sleep.

Unlocking his door, he could see there was a lantern on inside. Reaching for his pistol, he slowly walked in to see the Waitress sitting in a chair with a big smile on her face.

"I was wondering when you were going to get back." She said "I'm Karen, would you like some company for the night Deputy?" she asked with a big beautiful smile on her face.

"SORRY, but no thanks." Wapiti said, picking up the piece of pie.

"I'll help you relax faster and you can forget about your troubles for a couple hours." Karen said, starting to take her blouse off.

Wapiti set the pie down on the table, putting both hands on to the Young Lady's arm's stopping her. "I'm truly thankful Darlin', I'm just not that kind of man." Leading her towards the door. "It's not you, you are a very beautiful and sexy Young Lady. But my people feel that should only happen when two people are in love. Not just for enjoyment, but trust me, I'm sure it would be very enjoyable." She kept saying, all the way over to the door.

Wapiti's face was sweating from the heat this Young Lady was bringing alive inside himself. But he knew it was right, so he closed the door behind her, finished his pie and laid down to sleep.

CHAPTER 4

Before he knew it, the owner was in his room waking him up and handing him a cup of coffee. "Deputy Wapiti, here's your five A.M. wake-up call…Would you like the Mrs's to cook you something for breakfast?"

"Two, two hard eggs, sausage patty, a couple slices of bacon, those she can cut in half so they cover the entire sandwich, then slice of American cheese on toasted bread and butter only, NO mayonnaise on them." Wapiti said, taking the coffee and taking a sip.

"They'll be ready in five minutes, your coffee and hot plate are right there on the table." The Owner said, pointing and walking back towards the door. "I'll see you down stairs when you come down, Deputy." He said, closing the door behind himself.

Wapiti sat on the edge of the bed and slowly drank his first cup of coffee, thinking about where his best play be from? Standing up, he walked over to the table, refilled his cup of coffee and looked out the window to the street down below. With the street lantern's still burning, he could see all the street and the businesses on both sides of the street. The front of the Livery faced directly at the street just a half block further down from here. He could stay in there out of sight in the shadows till they all get out into the middle of the street. What would he do if someone got stuck in between them and I have to come out of hiding or they might get too close and see me waiting for them. An innocent person might get hit by a flying bullet that missed its target. He was starting to understand why the Marshal always had a couple shots of whiskey while he was playing out every different situation that might arise. Still looking out the window down at the street, Wapiti slowly got dress. Filling his coffee back up, he took a big drink then put his holster belt on and tied the holster down extra tight. Taking his pistol out, he looked it over, making sure it was fully loaded, it was. Putting it back in his holster, he picked up the rest of his gear, took one last drink of coffee and walked out the door and down the stairs. As soon as he got to the bottom he could smell the food cooking. Walking over to the Café he stuck his head inside the door. "Alright if I come in?"

"Sure Deputy, here's your breakfast in this paper bag, your sandwiches are wrapped inside wax paper so they won't dry out too fast on you." The Lady cook said "Here, let me get you another cup of coffee, we don't open until six, but we were more than happy to get up early to help you out Deputy."

"Who you chasing and where do you have to go to catch up to them at?" the Owner asked

Wapiti knew he couldn't tell them the truth, if they told ANYONE, even by mistake, an innocent person might get shot. "The Rustler's started out around Bend about a week ago and have been stealing cattle as they work their way north. I figure their only two days ahead of me at the most with them herding those slow cattle. Then trying to steal a few more as they work their way back north staying well off the beaten path." Wapiti said, taking a bite of one of the sandwiches.

"Why didn't you angle north coming out of Redmond?" the Owner asked

"Truthfully, I think they live around here and plan on bring-ing the herd back here to run up on the mountain somewhere for a couple years." Wapiti said "There's a hell of a lot of land out there for them to hide a few hundred head for a couple years. By then the majority of the brands are yours and the old brands have been removed from the rustled list."

Taking out his pocket watch he looked at it, it was just after five-thirty. "Well, I need to get going." Wapiti said, walking towards the door and outside. It was still dark out, if it wasn't for the street lamps being lit up, he wouldn't be able to see very far. Looking back over to the Broken Ranch Saloon, he saw a lamp come on in one of the room's.

Wapiti continued on into the Livery, lighting a lantern, he lit the paper and kindling already inside pot belly stove to cook a pot of coffee. After the fire was burning, he took the empty pot out to the pump to fill it up. Seeing the light on out of the corner of his eye, he was acting like he wasn't paying it any attention. Filling the pot up, he returned and filled it with coffee grounds, then put it back on the stove to cook, before opening the door up and adding a couple bigger pieces of wood. He needed Carl Marcs or one of his son's see him ride out of town first. So he knew he needed to take his time.

It only took him five minutes to saddle up and load all his gear on his horse. Leading him over to the door, he filled up one last cup of coffee standing in the doorway so he was easily visible for all to see. Glancing around, he could see a second room light up. It was also lighting up fast outside, the sun wasn't up over the mountains yet, but you could clearly see up and down the streets with ease.

Finishing his last cup of coffee, he put the cup back in the office then returned to his horse, climbed aboard then headed down the road at a slow trot going northwest. He also noticed that Carl was standing in the first lighted window when he rode out of town.

That was perfect, they needed to think I was long gone and didn't have a clue to the fact that they were the actual Bank Robberys he'd told them they didn't have a clue as to WHO robbed the Bank.

In no time at all he was well outside the town so he started working his way back out around Sisters. Making sure he was staying well out of sight of any houses. It actually only took him twenty minutes to work his way around town and be only a couple hundred feet from the back of the Livery. Dismounting, he put some hobbles around his horses front feet so he wouldn't wander off to fare.

Slowly working his way towards the Livery, he could see all three of their horses still tied up behind the hedges without their saddles on yet. That made Wapiti happy. Quickly and quietly he ran the last forty feet to the Livery Stables back door. Slowly opening it up, he looked around making sure nobody was inside, there wasn't anyone so walked inside.

Right off he could smell the coffee, he had only left the far side door open when he left. So he quickly crossed over to the other side of the Livery, staying hidden in the shadows. Reaching the other side and being behind the large closed door, he walked over to and inside the office. Filling himself a cup of coffee, staying way back he started looking out the office window towards the Saloon. The Saloon's Café didn't open till noon, but he could see people inside the Café eating. Looking back down at his pocket watch, he could see it was almost seven o-clock. Looking up at the two windows that had lit up before he left town, he wondered if one of them might still be upstairs. How much longer would they be...? Would there be a lot of people up and moving around by the time they're finally ready to leave. He was thinking to himself, still looking at as much of the street that he could safely look at.

He was just about to refill his third cup of coffee when the three came walking out the door just up the street from him. Putting his cup down, he quickly walked over to the closed door and looked around the edge from about ten feet back in the shadows. He could see all three packing their saddlebags over their left shoulders and Carl was packing the duffle bag in his left hand. They were all laughing and discussing how much fun they had had last night. When they were about thirty feet away and looking back at the Saloon, Wapiti walked out into the middle of the open front door and took his stance.

"Gentlemen, we all had a fun time last night. So how about you drop those saddlebags and your guns and maybe we'll be able to play cards again in a couple years." Wapiti said, catching them totally off guard.

All three men came to a sudden stop and looked over at Deputy Wapiti with his right hand next to his pistol. All three men instantly dropped their saddlebags to the ground and Carl also dropped the duffle bag. "Remember Deputy, one small hesitation and you'll be dead … So how about you just get back on your horse and tell the Judge you couldn't find us. Like you said, we too enjoyed your company last night as well, I sure wouldn't want to have to kill you, but there's no way you're out drawing all three of us.

"Maybe not, but I will take you out first Carl." Wapiti answered. Looking the three men over, Sam was to his left, Carl in the center and Chip to his right. He could see the fear in Chip's face and eyes, he'd be his last target, because he would be slowest on the draw.

Wapiti could see the sun coming up over the mountain top's behind them, which meant it would be shining into his eyes within a couple minutes most. "I'm going to ask you one more time to unbuckle and drop your holsters to the ground." Out of the corners of his eyes, he could see people coming out on the boardwalk to watch the shoot out to see if Wapiti was as fast with his pistol as he was with his feet, if not, he didn't have long to live cause they all had seen Carl and Sam outdraw and kill many men.

"You're just going to have to out shoot us son!" Carl said, as all three men started moving their right hands closer to their pistols.

Without hesitation, Wapiti pulled his pistol out and started firing, drilling both Carl and Sam dead center, killing them before they hit the ground. But Chip tried to jump out of the way, so he hit him just above the right nipple. Sending all three lifeless to the ground.

Slowly Wapiti started walking towards the three with his pistol still in hand. The closer he got, the more upset his stomach was getting. He couldn't hear anyone around him, he could only see the three men laying in the middle of the street. Walking up to them and looking down, he could see Sam's pistol was still in his holster, Carl's was laying on the ground next to him. Chip was saying something as he tried to crawl away backwards.

Wapiti looked at the holes in all three men one last time. The only reason Chip was still alive was because he tried to jump away. Slowly he could start hearing the people around him. Chip was hollering out, "DON'T SHOOT, DON'T SHOOT!"

"Throw your pistol as far as you can." Wapiti said, waving his pistol.

"YES SIR DEPUTY, PLEASE JUST DON'T SHOOT ME!" Chip yelled out, grabbing the handle grip of his pistol and tossing it as far as he could.

"I'm not going to shoot you." Wapiti said, putting his pistol away and started picking up all three pistols. Stopping and looking at all the notch's on Carl and Sam's pistols, it sent a small chill up his spin. Only seconds earlier he had killed these two men, if he had hesitated even a half second longer, he would be one of the dead ones lying on the street.

Starting to look around, he could see the people all walking over closer to him. They all wanted to see the dead men and congratulate Deputy Wapiti on a job well done. He couldn't understand what they were all laughing and cheering about. Two men were dead and a third was lucky to still be alive. Seeing Tom Chandler, he called him over.

"What can I do for you, Deputy?" Tom asked, grabbing his right wrist and shaking his hand.

Wapiti quickly pulled his hand back, looking back down at the two dead men, his stomach started churning again and his mouth got all watery like he was going to throw-up. "Would you please grab a couple men to help saddle their horses up, and send one man a couple hundred yards directly behind the Livery and bring my horse back as well please."

"Yes Sir Deputy, Hank, Rich you come with me, Junior, you go get the Deputy's horse." Tom said, as all four men took off running towards where they needed to go.

"Wapiti reached down and undid everyone's holster belts and put the pistols back inside each holster. He could see Chip was bleeding out of the right side of his chest, but he was breathing just fine. Which meant his bullet missed his lungs, so he'd be going back to face Judge Monson.

It only took five minutes most for Tom and the other's to return with all their horses.

Wapiti leaned down and picked Sam up over his shoulder and packed him over to the closest horse, then tossed him over the saddle. Somebody get a lariat, put the loop around his shoulders, then go under the horse's stomach and wrap the rope around their feet a couple times, then go up through their belt's and tie them off around their saddle horns. That way they won't slide off on me going back home." He said, walking back over and picking Carl up and packing him over to another horse and tossed him over the saddle. While men did as he asked, and were tying them down over the saddle.

Wapiti walked over to Chip and told him to stand up. Doing so, Wapiti pulled his shirt open so he could see the hole. "Somebody get the Doc. and tell him I need a couple pressure dressings."

"Already have a dozen ready Marshal, I mean, Deputy." Doc said, walking thru the crowd of people and over to Chip. "Take your shirt off Youngman."

Chip quickly unbuttoned his shirt using his left hand, it hurt too much to try and move his right arm. The Doc looked at the front wound, then turned him around and saw the exit hole. "You're lucky the bullet went all the way through Youngman." He said, putting a thick large gauze pad over the back hole and taped it down. Then taking a bandage half as big, he bandaged the much smaller front hole.

"Deputy, there's four more big gauze pads and four smaller ones. You'll need to change them if they fill up with too much blood, but this should be more than enough bandages to get you back to Prineville." Doc said, handing Wapiti a small bag.

"Thanks Doc." Wapiti said, putting a handcuff on Chip's left hand, then led him over to his horse. Pulling his arm up, he locked the other side around the saddle horn. "This way you can steer your own horse, but if you try to run on me, I'll shoot your horse and you will walk back to Prineville … Do I make myself clear!" He said, grabbing the lead rope to the two horses with the two dead men on them, then he climbed up into his saddle.

"I'm not going to try and do anything stupid, no-one was killed in that robbery, so the death sentence is off the table." Chip said, climbing up into the saddle.

Wapiti took the ten gauge out of his saddle bags and pulled one hammer back. "This is loaded with steel balls not Bee-Bee's, understand Mister."

"I already said I wouldn't give you any trouble, so you can go ahead and drop that hammer." Chip said, turning his horse down the road with Wapiti right beside him.

"Not Till We Get Back To Prineville, so you'd better hope my horse doesn't stumble." Wapiti said, looking over at Chip, then around at all the people in the street, he didn't think there were this many people in Sisters, but obviously there was.

When they hit the edge of town, Wapiti kicked them into a medium trot. Chip asked him one more time to please drop the hammer on that ten gauge, but again, Wapiti refused.

They had gotten out of town around eight o-clock and it was a long hot, quiet ride to Redmond No sooner had they entered Redmond and people were coming out of the wood works to see Deputy Wapiti bringing two men in over the saddle and one setting up, but bleeding from the right side of his chest.

Wapiti led them over to the Livery Stables to water the horses, before he even got off his horse there were more people than he could see thru. Grabbing his water bag, he started dumping it out.

"Can I get you anything?" Wapiti heard someone call out. Looking around, he saw the man walking towards them. "Yes Sir you could, would you please go to the nearest Café and get me two Bacon Cheese Burgers to go along with a couple beers."

"Can he get me a couple beers too?" Chip asked, trying to walk around and stretch his legs out a little.

"YEAH, grab him two to." Wapiti said, handing the man a twenty dollar bill. "Give the waitress that takes our order a two dollar tip if they cook our food next. But you bring those four beers out here while we're waiting for our food to cook."

"Yes Sir, Deputy." The Man said, taking the money and running towards the closest restaurant.

"Wapiti quickly refilled his water bag with cold water, took a long drink, then handed it over to Chip. He could hear the people talking about him and the men laying over the saddle. Were they really Carl and Sam Marcs, they were known for being fast on the draw and have been credited with killing over thirty people. How had Wapiti outdraw all three of them?

They could also see their holster's laying over Wapiti's saddle horn. On two of them they could see the notch's carved into two of the pistols' hand grips. Some were trying to count just how many notches were on each pistol.

The horses were just finishing up drinking when the man returned with their beers, which made both men happy. Wapiti opened the first and handed it over to Chip who 'thanked' him for it as he started drinking it.

They were just finishing up their first beer when the waitress came out with their food in a paper bag. "Here you go, Deputy, the cook also put in a couple pieces of apple pie." She said, handing him the bag and his change.

Wapiti took both, then telling the young Lady to take the five dollar bill out of his hand for her tip.

"Nobody tip's on a to-go order." The Waitress said, slowly reaching for the money.

"Why not, you still had to wait on me." Wapiti said, watching her shyly take the five dollar bill out of the change in his hand.

"Thanks Deputy." She said, looking at the two dead men tied up and lying over their saddles. She and everyone had seen the Marshal bring many men back in over the saddle. But this was Wapiti's first time, and he did it by outdrawing two of the fastest guns in this neck of the woods. Carl and Sam both were well known for having a fast draw, with over thirty kills between them, yet Wapiti had outdrawn them both.

Within a couple minutes Wapiti had them loaded back up and heading out of town at a slow walk while they ate their lunch.

Wapiti was still leading the two dead and having Chip rode out in front of him so he could more easily watch over him from trying to make a run for it. It only took them fifteen minutes at most to eat both the Hamburger and the piece of apple pie. Wapiti took out his pocket watch and could see it was just past one-thirty.

"Let's get going." Wapiti told Chip, kicking his horse back into a medium trot. "If everything goes right we should be back in time for dinner.

As usual, there was more traffic on this section of the road heading to Powell Butte then on to Prineville. All the westbound traffic would pull over and stop while they rode by, looking at them all. The man out front had a large blood stain on the right side of his shirt, followed by Deputy Wapiti sitting tall in the saddle with his famous ten gauge in one hand and his rein's in the other, and leading two horses that each had a dead man tied down laying over their saddles. They had all heard and read about the many fist fights he had been in, but this time it was a gun battle, and yet again he came out on top. How Had He Outshot Three Men?

Everyone made sure to look at Wapiti's entire body looking for blood on him, but just like his fist fights, he didn't have any visible blood anywhere on his clothes.

The people they passed from behind, all were wondering the same thing. Because it was early afternoon, the sun was high in the sky, making it hotter out. Making Wapiti slow them back down to a walk pace more than usual.

When he did slow them down, all the wagons close by would catch up to them and then slowly ride around them to be able to look them over better. The Marshal was KNOWN for bringing them in over the saddle, but to their knowledge, this was Wapiti's first two Real Scalp's he'd taken.

Sure, some of them had heard the story about him outshooting two Gunslinger's in Dayville last week, supposedly only shooting them in the shoulder. But most of them thought that was just some Bullshit Story someone had made up. But NOW, there he is, leading two dead and one wounded prisoners. They were also wondering about how many notches if any were on their pistol grips. The story from Dayville was one had nineteen and the other had seventeen.

Some of the wagons that rode past them, if they had kids in the back, they would all draw their hand pistols and start shooting Chip over and over.

"Don't look like Outlaw's are very welcome around here." Wapiti said, looking over at Chip "Can I ask you one question that's been bothering me?"

"Sure, go ahead and ask." Chip answered

"Why'd you jump sideways instead of pulling your pistol?" Wapiti asked "Are you really as bad a shot with your pistol as your Dad and Brother said?"

"I didn't want to die." Chip said, looking straight into Wapiti's face and eyes. "NO, I'M NOT…When we'd all practice with our pistols, I'd pick a different spot to shoot at, I can hit within an inch of my target at forty yards. But when we practiced I always purposely missed the target by at least a foot."

"Why would you purposely not shoot at the target they were shooting at?" Wapiti asked

"I wanted them to believe I couldn't hit the broad side of a barn, so they wouldn't expect me to kill anyone. I don't mind killing for food, but for MONEY! No, not even. Yes, I did enjoy spending all the money afterwords. Dad would always find Coach's or Banks that he knew had at least fifty thousand dollars or more on or in it.

Don't ask me how he knew which ones to hit, the Oregon Trust was the easiest, all's we had to do was wait in rented room for a week in Redmond, then got us a Hotel room in Prineville and waited for you and the Marshal to return with the two hundred plus pounds of gold that had been reported stolen off the Mine's guarded Stage Coach…We just didn't expect them to have twice that much gold in there at the same time. Dad said he knew we should have taken a couple extra saddle bags along."

"So, you've Never, killed anyone?" Wapiti asked

"No Sir, I always stayed outside holding the horses. Truthfully, I cringed with every shot I would hear them fire, cause I knew that bullet had killed an innocent person." Chip answered, with a sorrowful look on his face and in his eyes, and Wapiti could see it.

"Can they prove you robbed any other Coaches or Banks that people were killed in?" Wapiti asked

"HELL NO!" Chip said, chuckling. "The Posse's would always be looking for three horses with both the rocking A and the double zero brand on them. So we always kept those three horses on the far back side of our ranch, on a smaller ranch that's in Mom's name, that's why no-one ever found them."

"They can now." Wapiti said, pointing the ten gauge at the two brands. "Now they can tie you to all those past robbery's."

"Dad thought about that." Chip said, looking down at the brands, then back at his dead Dad and brother. "That's one reason why Dad bought the ranch on the back side of our ranch. Primarily to hide these three horses and the breedable mares on, while the ones that have that year's foals are on our front ranch should we actually get caught, we'd have a backup ranch to come back to.

"So how many of those notches on their pistols came from the robbery's?" Wapiti asked, looking down at the pistols.

"None, those were all fair gun duels. Usually a cheater at a poker game or later some Youngman wanting to make a name for himself as a Gunslinger who had drawn against either my Dad or Sam." Chip answered "Like you Deputy, I prefer settling my disagreements with my fists ... Are you putting these two notches on your pistol?"

"NOPE...!" Wapiti stated, looking back at the two dead men. "Fact, I'll give the Judge all your gun belts and you can pick them up when you get out of prison."

"No Thanks, I don't want the memories those guns would bring back." Chip firmly stated "If and when I get out, I'm the sole survivor and owner of our second ranch. Right now we have a good hundred plus brood Mare's and three other stallions, not to mention the hundred or so three year old's and younger. Them and three sections of land, I'll be able to start over real easy when I get out." He continued explaining, as he picked up his water bag and took a big drink before continuing. "We really didn't need to do this robbery. Over the years we never cashed in on any of the gold we got in the robbery, only the cash. But," starting to chuckle. "We just bought another couple sections, or almost fifty thousand dollars, and Dad found out they had scheduled four or five more big land deals last Friday. So we knew the bank was FAT for the taking." Chuckling a little harder. "Nobody knew how much gold those men had gotten away with. We figured like normal they'd only have three or four fifty pound satchels of gold, damned sure didn't figure. what, wasn't there eight satchels?" He asked seeing Wapiti nod his head in agreement saying, 'Something like that.' So we made sure our saddlebags and one extra set were empty going in. Dad said if he knew all that gold was in there he would go back and buy those two, just under his sixteen hand three fingers, or inches tall brood mares. As you can see, all these three are seventeen to seventeen hands two fingers tall.

Of course the tallest was dad's horse, and you threw his body over his horse, so just a Cavalry trooper, his horse is bringing his dead body back so it can be properly buried."

They'd been walking and talking longer than Wapiti had intended, but he was learning more about the men he was bringing in over the saddle. "Let's get moving." He said, dropping the hammer on that big ass ten gauge, then he jabbed it into the flank area on Chips horse, quickly jump starting him into a full out run at first, but Chip quickly got him back under control and slowed down as Wapiti came riding up alongside chuckling his head off. I didn't expect him to react that fidgety to getting poked in the flank area. Which brought Chip to start chuckling.

"Are you kidding, Dad enter this stud into a couple rodeos, he had an agreement with the stock owner, that he got the entry fee of his rider, then after the bull riding was over, or the usual ending point of the rodeo, Dad bet that eight men couldn't ride him for the full eight second ride at ten dollars a rider. Of course if anyone did ride him, they won the full eighty dollars and Dad and the remainder would also get their chance at winning an additional eighty dollars that he'd put up."

"The Larkin brother's, Larry, one of the I mean IDENTICAL twins. He had a big ass Roan, eighteen one, and lot's of fun." Larry claimed. "That was how them, three, really it was Randy, he logged up there around Sumpter and stabled his horses in an old abandon smokehouse that the tunnel from the banks came up at so they could load the real gold onto the train in the middle of the night and nobody would ever know they had actually loaded it. Cause like they did everyday during the daylight so everyone can see them load that load of worthless painted gold rocks. SO, to set up the robbery, Larry bet ten men couldn't ride his big ass Roan, eighty one, and lots of fun." chuckling harder, before continuing. "That

Larry Larkin is a character. All three of those Larkin men, and their Aunt Patty in Pendleton. She's a very beautiful lady, I didn't believe she was almost forty years old, her daughter Cassandra is a split younger version of her. One of the most beautifulest, sweetest, yet down to earth lady's I've had the pleasure of meeting. But their purse was five thousand dollars, five hundred a rider. So each man that wanted a chance spent the day before getting men to throw their money on their ability to ride that big ass Roan. They looked like Mutt and Jeff. That Roan is the biggest and tallest horse I have ever seen, and Larry is only about five-seven, maybe eight feet tall, and couldn't weigh more than one-fifty. So he looks like a kid riding a standard size horse. I guess the last man was the actual three time world champion bareback rider. This was saddle bronc style, but style of spurring was required. A bareback rider reaches his spurs down the front shoulders of the horse raking them straight upward back at himself everytime that horses front feet hit into the ground. Where as a saddle bronc rider plants his spurs in the horses front shoulders and rakes backward along the ribcage to the ascend of the horse, then get his spurs back up front before his front legs pound into the ground again. Larry said that man, a tall slender black man, I can't remember his name, C.R. HALL, it just hit me. Larry said he was the last rider and his only real worried about challenger. He said he watched C.R.'s ride play out in slow motion, said those eight second actually felt and played out well over a half hour in his mind. When finally at about seven seconds that big ass Roan man a move usually only a bull dose. Turn almost completely around, or doing a one-eighty, turning his front legs back towards his back legs and back legs around and quickly passed where the front legs had been sending C.R. literally flying over the top of the pole corral and up five rows into the grandstands crashing down onto the spectators." Starting to chuckle again. He said C.R.'s flight played out the same as he watched him fly thru the sky, he knew the horse had made his ride, but now he had to ride that horse out of the arena or everybody got their money back. BUT, he got to take the flank strap off. But again, none of the times that big ass Roan had bucked on him did he half a flank strap on, and would that big ass Roan be mad at him for putting him through that challenge. Said he could feel the nervousness and, it wasn't fear as much of fear of being in front of so many screaming, cheering people. Said when he first hit the saddle that big ass Roan instanted reared straight up leaping a good eight plus feet, landing on his hind feet, doing it two more times before taking off at a full run around and around that small arena area. Randy and Gary said, ``Larry was loudly and proudly cheering and bragging about the big horse's abilities." Wapiti was explaining, as they came riding back up to the wagons that had passed them when they were walking. The kid's again were pulling their hand pistols and shooting Chip over and over and over again for a s long as they could.

After another half hour they came riding into Powell Butte and Wapiti led them over to the water trough so the horses could drink. Wapiti was just about to dismount when he saw one of the boy's from yesterday go running inside the Merc.

The Blacksmith came slowly walking out, taking a drink off his pint. "I see they didn't give you much of a choice. Looks like you missed your target on this one." He said, looking over at Chip as he too got off his horse to stretch his legs out the best he could.

"He was my last target and he tried to jump out of the way." Wapiti said, dumping his warm water bag out, just as a boy came running up to him with two beers.

"Here's your beer, Deputy." The Boy said, handing them to him.

"Thanks Youngman." Wapiti said, reaching into his shirt pocket and took out some money. Looking thru it, he pulled out a ten dollar bill. "Go back inside and get me a couple pints of whiskey and two more beers. Tell the owner they're for my prisoner, so charge me the normal price for them."

"Yes Sir, Deputy." The Boy said, running back to the Merc.

Wapiti walked over and handed Chip a beer. "Drink it while you can, cause after we get in I have a feeling it's going to be many years before you get another one."

"Thank Deputy, you're the first Lawman that I know of who ever bought a prisoner something cold to drink." Chip said.

"I normally don't either, I usually make my prisoner's drink warm to hot water out of their water bags. But you haven't given me any trouble, so I figure I can be nice to you." Wapiti said, taking a long drink off his cold beer.

Wapiti was just finishing refilling up his water bag when the boy returned with two more beers and the two pints of whiskey that he had asked him to get for him.

"Here Ya go Deputy." The Boy said, handing them to him along with his change.

"Thanks." Wapiti said, setting them on the ground and looking through the change, taking out two one dollar bills and all the loose change he gave it to the boy as a tip for all his running.

"THANKS DEPUTY WAPITI!" the boy excitedly answered, walking away.

Wapiti ordered Chip to retighten his cinch strap as he tightened his. Then they both quickly drank down the last of their first beers, handing the Blacksmith their empty's, they climbed aboard their horses and headed back down the road. Just like in Sisters and Redmond, everyone in town had come out to see Deputy Wapiti lead two dead men down the road.

"He's turning into more like the Marshal everyday, look, he's bringing those prisoner's in lying over the saddle with only one setting up." Some of the people started saying as they rode by.

"Don't look like he had any other choice." A couple people started speaking up in his defense.

"Three men against one, that takes a lot of gut's." someone yelled out "He's lucky he's still alive."

"He could have brought a lot more in dead to if he'd wanted too, but he hasn't" Someone else yelled out in his defence.

Wapiti didn't say a word or even look towards the people, he just kept his eyes on Chip riding a half horse length in front of him. Looking down at his pocket watch, he could see it was ten after three. They were making good time and would be in just about dinner time.

He was actually going to have Carmen make him a couple big beef burritos with some of her hotter salsa in them. Just thinking about it made him instantly ten times hungrier, so he told Chip to kick it back up to a medium trot.

Once again, those going east would pull their wagons over to the side of the road and stop while they rode past them. They too wondered who the dead men were and were hollering back at Wapiti asking him to tell them who they were. But Wapiti just ignored them and kept riding down the road at a medium trot.

Also, all the wagons they came up behind, if there were kids in the back, they were pulling their hand pistols and pretending to shoot Chip over and over again.

It didn't take too many and they were making Chip's stomach feel real uneasy inside. Looking down at the bullet hole in his right side, then back to his Dad and brother again. He knew, if he'd stayed in and tried to draw against Wapiti, he too would be dead. All of a sudden he started getting cold, shivering sweats. He was getting sicker to his stomach, it was all he could do not to start throwing up. He kept running it over and over in his head. No matter how many times he thought about it, it always came up the same way. If he hadn't jumped sideways when he did, he would be dead too.

Before they knew it, they were at the top of the View Ridge going down into Prineville. Wapiti told him to pull-up and stop. So Chip did, looking back at Wapiti. "What's up?"

Wapiti rode up beside him and reached over and uncuffed his one hand cuff. "Put your coat on."

"Are you joking, it must still be eighty degree's out here." Chip said, looking at Wapiti.

"Look, I had that kid buy you a pints of whiskey. If you put one down your coat sleeve and keep them there until the jailer goes back to his desk. You should have enough to get good and drunk one last time." Wapiti said, taking the bottles out of his saddle bags.

"You're alright Deputy." Chip said, extending his right hand.

"I only treat people the way I'd hope they'd treat me." Wapiti said, shaking his hand.

Chip quickly untied his jacket and put it on and put a pint down each sleeve, then cuffed his right hand back around the saddle horn and headed on down the road.

Within twenty minutes they were at the bottom of the hill and entering the edge of Prineville. The people were coming from everywhere to see Deputy Wapiti bring in three more Outlaw's. But this time, two of them were dead and they all started talking about it as they followed them to the Courthouse where Judge Monson was standing outside on the boardwalk waiting for them to get to him.

They rode up to the hitchin' rail in front of the Courthouse and Wapiti grabbed all three holsters and quickly dismounted. Walking over to Chip, he unlocked his right hand leaving the hand-cuffs hanging off the saddle horn. "Walk towards that door." He said pointing.

"Yes Sir, Deputy." Chip answered, walking towards the door as it opened up.

"I got him Deputy." The Jailer yelled over to him.

"Thanks," Wapiti yelled back, walking over to Judge Monson, who was handing him a cold beer.

"I can see you had to be Judge, Jury, and Executioner." Judge Monson said, giving him the cold bottle of beer. "How do you feel?"

"I'm alright." Wapiti said, opening the beer. Looking over at all the people that were picking up the dead men's heads so they could see who they were. "I gave them two chances not to draw against me, but as you can see … they chose to make that decision for me."

"How'd you miss that one?" Judge Monson asked, looking over at Chip.

"I didn't then, nor do I now want to die Your Honor, so when they all went for their guns, I started jumping out of the way, as you can see, I just barely managed to succeed." Chip yelled out, just before he walked inside the outside jail door.

The people all started talking about the two dead men. They were none other than Carl and Sam Marcs, how the hell did Deputy Wapiti outdraw these two. They both were well known for being real fast on the draw, yet there they were, lying dead and Deputy Wapiti was handing Judge Monson their holsters and pistols.

"What do you want me to do with these?" Judge Monson asked, taking a hold of all three holsters.

"Hang them above your Courtroom desk with a sign saying 'Nobody is unbeatable', maybe that will detour some kid from wanting to be an Outlaw." Wapiti said, seeing the Undertaker come walking across the street. "I see you brought me some customer's Deputy Wapiti." The Undertaker said, with a big smile on his face and shaking his hand. "I'll get all the info on them that I need from the Judge." He said, leading the two horses with the dead men on them away.

"Thanks," Wapiti said, walking over and grabbing his and Chip's horses and headed towards the Livery.

Gordy was standing outside his Livery Stables looking over at the Courthouse watching everything going on. Walking back inside he grabbed his pint of whiskey and started walking back out, when Wapiti came leading the two horses in. Handing Wapiti the bottle of whiskey. "Need a pull to help calm your nerves?"

"Thanks," Wapiti said, dropping the reins and taking a hold of the bottle, pulling the cork, he took a big pull off the bottle and handed it back to Gordy.

Gordy took a quick pull and put the cork back in it. "You go on ahead and go relax and come to terms with killing those two men." Gordy said

"Thanks again." Wapiti said, shaking Gordy's hand, then headed across the street towards the shack. He could see everyone was stopping and watching him walk across the street until he was out of sight between the buildings.

www.ingramcontent.com/pod-product-compliance
Lightning Source LLC
Chambersburg PA
CBHW071701120626
46550CB00001B/67